PREVENTION'S

COOKING FOR
GOOD
HEALTH

easy recipes for low-fat living

Edited by Jean Rogers, Food Editor,
Prevention Magazine Health Books

RODALE

Rodale Press, Emmaus, Pennsylvania

This book was previously published by Rodale Press as *Prevention's Natural Healing Cooking School.*

Printed in the United States of America on acid-free ∞, recycled paper containing a minimum of 20% post-consumer waste ♻

Cover Photographer: Jerry Simpson

Library of Congress Cataloging-in-Publication Data

Prevention's cooking for good health: easy recipes for low-fat living /
    edited by Jean Rogers, food editor, Prevention Magazine Health Books.
        p.   cm.
    Includes index.
    ISBN 0-87596-210-6 hardcover
     1. Low-fat diet — Recipes.   I. Rogers, Jean [date].
  II. Prevention Magazine Health Books.
  RM237.7.P73   1994
  641.5′638 — dc20
                                   94-4881
                                     CIP

Distributed in the book trade by St. Martin's Press

2   4   6   8   10   9   7   5   3   1   hardcover

OUR MISSION

We publish books that empower people's lives.

RODALE ❧ BOOKS

PREVENTION'S *COOKING FOR GOOD HEALTH* STAFF

Editor: Jean Rogers

Editor, *Prevention* Magazine: Mark Bricklin

Book and Cover Designer: Debra Sfetsios

Additional Design: Faith Hague and Karen C. Heard

Recipe Development: Laura Barton, Erin Bause-Landry, JoAnn Brader, Marlene Brown, Kathy Casey, Sharon Faelten, Aliza Green, Judith Benn Hurley, Jeanne Jones, Sandy Kapoor, Tom Ney, Jean Rogers, Miriam Rubin, Marie Simmons, Nancy Zelko

Photographers: Angelo Caggiano, Zeva Oelbaum, Jerry Simpson

Photo Editor: Barbara Fritz

Food Stylists: Anne Disrude, Karen Hatt, Mariann Sauvion

Prop Stylists: Betty Alfenito, Denise Canter, Valorie Fisher

Illustrator: David Flaherty

Home Economist, Rodale Food Center: JoAnn Brader

Research Associates: Christine Dreisbach, Karen Lombardi Ingle

Copy Editor: Jane Sherman

Prevention Magazine Health Books

Editor-in-Chief: Bill Gottlieb

Executive Editor: Debora A. Tkac

Art Director: Jane Colby Knutila

Research Manager: Ann Gossy Yermish

Copy Manager: Lisa D. Andruscavage

CONTENTS

INTRODUCTION

■ ■ ■ ■ ■ ■ ■ ▬▬▬▬

Cooking for good health has become a priority with those who recognize the very real link between diet and physical well-being. Every day, new scientific studies further strengthen that link. But it's one thing to know intellectually that a low-fat diet, for instance, can help prevent heart disease, some types of cancer and other devastating ills. Or that a low-sodium diet can help some individuals manage their high blood pressure. It's quite another thing to incorporate that information into your daily diet.

That's what this book is designed to do — to help you tap into the amazing power of good, wholesome food every day and at every meal. And the best part? You'll love every bite.

These dishes were developed especially for the way you cook today. You don't want to serve your family food that's loaded with fat, cholesterol and sodium. You want recipes that will help build their health — without sacrificing good taste.

This book gives you the best of both worlds. So you *can* eat such favorites as kabobs, quiches, sundaes, meat loaf with mashed potatoes, stuffed mushrooms, turkey tetrazzini, enchiladas, peach upside-down cake and more. (And as extra proof of just how appealing healthy food can be, we've accompanied every recipe with a color photo.)

SIGNS OF HEALTH

We'd like to take this opportunity to acquaint you with some special features that accompany the recipes. First are the good-health symbols found at the top of the recipe pages. They show you at a glance which recipes are especially low in cholesterol, calories and sodium so you can zero in on those dishes that meet your most pressing health goals.

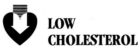 **LOW CHOLESTEROL**

You'll find this symbol on recipes that are low in dietary cholesterol. The exact amount varies according to what food category a dish fits into. Entrées and one-dish meals, for example, have less than 100 milligrams of cholesterol per serving. Side dishes, light soups, breads, muffins and desserts contain less than 15 milligrams. Snacks have less than 25.

To control cholesterol intake in general, rely less on meat and full-fat dairy products and eat more plant foods, such as grains, vegetables and cereals, which contain no cholesterol at all. Take advantage of egg substitutes and egg whites for omelets, casseroles, sauces, baked goods and other dishes that ordinarily use whole eggs. Remember that each egg yolk that you eliminate from your diet saves you 213 milligrams of dietary cholesterol.

According to guidelines from the American Heart Association, your goal should be to limit your cholesterol intake to less than 100 milligrams for each 1,000 calories you consume, with an upper limit of 300 milligrams per day.

Keep in mind that dietary cholesterol isn't the only thing that influences your blood cholesterol. So cutting back on your intake of cholesterol — which is found only in animal products — is only part of the picture. Saturated fat plays a large role in raising cholesterol levels. And many doctors consider it to have a greater effect than that of the cholesterol you eat.

So make an effort to keep your consumption of saturated fat low. (The current recommendation is that no more than 10 percent of your calories should come from saturated fat.) That means cutting way back on the foods that are highest in saturated fat, such as fatty meats, butter, whole milk, cream and full-fat cheeses. Use the nutrient analyses that accompany the recipes in this book to pinpoint those dishes that are especially low in saturated fat.

On the positive side, there are certain dietary components that can help you to lower your blood cholesterol if it is high. Among them are such proven cholesterol fighters as:

- fiber — especially the soluble fiber found in beans, oats and fruit
- monounsaturated fats — found in olive oil, avocados and nuts, for example
- omega-3 fatty acids — heart-healthy fats abundant in many types of seafood

Good news for shellfish lovers is that shrimp, lobster, oysters, scallops and other such seafoods are not off-limits to those watching their cholesterol intake. These crustaceans and mollusks were formerly thought to be prohibitively high in cholesterol. Newer ways of measuring cholesterol have found that not to be the case. Further, these seafoods are very low in both total fat and saturated fat, so they fit quite nicely into a cholesterol-lowering diet. Just be certain not to serve these lean shellfish in high-fat creamy sauces and pools of butter.

 **LOW CALORIE**

Look for this symbol on recipes that have only a moderate amount of calories (some examples: less than 300 for entrées, less than 450 for one-dish meals and less than 150 for desserts, side dishes and snacks).

Remember that if you are overweight, more than your physique is at stake. Your chances of developing high blood pressure, elevated blood cholesterol, diabetes, heart disease and stroke increase greatly with extra pounds. Doctors have even linked certain types of cancer to obesity. Fortunately, losing excess weight often reduces your risk of falling prey to these and other serious health threats.

When trying to lose weight, don't bite off more than you can chew. In other words, look for a diet you can *live* with — day after day, year after year. For a ballpark figure of how many calories you should consume a day, use this formula: If you're a moderately active person (meaning that you exercise once or twice a week and walk a fair amount), multiply your ideal weight by 15. So if you weigh (or want to weigh) 120 pounds, for example, multiply 120×15 to get a maximum intake of 1,800 calories a day.

For best weight-loss results — and optimum health — make sure that no more than 30 percent of those calories come from fat. In the example above, that means an upper limit of 540 fat calories per day. In terms of fat *grams,* which is how fat is generally expressed on labels and recipe analyses, that translates to 60 grams of fat (there are 9 calories in each gram of fat).

 LOW SODIUM

If you have elevated blood pressure or if your doctor has told you you're at risk for developing it, watch for this symbol. It earmarks recipes that are low in sodium. Examples include less than 200 milligrams for main courses and one-dish meals, less than 100 milligrams for desserts and less than 50 milligrams for side dishes, breads and muffins.

Doctors know that there is an association between too much sodium in the diet and high blood pressure in some individuals. Although only certain people react badly to sodium, Americans in general consume far too much salt. Many experts advise a total daily intake of only 1,500 to 2,000 milligrams. So our recipes contain no added salt — with one exception: yeast-risen breads. Many bakers feel that a small amount of salt helps the yeast work better. We'll list salt as an optional ingredient in these recipes and leave the saltshaker in *your* hands.

THE FINAL ANALYSIS

Along with each recipe you'll find "Nutrition at a Glance." It gives you the amount of calories, fat, saturated fat, cholesterol and sodium contained in each serving. You'll also find the percentage of calories from total fat and from saturated fat. In general, of course, the lower those numbers, the better. The American Heart Association recommends an upper limit of 30 percent total fat and no more than 10 percent saturated fat. Some nutrition experts recommend even lower amounts. Check with your doctor to find out what numbers you should aim for.

Do, however, keep one thing in mind: *It's your day-to-day diet that counts, not the percent figures for any single dish.* The majority of the recipes in *Prevention's Cooking for Good Health* do get less than 30 percent of their calories from fat. But some do not. Sometimes, for instance, even the barest amount of fat in a low-calorie dish will make the percent figure high. Other times, an essentially lean entrée, such as a red-meat dish, will have an elevated percent. However, if you pair the meat with low-fat vegetables, bread and a side dish of rice, pasta or potatoes — as you normally would when planning meals — the percent for the entire meal will be much lower.

Probably the easiest way for you to get a handle on the percentage question is for you to figure out what your total maximum intake of fat *grams* should be each day and aim for that. To do that, multiply your ideal daily calorie intake by 30 percent (0.30), then divide that number by 9. For example, if you consume 1,800 calories a day, multiply that by 0.30 to get 540 calories. Divide the calories by 9 to get 60 grams of fat. (If you're aiming for a diet that gets 25 percent of calories from fat, multiply your calories by 0.25 instead.)

The nutritional values given in this book are obtained from a computer software program used by nutritionists at the Rodale Food Center. This program is supplemented with information from manufacturers so that we may use the latest low-fat, low-sodium products. When analyzing recipes, we use the following guidelines:

- Meat is trimmed of all visible fat before cooking.
- If poultry is cooked with the skin on (as it sometimes is to retain moisture), the skin is removed before eating.
- Recipes calling for fresh ingredients, such as raw meats, fruits, vegetables and so forth, are analyzed using data for uncooked foods.
- All stock is assumed to be low-sodium homemade or store-bought broth. (If no particular type of stock is specified, you may use whatever's on hand, which for most people is chicken stock.)
- When a range of ingredients is given (such as 4 to 5 cups flour), the lesser number is used for calculations.
- Optional ingredients are not included in the analyses.
- When ingredient choices are given (such as nonfat or low-fat sour cream), the first one mentioned is used.
- Any accompanying pasta, rice or other grain that appears in the ingredients list is factored into the analysis. Suggested accompaniments that appear under the Chef's Notes are not used in the analyses.
- When no amount is specified, as in a garnish, a reasonable amount is assigned.

A NOTE ABOUT NOTES

We've tried to include as much information as possible with each recipe to make meal preparation easier for you. The heading "Do First" lets you see at a glance if there's anything you need to do before you can make a recipe. Some recipes, for instance, call for already-cooked rice, chicken or beans. Or they require you to roast peppers, peel tomatoes or drain yogurt for yogurt cheese. If you're in a hurry, you'll be forewarned to choose other recipes.

The Chef's Notes also give you ideas for accompaniments, variations and ways to attractively present food. And they sometimes clue you in to kitchen tricks, make-ahead tips and microwave options that will save you time or expand your culinary skills.

IT'S ABOUT TIME

One other important feature of this book is the preparation-time information found at the end of each recipe. This gives you a rough estimate of how much cooking time to allow for each dish, plus how much time you'll need for up-front preparation work such as slicing, dicing, measuring, mixing, stirring and such.

Many dishes can be ready for the stove or oven in 20 minutes or less. Then they can cook unattended while you relax or work on other things. Some foods, such as meats, benefit from marinating before cooking, and we alert you to recipes in which that is the case. Certain desserts, such as ices and homemade frozen yogurt, need additional time in the freezer or an ice-cream maker. Yeast breads need time to rise. All of those situations are indicated by the phrase "standing time."

APPETIZERS AND HORS D'OEUVRES

HEAVENLY STUFFED EGGS

These deviled eggs have a healthy secret—a savory, low-cholesterol filling made from garlic-scented potatoes and just one hard-cooked yolk for the whole batch. They're a heavenly addition to picnics, barbecues and party buffets.

HEAVENLY STUFFED EGGS

5 hard-cooked eggs
1 baking potato, cooked, peeled and cubed
1-2 cloves garlic, minced
3 tablespoons defatted chicken stock
2 tablespoons lemon juice
1 tablespoon white-wine vinegar
1 teaspoon olive oil
2 tablespoons minced scallion greens
¼ teaspoon ground black pepper

1. Peel the eggs and cut them in half lengthwise. Lift out the yolks. Set aside 2 yolk halves for use in the filling. Discard the remaining yolks or reserve them for another use.

2. Shave a thin slice off the bottom of each white so it will stand upright. Arrange the whites, cut side up, on a large plate.

3. In a medium bowl, combine the potatoes, garlic and the 2 yolk halves. Mash with a potato masher or the back of a fork until well-blended. Stir in 2 tablespoons stock, 1 tablespoon lemon juice and 1 teaspoon vinegar until well-blended.

4. Add the oil and the remaining 1 tablespoon stock, 1 tablespoon lemon juice and 2 teaspoons vinegar. Beat with a spoon until smooth and fluffy. Fold in 1 tablespoon of the scallions and the pepper.

5. Using a teaspoon or a pastry bag fitted with a large star tip, fill the egg whites with the potato mixture. Sprinkle the tops with the remaining scallions.

MAKES 10.

Preparation Time: 15 min.

CHEF'S NOTES

■ ■ ■ ■ ■ ■ ■ ■ ■

DO FIRST:
Cook the eggs: Bring about 3'' of water to a boil in a deep saucepan. Add the eggs, cover and reduce the heat. Simmer the eggs for 15 minutes. Plunge into cold water and peel when cool enough to handle.
Cook the potato: Boil the potato for about 15 minutes.

■

NUTRI-NOTE:
Dietary cholesterol does not pose health problems for pets, so you may feed leftover cooked yolks to your dog or cat.

■

CHEF'S SECRET:
If making these eggs to take along on a picnic or other outing, slice them crosswise. The filled halves will easily fit into the slots of the washed empty egg carton.

NUTRITION AT A GLANCE ■■■

PER HALF EGG:
Calories 32
Fat . . . . 1 g. (28% of cal.)
Sat. fat . . . . . 0.2 g. (6% of cal.)
Cholesterol . . . . 21 mg.
Sodium . . . . 29 mg.

SPINACH AND FETA STUFFED MUSHROOMS

Stuffed mushrooms are perennial favorites on the party scene—and rightly so. They are a perfect finger food and can accommodate a wide variety of healthy stuffings. This version of low-cal Greek-style appetizers includes vitamin C–rich spinach and a small amount of very flavorful feta cheese.

SPINACH AND FETA STUFFED MUSHROOMS

2 pounds fresh spinach
16 large mushrooms (2″–2½″)
1 large onion, minced
1 tablespoon minced garlic
2 tablespoons defatted chicken stock
¼ cup crumbled feta cheese
1 cup soft bread crumbs
2 teaspoons olive oil

1. Wash the spinach in lots of cold water to remove any grit. Remove thick stems and coarsely chop large leaves. Shake off the excess water and set aside in a colander to drain further.

2. Carefully remove the stems from the mushrooms. Finely chop the stems and set aside. Place the caps, stem side up, on a baking sheet and set aside.

3. In a large no-stick frying pan over medium heat, sauté the onions, garlic and chopped mushroom stems in the stock for 5 minutes. Reduce the heat to low and add the spinach. Cover and cook for 2 minutes, or until the spinach is wilted.

4. Place the mixture in a large strainer and press with the back of a spoon to remove excess liquid. Transfer to a medium bowl and set aside to cool. Stir in the feta cheese.

5. Wipe out the frying pan with paper towels. Add the bread crumbs and oil. Sauté over medium heat for 8 minutes, or until lightly browned.

6. While the bread crumbs are browning, bake the mushroom caps at 400° for 10 minutes, or until softened. Divide the spinach filling among the caps. Sprinkle with the bread crumbs. Bake for 8 minutes.

MAKES 16.

Preparation Time: 15 min.
Cooking Time: 35 min.

CHEF'S NOTES

DO FIRST:
Prepare soft bread crumbs by tearing 4 or 5 slices of fresh or slightly stale bread into pieces. Place in a blender or food processor and chop with on/off turns.

INGREDIENTS NOTE:
You may use frozen spinach in place of the fresh. Thaw two boxes (10 ounces each) and squeeze out all the excess moisture. You may use smaller or larger mushrooms, according to what's available.

VARIATION:
Use other greens, such as kale, collards or mustard.

MAKE-AHEAD TIP:
You may prepare the filling and stuff the mushrooms several hours ahead. Add the bread crumbs just before baking.

NUTRITION AT A GLANCE

PER MUSHROOM:
Calories 37
Fat . . . . 1.3 g. (32% of cal.)
Sat. fat . . . . 0.4 g. (10% of cal.)
Cholesterol . . . . 2 mg.
Sodium . . . . 68 mg.

GARDEN-JEWEL HORS D'OEUVRES

These beautiful little tidbits make superbly healthy party food. The fillings taste rich and creamy, yet they're amazingly low in fat, calories and cholesterol. And if you team them with a wide variety of colorful vegetables as we have here, you'll add nice amounts of cancer-fighting vitamin A.

GARDEN-JEWEL HORS D'OEUVRES

BASIL AND SPINACH SPREAD

- ½ cup coarsely chopped fresh spinach
- 1 clove garlic, minced
- 1 shallot, minced
- 3 tablespoons minced fresh basil or 1 teaspoon dried
- 1 cup low-fat cottage cheese
- 1 teaspoon olive oil

1. In a food processor or blender combine the spinach, garlic, shallots and basil. Process until the mixture is almost a paste. With the motor running, add the cottage cheese and oil. Process until the mixture is smooth. Use as a spread on vegetables, crackers and small pieces of toast.

MAKES ABOUT 1 CUP.

Preparation Time: 5 min.

SMOKED SALMON AND CHIVE SPREAD

- 2 cups nonfat yogurt
- 4 ounces lightly smoked salmon, minced
- 2 tablespoons snipped chives
- 1 teaspoon lemon juice
- 1 teaspoon Dijon mustard

1. Spoon the yogurt into a strainer lined with cheesecloth or a paper coffee filter. Allow to drain for about 20 minutes to thicken. You should have about 1⅔ cups yogurt. Transfer to a medium bowl. With a fork stir in the salmon, chives, lemon juice and mustard until just combined.

MAKES ABOUT 2 CUPS.

Preparation Time: 25 min.

CHILI-BEAN SPREAD

- 1 cup cooked white or red beans
- 2 scallions, coarsely chopped
- 2 teaspoons olive oil
- 1 teaspoon dried oregano
- ½ teaspoon chili powder
- Dash of hot-pepper sauce

1. In a food processor or blender puree the beans, scallions, oil, oregano, chili powder and hot-pepper sauce until smooth. Use as a spread or place filling in a pastry bag fitted with a medium star tip. Pipe onto vegetables, crackers or small pieces of toast.

MAKES ABOUT 1 CUP.

Preparation Time: 5 min.

CHEF'S NOTES

PRESENTATION:

Choose vegetables that are crisp and colorful, such as red and yellow cherry tomatoes (scoop out seeds and spoon in spreads), carrots (slice into rounds or sticks), snow peas (blanch briefly and slit open to fill), cucumbers (cut rounds), button mushrooms (remove stems) and broccoli (break into florets).

NUTRITION AT A GLANCE

PER TABLESPOON:

BASIL AND SPINACH SPREAD

Calories	16
Fat	0.4 g. (23% of cal.)
Sat. fat	0.1 g. (6% of cal.)
Cholesterol	0 mg.
Sodium	59 mg.

SMOKED SALMON AND CHIVE SPREAD

Calories	16
Fat	0.4 g. (23% of cal.)
Sat. fat	0 g.
Cholesterol	1 mg.
Sodium	81 mg.

CHILI-BEAN SPREAD

Calories	15
Fat	<0.1 g. (4% of cal.)
Sat. fat	0 g.
Cholesterol	0 mg.
Sodium	1 mg.

SPICY CHICKEN HORS D'OEUVRES

These little appetizers are a delicious stand-in for cocktail meatballs, which can be high in fat. By substituting low-fat chicken breast for ground beef and serving it with a simple yogurt-based sauce, we slashed calories and fat to the bone!

SPICY CHICKEN HORS D'OEUVRES

- **1 pound boneless skinless chicken breast**
- **¾ teaspoon chili powder**
- **¼ teaspoon hot-pepper sauce**
- **3 cloves garlic, minced**
- **1 tablespoon snipped chives**
- **1½ teaspoons red-wine vinegar**
- **½ cup nonfat yogurt**
- **1½ teaspoons Dijon mustard**

1. Trim the chicken of all fat and remove the white tendon running through each breast. Cut meat into 1″ cubes.

2. Transfer to a food processor. Add the chili powder, hot-pepper sauce, garlic, chives and vinegar. Using on/off turns, process until finely chopped, about 12 to 15 seconds.

3. Form the mixture into little balls, patties or logs.

4. Coat a no-stick frying pan with no-stick spray. Heat on medium high. Add the meat and sizzle until lightly browned and cooked through, about 4 minutes on each side.

5. In a small bowl combine the yogurt and mustard.

6. Serve the hors d'oeuvres warm with mustard sauce for dipping.

SERVES 6.

Preparation Time: 20 min.
Cooking Time: 10 min.

CHEF'S NOTES

PRESENTATION:
Line a serving tray with colorful lettuce or kale cups. Place hors d'oeuvres in the cups. Use another cup for sauce. Garnish with chive blossoms or parsley sprigs.

VARIATIONS:
Serve with tomato salsa or honey-mustard sauce for dipping. You may also use boneless turkey breast in place of the chicken.

KITCHEN TRICK:
For easier handling, wet your hands before forming balls.

MAKE-AHEAD TIP:
You may prepare the meat mixture and store, tightly covered, in the refrigerator for up to a day.

NUTRITION AT A GLANCE

PER SERVING:
Calories 93
Fat . . . . 1 g. (10% of cal.)
Sat. fat . . . . . 0.3 g. (3% of cal.)
Cholesterol . . . . 44 mg.
Sodium . . . . 75 mg.

SMOKED TURKEY AND FRUIT APPETIZERS

Treat your family right with these tasty morsels. Because they're mostly fruit and extra-lean turkey breast, they're lower in calories than many popular hors d'oeuvres. The fresh fruits we've chosen are high in disease-fighting beta-carotene and vitamin C.

SMOKED TURKEY AND FRUIT APPETIZERS

APPETIZERS

12 ounces lightly smoked turkey breast, sliced paper thin

3 tablespoons smooth mango chutney

3 honeydew or yellow watermelon wedges, 1″ wide

3 cantaloupe wedges, 1″ wide

3 papaya slices, 1″ wide

3 lengthwise pineapple slices, 1″ wide

12 strawberries or figs

CURRY SAUCE

2 teaspoons curry powder

½ cup nonfat yogurt

TANGY ORANGE SAUCE

½ cup all-fruit orange marmalade

¼ cup orange juice

2 teaspoons lemon juice

1. *To make the appetizers:* Lightly brush the top surface of each turkey slice with the chutney.

2. Wrap the turkey around each piece of fruit or simply fold the turkey and attach to the fruit with a food pick. If desired, slice the honeydew or watermelon, cantaloupe, papaya and pineapple into bite-size pieces; leave the strawberries or figs whole.

3. *To make the curry sauce:* Heat the curry powder in a small no-stick frying pan over medium heat until fragrant, about 1½ minutes. Stir into the yogurt and use as a dipping sauce for the fruit.

4. *To make the tangy orange sauce:* In a 1-quart saucepan combine the marmalade, orange juice and lemon juice. Bring to a boil, stirring constantly. Remove from the heat and let cool before using as a dipping sauce.

SERVES 12.

Preparation Time: 15 min.
Cooking Time: 2 min.

CHEF'S NOTES

■ ■ ■ ■ ■ ■ ■ ■ ■

ACCOMPANIMENTS:

Serve with lime and orange wedges. Squeeze the lime over the fruit before eating.

■

VARIATIONS:

Use other fruit, such as sliced mangoes, bananas, peaches and nectarines. Or use lightly cooked vegetables, such as asparagus or spears of broccoli, carrots or sweet potatoes. Serve with a mixture of honey and mustard instead of the curry sauce.

■

MICROWAVE OPTION:

If the chutney is too thick to spread, soften it in the microwave for about 20 seconds.

NUTRITION AT A GLANCE ■■■■

PER SERVING:

Calories 111
Fat . . . . . . .1.2 g. (10% of cal.)
Sat. fat . . . . .0 g.
Cholesterol . . . . .15 g.
Sodium . . . . .211 mg.

SALMON BITES

This is a wonderfully simple way to incorporate salmon into your diet. These tidbits are more than just savory—the omega-3 fats in salmon are credited with helping avoid heart attacks. These good fats make the blood less prone to dangerous clotting.

SALMON BITES

TOAST
- 4 teaspoons coarse mustard
- 1 teaspoon olive oil
- 4 large slices bread

SALMON
- 1½ pounds salmon fillet
- 1 teaspoon olive oil
- 2 teaspoons fennel seed
- Ground black pepper (to taste)
- Sprigs of thyme or dill

1. *To make the toast:* In a small bowl combine the mustard and oil. Spread the mixture on both sides of the bread.

2. Position an oven rack in the middle of the oven. Place the bread directly on the rack. Bake at 400° for 7 minutes, or until lightly browned.

3. Remove the bread from the oven and cut into desired shapes (squares, triangles or rectangles).

4. *To make the salmon:* Carefully remove any bones from the salmon. Rub the top surface of the fish with the oil.

5. In a small pan heat the fennel seeds on medium high until fragrant, about 2 minutes; stir frequently to keep the seeds from scorching. Transfer the seeds to a mortar and grind with a pestle until fine. Sprinkle on top of the salmon, along with the pepper.

6. Arrange the salmon, skin side down, on an oiled broiler pan. Broil about 4″ from the heat until cooked through, 9 to 10 minutes. Let cool for a few minutes, then remove and discard the skin.

7. Cut or break the salmon into pieces to fit the toast. Set each piece of salmon on a piece of toast and top with thyme or dill. If desired, secure the salmon with food picks. Serve warm.

SERVES 8.

Preparation Time: 15 min.
Cooking Time: 20 min.

CHEF'S NOTES

DO FIRST:

Remove any bones from the salmon: A small pair of needle-nose pliers reserved for kitchen use makes this job easier.

VARIATION:

Grill the fish: Place it in a fine-mesh basket and grill for about 10 minutes (cover the grill and close the bottom vents for more even cooking).

KITCHEN TRICK:

At the fish market, ask for salmon tail; it's less fatty than flesh nearer the head and tends to have fewer bones.

MAKE-AHEAD TIP:

Make the toast a day ahead and store it in a tightly covered container.

NUTRITION AT A GLANCE

PER SERVING:

Calories 134
Fat . . . . 5.1 g. (34% of cal.)
Sat. fat . . . . . 0.9 g. (6% of cal.)
Cholesterol . . . . 39 mg.
Sodium . . . . 108 mg.

SWEET POTATO HORS D'OEUVRES

Here's an intriguing variation on party chips. These tasty rounds are actually vitamin A–rich sweets, baked until lightly browned and tender. Complement their subtle flavor with a bold low-fat topping, such as piquant horseradish or creamy pimento.

Sweet Potato Hors d'Oeuvres

½ cup dry-curd cottage cheese

½ cup crumbled farmer's cheese

1 tablespoon minced fresh dill

2 teaspoons prepared horseradish

¼ cup chopped pimento

1 tablespoon minced fresh basil

1 large orange sweet potato

1–2 large yellow sweet potatoes

1½ teaspoons olive oil

Sliced pimentos and herb sprigs

1. In a food processor, blend the cottage cheese and farmer's cheese until smooth. Transfer half the mixture to a small bowl; stir in the dill and horseradish. Set aside.

2. Add the chopped pimentos and basil to the remaining cheese in the food processor. Process until smooth. Transfer to a small bowl and set aside.

3. If desired, peel the sweet potatoes. Cut crosswise into ¼'' slices. Coat a jelly-roll pan with no-stick spray. Add the sweet potatoes and oil. Coat the potatoes well on all sides. Place in a single layer in the pan.

4. Bake at 400° for 15 minutes. Flip the pieces and bake another 10 minutes, or until the rounds are tender and lightly browned but still hold their shape.

5. Serve the chips warm or at room temperature topped with the cheese spreads and pieces of pimentos or herbs.

SERVES 6.

Preparation Time: 10 min.
Cooking Time: 25 min.

CHEF'S NOTES

PRESENTATION:

For the most attractive presentation, mix and match toppings. Try the pimento cheese on the yellow potatoes and garnish with herbs. Put the horseradish spread on the orange potatoes and top with pieces of pimento (cut into decorative shapes with tiny canapé cutters).

VARIATIONS:

Replace the cheese spreads with layers of nonfat yogurt cheese, sliced jalapeño peppers and mild salsa. Or use one of the spreads from page 7.

NUTRITION AT A GLANCE

PER SERVING:

Calories 85
Fat . . . . 2.4 g. (25% of cal.)
Sat. fat . . . . . 0.2 g. (2% of cal.)
Cholesterol . . . . 1 mg.
Sodium . . . . 36 mg.

SPICY RICE BITES

These mini-timbales are an attractive addition to party buffets. Made with two kinds of rice, they're satisfying little mouthfuls. Better yet, they're super-low in fat, with no cholesterol and only 31 calories apiece.

SPICY RICE BITES

- **1 tablespoon unbleached flour**
- **1 cup skim milk**
- **½ cup fat-free egg substitute**
- **2 tablespoons snipped chives**
- **½ teaspoon dried thyme**
- **½ teaspoon dried marjoram**
- **½ teaspoon hot-pepper sauce**
- **2 tablespoons Dijon or coarse mustard**
- **1 cup cooked long-grain white rice**
- **1 cup cooked wild rice**
- **1 jar (3–4 ounces) pimentos**
- **½ cup nonfat yogurt**
- **½ cup nonfat or low-fat sour cream**
- **Lettuce, kale or spinach leaves**

1. Place the flour in a 2-quart saucepan. Gradually whisk in the milk until smooth. Whisk over medium heat until thickened, about 5 minutes.

2. Remove from the heat and whisk in the egg, chives, thyme, marjoram, hot-pepper sauce and 1 tablespoon of the mustard. Fold in the white rice and wild rice.

3. Coat 24 small muffin cups (about 1¾'') with no-stick spray. Spoon the rice mixture into the cups, filling them almost to the top. Place the muffin tins in a broiler pan. Add enough hot water to the pan to come about two-thirds of the way up the outside of the muffin tins. Bake at 400° for 20 minutes.

4. Remove the tins from the water and let cool for 5 minutes on wire racks. Run a knife around the edge of each rice hors d'oeuvre to loosen and remove from the pans.

5. While the rice hors d'oeuvres are baking, drain the pimentos and pat dry with paper towels. Cut into decorative shapes with a knife or small canapé cutters.

6. In a small bowl, whisk together the yogurt, sour cream and the remaining 1 tablespoon mustard.

7. Line a platter with the lettuce, kale or spinach. Place the hors d'oeuvres, upside down, on the plate. Decorate with the pimentos. Serve the mustard sauce as a dipping sauce or spoon a dollop on each hors d'oeuvre.

MAKES 24.

Preparation Time: 15 min.
Cooking Time: 25 min.

CHEF'S NOTES

DO FIRST:
Cook the rice: Start with about ½ cup each of white and wild rice. Cook the white rice for about 20 minutes, the wild for about 35. For best results, fluff the rice and chill before measuring and proceeding with the timbales.

VARIATIONS:
You may substitute brown rice for either the white or wild rice. You may use other seasonings, such as basil, oregano, sage or coriander. You may also replace the pimento garnish with small cooked shrimp, tiny olives or whole fresh herb leaves.

NUTRITION AT A GLANCE

PER TIMBALE:

Calories	31
Fat	0.1 g. (3% of cal.)
Sat. fat	0 g.
Cholesterol	0 mg.
Sodium	37 mg.

TUNA TAPÉNADE

Albacore tuna is a good source of heart-healthy omega-3 fatty acids. This Mediterranean appetizer pairs the fish with low-cal cottage cheese, fresh herbs and a little olive oil to produce a very rich-tasting but slimming dip. Serve with high-fiber vegetables.

Tuna Tapénade

- 6½ ounces water-packed albacore tuna, well-drained
- ½ cup dry-curd cottage cheese
- 2 tablespoons lemon juice
- 2 tablespoons nonfat mayonnaise
- 1 tablespoon olive oil
- 1 tablespoon minced fresh parsley
- 1 tablespoon minced fresh tarragon
- 1 teaspoon Dijon mustard
- 8 ounces carrot sticks
- 8 ounces broccoli florets or asparagus spears
- 8 ounces celery sticks or radish slices
- 2 Belgian endive or radicchio, separated into leaves
- 1 pint cherry tomatoes (optional)

1. In a food processor or blender, blend the tuna, cottage cheese, lemon juice, mayonnaise, oil, parsley, tarragon and mustard until smooth. Stop and scrape down the sides of the container as necessary. Transfer to a small serving bowl and chill until needed.

2. Steam the carrots and broccoli or asparagus until just crisp-tender, about 5 minutes; do not overcook. Transfer to a large platter and refrigerate until chilled, about 30 minutes.

3. To serve, arrange the carrots, broccoli or asparagus, celery or radish slices, endive or radicchio and tomatoes on the platter. Use to dip in the tuna mixture.

SERVES 8.

Preparation Time: 10 min. + standing time
Cooking Time: 5 min.

CHEF'S NOTES

VARIATIONS:

Replace the tuna with canned salmon. Use any other vegetables, such as whole button mushrooms, cauliflower florets, zucchini strips or pepper slices. Or spread the dip on croutons.

MICROWAVE OPTION:

You may cook the carrots and broccoli in the microwave. Place in separate glass pie plates. Arrange the broccoli with the tender florets facing toward the center. Cover each plate with vented plastic wrap. Microwave separately 3 to 4 minutes.

NUTRITION AT A GLANCE

PER SERVING:

Calories 91
Fat . . . . . . 2.5 g. (25% of cal.)
Sat. fat . . . . . 0.4 g. (4% of cal.)
Cholesterol . . . . 9 mg.
Sodium . . . . 139 mg.

CALIFORNIA DIPS AND CHIPS

Black beans and avocados are an excellent combo—as a source of both great taste and dietary fiber. High-fiber foods are essential to digestive health. They also help control high cholesterol and protect against certain types of cancer.

Appetizers and Hors d'Oeuvres

CALIFORNIA DIPS AND CHIPS

GUACAMOLE

- **1 cup chopped or coarsely mashed ripe avocado**
- **1 cup peeled, seeded and diced tomato**
- **¼ cup light sour cream or nonfat yogurt**
- **¼ cup minced scallions**
- **1-3 tablespoons minced fresh coriander**
- **2 teaspoons lime juice**
- **1-3 teaspoons chili powder**
- **1 clove garlic, minced**
- **1-2 sweet red, green or yellow peppers, halved and seeded**

SPICY BLACK BEAN DIP

- **1½ cups cooked black beans**
- **¼ cup minced red onion**
- **2-4 tablespoons lime juice**
- **2-4 tablespoons chopped fresh coriander**
- **1 clove garlic, minced**
- **⅛-¼ teaspoon hot-pepper sauce**
- **1-2 tablespoons water or defatted chicken stock (optional)**
- **1-2 yellow peppers, halved and seeded**

TORTILLA CHIPS

- **8 flour tortillas**
- **1 tablespoon oil**

1. *To make the guacamole:* In a large bowl, mix the avocado, tomatoes, sour cream or yogurt, scallions, coriander, lime juice, chili powder and garlic until blended but not smooth.

2. Spoon the guacamole into the pepper halves for serving.

3. *To make the spicy black bean dip:* In a food processor, mix the beans, onions, lime juice, coriander, garlic and hot-pepper sauce with on/off turns until well-combined but not smooth. If the dip is very thick, thin it with a little water or stock.

4. Spoon the dip into the pepper halves for serving.

5. *To make the tortilla chips:* Brush the tortillas with the oil. Cut each into 12 wedges. Bake in a single layer on cookie sheets at 400° for 5 to 6 minutes, or until crisp and beginning to brown at the edges. Serve with guacamole and bean dip.

SERVES 12.

Preparation Time: 15 min.
Cooking Time: 6 min.

CHEF'S NOTES

■ ■ ■ ■ ■ ■ ■ ■ ■

DO FIRST:
Cook the beans (see page 354); start with about ¾ cup dried black beans. If using canned beans, rinse well to remove excess sodium.

■

NUTRI-NOTE:
When most of the dips have been scooped from the pepper halves, cut up the peppers and eat them with the remainder. They're much too high in vitamins to simply be discarded.

NUTRITION AT A GLANCE ▬▬

PER SERVING:

Calories	151
Fat	6.5 g. (39% of cal.)
Sat. fat	0.6 g. (4% of cal.)
Cholesterol	0 mg.
Sodium	10 mg.

PARTY PIZZAS

These mini-pizzas are just the right size for party hors d'oeuvres. And they're quite easy to make. The homemade dough takes only a few minutes. And the vitamin-rich toppings can be prepared in the short time that the dough needs to "rest."

PARTY PIZZAS

PIZZAS

1 tablespoon quick-rising active dry yeast	**¼ cup rye flour (optional)**
1⅓ cups warm water (115°)	**2–3 cups unbleached flour**
1 tablespoon olive oil	**1–2 tablespoons cornmeal (optional)**
1 teaspoon salt (optional)	**Pepper Topping (below)**
1 cup whole wheat flour	**Broccoli Topping (below)**

1. In a large bowl, mix the yeast with the water. Set aside for a few minutes to dissolve. Stir in the oil and salt. Add the whole wheat flour and rye flour. Stir in enough of the unbleached flour to make a kneadable dough. On a lightly floured surface, knead until smooth and elastic, about 10 minutes. Divide into 16 pieces. Cover and let rest for 15 minutes.

2. Preheat the oven to 450°. Form the pieces into small pizzas about 4″ in diameter. Coat 2 large cookie sheets with no-stick spray. Sprinkle lightly with the cornmeal. Place the pizzas on the sheets. Top 8 with the pepper topping and 8 with the broccoli topping.

3. Bake for 10 to 12 minutes, or until the crusts are browned.

SERVES 16.

Preparation Time: 40 min.
Cooking Time: 12 min.

PEPPER TOPPING

2 teaspoons olive oil	**3 ounces part-skim mozzarella cheese, shredded**
1 clove garlic, minced	**1 cup sliced canned roasted peppers**
2 Italian tomatoes, thinly sliced	**¼ cup sliced black olives**
1 tablespoon minced fresh oregano	

1. In a small cup, combine the oil and garlic. Brush over 8 of the pizza crusts. Top with the tomatoes, oregano, mozzarella, peppers and olives.

Preparation Time: 5 min.

BROCCOLI TOPPING

1 cup sliced or diced onions	**2–3 cups small broccoli florets, lightly steamed**
1 teaspoon olive oil	**1 cup shredded reduced-fat Cheddar cheese**
1 cup nonfat sour cream	
1 teaspoon minced fresh dill	

1. In a small no-stick frying pan over low heat, cook the onions in the oil until soft. Stir in the sour cream and dill. Spread over 8 of the pizza crusts, leaving a ⅜″ border. Top with the broccoli and Cheddar.

Preparation Time: 5 min.
Cooking Time: 10 min.

CHEF'S NOTES

■ ■ ■ ■ ■ ■ ■ ■

DO FIRST:
Steam the broccoli for 5 to 8 minutes.

■

VARIATIONS:
Make two large pizzas (bake for 20 minutes) or eight medium ones (bake for 12 to 15 minutes).

NUTRITION AT A GLANCE ▬▬

PER SERVING:

PEPPER PIZZA
Calories 149
Fat . . . . . . 4.6 g. (19% of cal.)
Sat. fat . . . . .1.5 g. (9% of cal.)
Cholesterol . . . . .6 mg.
Sodium . . . . .67 mg.

BROCCOLI PIZZA
Calories 164
Fat . . . . . . 3.4 g. (19% of cal.)
Sat. fat . . . . .0.3 g. (2% of cal.)
Cholesterol . . . . .8 mg.
Sodium . . . . .253 mg.

MINI EGG FO YONGS

You'll love these healthy versions of classic Chinese omelets. They're made with cholesterol-free egg whites and a wide variety of crunchy, fiber-filled vegetables. Make all three kinds for an interesting array of low-fat, low-cal party hors d'oeuvres.

MINI EGG FOO YONGS

GARDEN FOO YONGS

- **4 egg whites**
- **1 cup finely chopped mushrooms**
- **½ cup bean sprouts, chopped**
- **½ cup diced snow peas**
- **⅓ cup shredded carrot**
- **1 scallion, thinly sliced**
- **½ teaspoon minced fresh ginger**
- **¼ teaspoon ground black pepper**

1. In a medium bowl, beat the egg whites with a fork until frothy. Add the mushrooms, sprouts, peas, carrots, scallions, ginger and pepper.

2. Coat a no-stick frying pan with no-stick spray and warm over medium heat. Drop small rounded tablespoons of the egg mixture into the pan and cook until browned underneath. Flip and cook until just set.

Preparation Time: 10 min.
Cooking Time: 10 min.

BROCCOLI FOO YONGS

- **4 egg whites**
- **½ cup finely chopped broccoli**
- **½ cup chopped mushrooms**
- **½ cup small cooked shrimp, chopped**
- **½ cup diced sweet red pepper**
- **⅓ cup bean sprouts, chopped**

1. In a medium bowl, beat the egg whites with a fork until frothy. Add the broccoli, mushrooms, shrimp, peppers and sprouts. Cook as above.

Preparation Time: 10 min.
Cooking Time: 10 min.

CABBAGE FOO YONGS

- **4 egg whites**
- **1 cup shredded red cabbage**
- **⅔ cup bean sprouts, chopped**
- **¼ cup diced green pepper**
- **¼ teaspoon minced fresh ginger**
- **¼ teaspoon ground black pepper**

1. In a medium bowl, beat the egg whites with a fork until frothy. Add the cabbage, sprouts, green peppers, ginger and black pepper. Cook as above.

Preparation Time: 10 min.
Cooking Time: 10 min.

EACH RECIPE MAKES ABOUT 18.

CHEF'S NOTES

PRESENTATION:
Arrange on bright leafy greens, such as kale or romaine lettuce. If desired, sprinkle with toasted sesame seeds and garnish with blanched snow peas.

ACCOMPANIMENT:
Serve with Foo Yong Sauce: In a 1-quart saucepan, dissolve 2 tablespoons cornstarch in 2 tablespoons water. Stir in 1 cup chicken stock, 1 tablespoon reduced-sodium soy sauce, 2 teaspoons vinegar and 2 teaspoons honey. Stir over medium heat until thickened. Makes 1¼ cups.

MICROWAVE OPTION:
You may reheat leftover Egg Foo Yongs in the microwave. Four will take about 30 seconds.

NUTRITION AT A GLANCE

PER SERVING (1 OF EACH):

Calories 24
Fat . . . . 0.2 g. (8% of cal.)
Sat. fat . . . . 0 g.
Cholesterol . . . . 7 mg.
Sodium . . . . 48 mg.

CHILLED SCALLOP COINS

This lean appetizer is perfect for *everyone.* It's light on calories and cholesterol but high in infection-fighting vitamins A and C. And the low-fat scallops and high-fiber vegetables are the kind of foods doctors recommend for diabetics.

CHILLED SCALLOP COINS

12 ounces sea scallops
3 tablespoons defatted chicken stock
½ teaspoon grated fresh ginger
2 cloves garlic, minced
4 ounces snow peas

1 teaspoon cornstarch
1 sweet red or yellow pepper, slivered
1 tablespoon rice-wine vinegar
Pinch of grated orange rind

1. Slice the scallops crosswise to make coin shapes about ⅜″ thick.

2. In a large bowl combine the stock, ginger and garlic. Add the scallops and toss to coat. Let stand for 15 minutes.

3. Prepare the snow peas by removing their strings and cutting the pods into thirds on the diagonal or into other decorative shapes. Set them in a colander and pour 1 quart of boiling water over them. Let drain.

4. Drain the scallops, reserving the liquid.

5. Coat a large no-stick frying pan with no-stick spray. Heat the pan and sauté the scallops for 2 minutes. Add the peas and toss to combine.

6. In a cup combine the reserved liquid with the cornstarch. Pour over the scallops. Cook over high heat, constantly tossing and turning the mixture, until the sauce is shiny and thick, about 1 minute.

7. Transfer to a bowl, cover loosely and refrigerate until chilled.

8. Just before serving, add the peppers, vinegar and orange rind.

SERVES 4.

Preparation Time: 25 min.
Cooking Time: 5 min.

CHEF'S NOTES

PRESENTATION:
Serve as an appetizer course with an oriental dinner or as a party dish on a buffet table.

VARIATION:
Replace the scallops with shrimp or firm-fleshed fish such as monkfish, cut into bite-size pieces.

NUTRI-NOTE:
Red peppers, which are just green peppers that have ripened fully, contain much more vitamin A than green or even yellow ones.

KITCHEN TRICK:
If you don't have a special ginger grater, use a nutmeg grater or the fine holes of a standard kitchen grater.

NUTRITION AT A GLANCE

PER SERVING:
Calories 98
Fat . . . . .0.8 g. (8% of cal.)
Sat. fat . . . . .0.1 g. (1% of cal.)
Cholesterol . . . . .28 mg.
Sodium . . . . .143 mg.

BUCKWHEAT CRÊPES WITH ASPARAGUS

The rich, nutty flavor of buckwheat shines through in these tasty, low-fat crêpes. Scientists say buckwheat is digested more slowly than many other carbohydrates, which keeps blood-sugar levels on an even keel. In practical terms, that means a meal containing buckwheat leaves you feeling full longer.

BUCKWHEAT CRÊPES WITH ASPARAGUS

BUCKWHEAT CRÊPES
- 1½ cups low-fat milk
- ¼ cup fat-free egg substitute or 1 egg
- 2 tablespoons oil
- ½ teaspoon honey
- ½ cup buckwheat flour
- ½ cup unbleached flour

ASPARAGUS FILLING
- ½ clove garlic
- 36 asparagus spears
- 2 teaspoons olive oil
- ⅛ teaspoon ground black pepper
- 1 cup low-fat cottage cheese
- ½ cup nonfat yogurt
- 2 tablespoons snipped chives
- Whole chives (optional)

1. *To make the buckwheat crêpes:* In a medium bowl whisk together the milk, eggs, oil and honey.

2. Sift together the buckwheat flour and the unbleached flour. Gradually stir the flour into the liquid ingredients until just blended. Cover the bowl and let stand at room temperature for 2 hours. (This allows the flour particles to swell and soften to produce lighter crêpes.)

3. Coat a small no-stick frying pan with no-stick spray. Heat it over medium heat until a drop of water sizzles and evaporates upon contact.

4. Holding the pan in one hand, ladle about 3 tablespoons of batter into it with the other. Immediately rotate the pan so the batter forms an even circle in the bottom of the pan. Cook until the edges begin to brown and the batter is set, 1 to 2 minutes. Using a rubber spatula, loosen the edges and carefully flip the crêpe. Cook the other side about 45 seconds. Transfer it to a plate. Repeat to make about 18 crêpes.

5. *To make the asparagus filling:* Rub the bottom of a shallow baking dish with the cut side of the garlic. Trim the tough ends off the asparagus. Place the spears in the baking dish and drizzle with the oil. Bake uncovered at 400° for 10 to 12 minutes, stirring at least once, until the asparagus is crisp-tender. Sprinkle with the pepper. Set aside.

6. In a food processor or blender puree the cottage cheese and yogurt until smooth. Transfer to a small bowl and fold in the chives. Place 1 rounded tablespoon of the chive mixture in the center of each crêpe. Spread it out slightly with the back of a spoon. Top with 2 asparagus spears and, if desired, some whole chives. Roll up each crêpe to enclose the spears.

SERVES 9.

Preparation Time: 15 min. + standing time
Cooking Time: 30 min.

CHEF'S NOTES

VARIATIONS:
Make smaller crêpes, about 3'' in diameter, to serve as finger food. Replace the asparagus with steamed broccoli spears, long carrot sticks or other crisp-tender vegetables. For sweet crêpes, add honey to the filling and replace the chives with cinnamon or nutmeg. Fill the crêpes with sautéed apple slices, fresh berries or peach slices.

NUTRI-NOTE:
Buckwheat flour comes in light and dark varieties. The dark, which contains more of the outer bran, has a stronger flavor and contains more protein and various other nutrients.

KITCHEN TRICK:
If you make the crêpes ahead, layer them between squares of waxed paper so they won't stick together.

NUTRITION AT A GLANCE

PER SERVING:

Calories	131
Fat	5.1 g. (35% of cal.)
Sat. fat	1.1 g. (8% of cal.)
Cholesterol	4 mg.
Sodium	141 mg.

SOUPS AND STEWS

SEAFOOD AND VEGETABLE HARVEST CHOWDER

You won't believe how creamy this chowder is—without the use of half-and-half or heavy cream! That's because 2% milk thickened with a little flour gives it all the rich body you could ask for—and it's a great low-fat way to put bone-building calcium into your diet.

SEAFOOD AND VEGETABLE HARVEST CHOWDER

- **1 pound fresh mussels, washed and debearded**
- **1 cup water**
- **1 cup bottled clam juice**
- **2 teaspoons lemon juice**
- **2 teaspoons minced garlic**
- **2 tablespoons margarine**
- **¼ cup unbleached flour**
- **2 cups low-fat milk**
- **½ cup diced celery**
- **½ cup diced green pepper**
- **½ cup corn**
- **¼ cup diced sweet red pepper**
- **¼ cup diced carrot**
- **4 ounces small shrimp, peeled, deveined and chopped**
- **4 ounces fish fillet, cut into small cubes**
- **1 cup diced cooked red-skinned potato**
- **1 tablespoon minced fresh parsley**
- **¼ teaspoon reduced-sodium soy sauce**
- **¼ teaspoon ground black pepper**
- **Hot-pepper sauce (to taste)**

1. In a large heavy pot or 6-quart Dutch oven, combine the mussels, water, clam juice, lemon juice and garlic. Bring to a boil over medium heat, cover and cook until the mussels open, about 10 minutes.

2. Strain the broth from the mussels and reserve. Remove the mussels from the shells and reserve.

3. Wash and dry the pot. Add the margarine and melt over medium heat. Stir in the flour to make a smooth paste. Whisk in the reserved mussel broth (if there is sandy sediment at the bottom of the broth, be careful not to add it). Whisk in the milk.

4. Whisk over medium-low heat 5 minutes, or until thickened.

5. Add the celery, green peppers, corn, red peppers and carrots. Cook over medium-low heat for 10 to 15 minutes, or until the vegetables are tender.

6. Add the shrimp, fish, potatoes, parsley, soy sauce, black pepper and hot-pepper sauce. Cook for 4 to 5 minutes, or until the fish is opaque. Add the mussels and heat briefly. Serve immediately.

SERVES 4.

Preparation Time: 20 min.
Cooking Time: 45 min.

CHEF'S NOTES

DO FIRST:

Cook the potatoes: Steam small red potatoes until tender.
Peel and devein the shrimp.

ACCOMPANIMENTS:

Generous amounts of seafood and vegetables make this a meal in itself. All you need to add is bread and a simple green salad.

VARIATIONS:

Use clams instead of mussels. Use any variety of white-fleshed fish, such as flounder, cod or haddock.

MICROWAVE OPTION:

Place the diced potatoes in a pie plate or ring pan, sprinkle with water, cover and cook about 2 minutes, or until tender.

NUTRITION AT A GLANCE

PER SERVING:

Calories 281
Fat . . . . 10 g. (32% of cal.)
Sat. fat . . . . . 2.8 g. (9% of cal.)
Cholesterol . . . . 72 mg.
Sodium . . . . 282 mg.

CREAMY MUSSEL SOUP

Mineral-rich mussels are a great seafood that people often overlook. They have iron for protection against anemia, potassium to help prevent strokes and even some zinc for proper wound healing.

CREAMY MUSSEL SOUP

2 pounds fresh mussels, washed and debearded
½ cup fish stock or water
1 piece orange rind (2″ × ½″)
1 thin slice fresh ginger
1 bay leaf
1 clove garlic, crushed
1 sprig fresh basil or flat-leaf parsley
1 scallion

2 teaspoons olive oil
2 teaspoons curry powder
½ teaspoon ground turmeric
1 large russet potato, diced
2½ cups low-fat milk
¼ cup peeled, seeded and diced tomato
Ground black pepper (to taste)

1. Sort the mussels and discard any with shells that are cracked or that won't close tightly when you gently tap them with your finger. Place in a large bowl of cold water and let stand 10 minutes. Drain, pull or cut off the beards and scrub the shells with a brush. Rinse well and drain.

2. In a 3- or 4-quart saucepan, combine the stock or water, orange rind, ginger, bay leaf, garlic and basil or parsley. Chop the white part of the scallion and add to the pan. (Finely chop the green part and reserve for garnish.) Bring the liquid to a hard boil. Cover and simmer 5 minutes. Add the mussels; cover and cook over high heat 3 to 5 minutes, or until all the mussels open.

3. Using tongs, transfer the mussels to a platter and let cool. Discard any that haven't opened. Remove the remaining mussels from their shells and set aside.

4. Line a sieve with cheesecloth and set it over a bowl. Use it to strain the broth left in the pan. Retrieve the rind and mince enough to equal 1 teaspoon. Retrieve the herb sprig and separate it into individual leaves. Set both aside.

5. In a 2-quart saucepan over low heat, warm the oil. Add the curry powder and turmeric. Stir over heat until fragrant, about 1 minute. Add the reserved mussel broth and the potatoes. Bring to a boil, cover and cook over low heat, stirring often, until the potatoes are very tender, about 10 minutes.

6. Using a slotted spoon, transfer the potatoes to the bowl of a food processor. Add half the liquid. Puree the potatoes, then return to the saucepan.

7. Add the milk and tomatoes. Stir in the reserved mussels, rind and herb leaves. Heat, stirring, over low heat just until hot; do not boil. Season with pepper. Ladle into individual bowls and sprinkle with the scallion greens.

SERVES 4.

Preparation Time: 25 min.
Cooking Time: 25 min.

CHEF'S NOTES

VARIATION:
Use other shellfish, such as clams or oysters.

KITCHEN TRICKS:
Buy mussels with tightly closed shells or those that snap shut when tapped — otherwise they're not fresh and alive.

Briefly twist the two shells of every mussel in opposite directions when cleaning to ferret out any shells that are filled with mud.

NUTRITION AT A GLANCE

PER SERVING:

Calories 183
Fat . . . . 5.7 g. (28% of cal.)
Sat. fat . . . . . 1.3 g. (6% of cal.)
Cholesterol . . . . 24 mg.
Sodium . . . . 274 mg.

ORIENTAL SHRIMP SOUP

This light soup is brimming with vegetables, including a nice portion of cabbage. Cabbage is a member of the crucifer family, and studies have suggested that people who eat lots of cruciferous vegetables may reduce their risk of cancer of the gastrointestinal and respiratory tracts. And a super soup like this is a tasty way to enjoy your cabbage.

Oriental shrimp soup

1 teaspoon sesame oil

2 tablespoons minced onion

2 teaspoons minced garlic

1½ teaspoons minced fresh ginger

6 cups defatted chicken stock

1 teaspoon reduced-sodium soy sauce

1 teaspoon lemon juice

½ teaspoon grated lemon rind

1 cup diced Napa cabbage

⅓ cup bean sprouts

¼ cup shredded carrot

¼ cup thinly sliced celery

¼ cup thinly sliced mushrooms

¼ cup diced sweet red pepper

8 ounces small shrimp, peeled, deveined and cooked

1 tablespoon minced fresh coriander

Dash of hot-pepper sauce

1. In a 3-quart saucepan heat the oil over medium heat. Add the onions, garlic and ginger. Cook for 1 minute, stirring; do not brown.

2. Add the stock, soy sauce, lemon juice and lemon rind. Bring to a boil.

3. Add the cabbage, bean sprouts, carrots, celery, mushrooms and peppers. Cook for 1 to 2 minutes.

4. Stir in the shrimp, coriander and hot-pepper sauce. Cook an additional 1 to 2 minutes to heat through.

SERVES 6.

Preparation Time: 25 min.
Cooking Time: 7 min.

CHEF'S NOTES

DO FIRST:

Prepare the shrimp: Peel and devein the shrimp, then cook in water for 5 minutes, until just opaque. Do not overcook the shrimp because they become tough.

ACCOMPANIMENT:

Serve with oven-toasted pita chips. Cut pita pockets into wedges and separate the tops from the bottoms. Very lightly brush the inner surface of each wedge with olive oil. Bake at 375° until just crisp, about 5 minutes.

VARIATIONS:

Substitute any seasonal vegetables. Try bok choy, rutabagas, snow peas, sugar snap peas, turnips, or zucchini.

KITCHEN TRICK:

An easy way to peel garlic is to smash it with the broad side of a cleaver. The peel will slip right off.

NUTRITION AT A GLANCE

PER SERVING:

Calories 93
Fat . . . . .0.9 g. (9% of cal.)
Sat. fat . . . . .0.2 g. (2% of cal.)
Cholesterol . . . . .74 mg.
Sodium . . . . .211 mg.

PORK AND SWEET POTATO STEW

This is our version of a stew popular in South America. It combines lean pork loin with vitamin A-rich sweet potatoes for a hearty main course soup. In addition, the iron and B vitamins in this dish help form the healthy red blood cells so vital for energy and stamina.

Pork and sweet potato stew

12 ounces lean pork loin, cut into ¾" cubes

2 teaspoons olive oil

2 cups diced onion

½ cup thinly sliced carrot

½ cup thinly sliced celery

1 tablespoon minced garlic

2 teaspoons ground cumin

1 can (28 ounces) imported peeled Italian tomatoes, chopped or pureed

1 large sweet potato, cubed

2 tablespoons currants or raisins

2 cups packed chopped escarole

1 tablespoon water

¼ teaspoon ground black pepper

2 tablespoons minced fresh coriander

1. In a Dutch oven over medium heat, brown the pork in the oil, about 10 minutes. Add the onions, carrots, celery and garlic. Cover and cook over low heat for 10 minutes. Stir in the cumin. Cover and cook for 10 minutes, or until the vegetables are tender.

2. Add the tomatoes (with juice), sweet potatoes and currants or raisins. Cover and cook over medium-low heat for 1 to 1½ hours, or until the meat and potatoes are tender.

3. Place the escarole and water in a large no-stick frying pan. Cover and cook over low heat for 12 minutes, or until wilted and almost tender.

4. Stir the escarole (with any pan juices) and pepper into the stew. Cover and simmer for 10 minutes. Serve sprinkled with the coriander.

SERVES 4.

Preparation Time: 25 min.
Cooking Time: 1¼ hr.

CHEF'S NOTES

■ ■ ■ ■ ■ ■ ■ ■

DO FIRST:

Remove any visible fat from the pork. An easy way is to freeze the meat for 20 minutes. Use a paring knife to shave off the solidified fat. Partial freezing will also make cutting the meat easier.

■

ACCOMPANIMENT:

This is pretty much a meal in itself. All it needs is warm rolls or slices of a hearty bread. Try Wild Rice Rolls (page 277) or Golden Grain and Herb Loaves (page 273).

■

VARIATION:

Replace the pork with cubes of veal, lamb or beef. Or use chicken or turkey; reduce the cooking time to 30 minutes.

NUTRITION AT A GLANCE

PER SERVING:

Calories 268
Fat . . . . . . .7.5 g. (25% of cal.)
Sat. fat . . . . .2.4 g. (8% of cal.)
Cholesterol . . . . .47 mg.
Sodium . . . . .101 mg.

ITALIAN MINESTRONE

This no-cholesterol soup is quite light on calories, especially when you consider that it's virtually a meal in itself. The combination of beans and pasta makes it hearty and filling. And the beans have an added benefit: They've been shown to actually help *lower* cholesterol.

ITALIAN MINESTRONE

- ½ **cup coarsely chopped onion**
- ½ **cup coarsely chopped celery**
- ½ **cup coarsely chopped carrot**
- 2 **tablespoons water**
- 1 **tablespoon olive oil**
- 5 **cups defatted beef or chicken stock**
- 1 **can (14 ounces) imported peeled Italian tomatoes**
- 1½ **cups cooked red kidney beans**
- 1 **cup packed chopped escarole**
- ¼ **cup orzo (small rice-shaped pasta)**
- ½ **cup diced zucchini**
- ½ **cup peas**
- ½ **cup thinly sliced (¼″) green beans**
- **Ground black pepper**
- ½ **cup chopped fresh parsley**
- 2 **strips (½″ × 2″) lemon rind**
- 1 **clove garlic, chopped**

1. Combine the onions, celery, carrots, water and oil in a 3-quart saucepan or Dutch oven; stir to blend. Cover and place over low heat to gently cook vegetables until tender but not browned, about 15 minutes.

2. Add the stock, tomatoes (with juice), kidney beans, escarole and orzo. Bring to a boil, stirring occasionally. Then reduce heat to medium low. Simmer uncovered until vegetables and pasta are tender, about 25 minutes.

3. Add the zucchini, peas and green beans. Simmer, partially covered, until vegetables are tender, about 20 minutes. Add black pepper to taste.

4. In a food processor or by hand, finely chop the parsley, lemon rind and garlic together. Stir into the soup for last 5 minutes of cooking.

SERVES 6.

Preparation Time: 20 min.
Cooking Time: 1 hr.

CHEF'S NOTES

DO FIRST:

Cook dried beans or use canned beans (rinse well to remove excess sodium).

ACCOMPANIMENTS:

Serve with a loaf of crusty whole-grain bread and a green salad tossed with grated Parmesan cheese. Have frozen yogurt for dessert.

VARIATIONS:

Use other vegetables, such as Swiss chard, savoy cabbage, lima beans and yellow squash. Use rice instead of pasta.

KITCHEN TRICK:

Use a swivel-bladed potato peeler to remove strips of lemon rind. Be sure to take off only the yellow part, not the underlying bitter white pith.

NUTRITION AT A GLANCE

PER SERVING:

Calories 159
Fat . . . . .4 g. (23% of cal.)
Sat. fat . . . . .0.4 g. (2% of cal.)
Cholesterol . . . . .0 mg.
Sodium . . . . 249 mg.

CURRIED YELLOW SPLIT-PEA SOUP

While this thick and hearty soup is warming you to the bones, it may also be helping your blood pressure. That's because it's low in sodium and high in potassium —a combination that helps reduce high blood pressure.

CURRIED YELLOW SPLIT-PEA SOUP

SOUP

1 cup chopped onion
½ cup chopped celery
1 clove garlic, minced
1 tablespoon water
2 teaspoons olive oil
1 tablespoon curry powder
8 cups water
1 cup dried yellow split peas, sorted and rinsed
1 large carrot
½ cup green peas
½ cup diced sweet red pepper

Pinch of ground black pepper

TOPPING

½ cup low-fat yogurt
¼ cup packed parsley sprigs
¼ cup packed dill sprigs
1 tablespoon chopped onion
Dash of hot-pepper sauce

1. *To make the soup:* Combine the onions, celery, garlic, 1 tablespoon water and oil in a 3- or 4-quart saucepan. Sauté the vegetables over low heat until tender but not browned, about 10 minutes. Add the curry powder; sauté 1 minute.

2. Add 8 cups water, split peas and the carrot (whole). Bring to a boil, reduce heat to medium low and cook uncovered until the split peas are tender and the soup is thickened, about 2 hours. (Add additional liquid if the soup gets too thick.)

3. Lift out the carrot, cool slightly, then dice into ¼″ pieces. Return the carrots to the saucepan.

4. Add the green peas, red peppers and black pepper. Cook uncovered until the vegetables are tender, about 5 minutes.

5. *To make the topping:* In a blender or food processor puree the yogurt, parsley, dill, onions and hot-pepper sauce until smooth.

6. Ladle the soup into shallow bowls and swirl a spoonful of the yogurt mixture in the center of each bowl.

SERVES 8.

Preparation Time: 15 min.
Cooking Time: 2¼ hr.

CHEF'S NOTES

DO FIRST:

Pick through the split peas to remove any stones and other foreign objects that might be mixed in. Then rinse the peas well to remove surface dirt.

VARIATIONS:

Use green split peas or lentils. If desired, add some chopped cooked chicken during the last few minutes of cooking.

MAKE-AHEAD TIP:

Like most bean soups, this one benefits from being made a day ahead. That gives flavors time to meld nicely. Reheat over low heat. If the soup is too thick, add a little stock or water.

NUTRITION AT A GLANCE

PER SERVING:

Calories 148
Fat . . . . 2 g. (12% of cal.)
Sat. fat . . . . . 0.4 g. (2% of cal.)
Cholesterol . . . . 1 mg.
Sodium . . . . 30 mg.

MINTED GREEN-PEA SOUP

With a hefty dose of cholesterol-lowering soluble fiber and little or no fat, cholesterol and sodium, peas do their share to promote heart health. They also contribute cancer protection, thanks to generous amounts of vitamins A and C. And their low-fat, high-fiber makeup can help to control diabetes. So count on easy soups like this to make peas a frequent addition to your diet.

MINTED GREEN-PEA SOUP

4 cups defatted chicken stock

4 ounces boneless skinless chicken breast

½ cup peas

1 cup diced carrot

1 teaspoon minced shallot

1 teaspoon lemon juice

2 teaspoons minced fresh mint or ½ teaspoon dried

1. Combine the stock and chicken in a 2-quart saucepan. Poach over medium-high heat until the chicken is cooked through, about 5 minutes. Remove from the stock with a slotted spoon; reserve the stock. Dice the chicken.

2. In a blender puree ¼ cup of the peas with ½ cup of the stock.

3. Add the carrots, shallots and lemon juice to the stock in the saucepan. Bring to a boil and cook for 2 to 3 minutes.

4. Add the remaining ¼ cup peas, chicken and mint. Heat briefly. Stir in pureed peas.

SERVES 4.

Preparation Time: 10 min.
Cooking Time: 10 min.

CHEF'S NOTES

DO FIRST:
If using fresh peas, shell them. Count on 1 pound of pods to yield 1 cup of shelled peas.

ACCOMPANIMENTS:
Sprinkle the soup with whole-grain croutons. To make your own, lightly brush bread slices with a mixture of olive oil and your choice of dried herbs. Cut the bread into cubes and bake at 300°, stirring often, until crisp, 10 to 20 minutes.

VARIATION:
Add ¼ cup of cooked rice to the soup.

MAKE-AHEAD TIP:
Prepare through step 3. Reheat and add remaining ingredients just before serving.

NUTRITION AT A GLANCE

PER SERVING:
Calories 92
Fat . . . . . . .1.3 g. (13% of cal.)
Sat. fat . . . . .0.1 g. (1% of cal.)
Cholesterol . . . . .17 mg.
Sodium . . . . .54 mg.

GINGERED CARROT SOUP

This soup is a powerhouse of vitamin A. In fact, one serving contains almost five times the RDA! That's a boon for your eyes because this nutrient is vital for sharp vision, especially at night. And older folks are particularly well advised to get an adequate intake: Daily consumption of high-A produce may lower the risk of macular degeneration.

GINGERED CARROT SOUP

- **2 cups defatted chicken stock**
- **1 pound carrots, chopped**
- **1 potato, cubed**
- **½ cup orange juice**
- **¼ cup chopped onion**
- **1 tablespoon grated fresh ginger**
- **1 teaspoon grated orange rind**
- **1 cup buttermilk**
- **1 cup nonfat yogurt**
- **2 tablespoons honey**
- **½ teaspoon reduced-sodium soy sauce**
- **¼ teaspoon ground cinnamon**
- **Pinch of ground red pepper**

1. In a 3-quart saucepan combine the stock, carrots, potatoes, orange juice, onions, ginger and orange rind. Cover and cook over medium-high heat until the carrots and potatoes are tender, about 25 minutes. Let cool 5 minutes.

2. Transfer half of the soup to a blender. Add half of the buttermilk and half of the yogurt. Puree until smooth. Transfer to a serving bowl or saucepan. Repeat with remaining soup, buttermilk and yogurt.

3. Stir in the honey, soy sauce, cinnamon and pepper.

SERVES 6.

Preparation Time: 15 min.
Cooking Time: 25 min.

CHEF'S NOTES

ACCOMPANIMENT:
Serve with toasted sesame pitas.

VARIATIONS:
Replace the carrots with chunks of pumpkin or winter squash. Replace the cinnamon with cardamom or nutmeg. For a dairy-free soup replace the buttermilk with additional stock or orange juice.

NUTRI-NOTE:
If you garden, be aware that A-Plus Hybrid carrots have 75% more carotene (the plant form of vitamin A) than other varieties. A single carrot contains a day's supply of vitamin A.

MICROWAVE OPTION:
Place the stock, vegetables, orange juice, ginger and orange rind in a 3-quart casserole. Cook uncovered on full power until the vegetables are tender, about 10 minutes.

NUTRITION AT A GLANCE

PER SERVING:
Calories 136
Fat . . . . .1.1 g. (7% of cal.)
Sat. fat . . . . .0.3 g. (2% of cal.)
Cholesterol . . . . .2 mg.
Sodium . . . . .144 mg.

FRENCH ONION SOUP

Onions are excellent health boosters, helping to lower cholesterol and maybe even prevent dangerous blood clots. One way to increase your consumption of these noteworthy vegetables is with onion soup. This tasty version is low in saturated fat and calories.

FRENCH ONION SOUP

6 cups thinly sliced onion
1 tablespoon olive oil
2 tablespoons whole wheat flour
2 cups defatted beef stock
2 cups defatted chicken stock
1 bay leaf
½ teaspoon dried thyme
¼ teaspoon ground black pepper
Hot-pepper sauce (to taste)
4 slices French bread
¼ cup minced fresh parsley
4 teaspoons grated Parmesan cheese

1. In a 3-quart saucepan, combine the onions and oil. Mix well, cover and cook over medium-low heat until soft, about 15 minutes.

2. Uncover the pan and raise the heat to medium. Cook, stirring every 2 to 3 minutes, until the onions are golden and almost caramel colored, about 30 minutes. Make sure to stir often so the onions slowly caramelize rather than scorch.

3. Sprinkle with the flour and stir to combine. Add the beef and chicken stocks. Stir well to smooth out the lumps. Add the bay leaf, thyme, pepper and hot-pepper sauce.

4. Cover the pan and simmer over medium-low heat for 30 minutes. Stir occasionally to prevent sticking. Remove the bay leaf before serving.

5. *To make the croutons:* While the soup is cooking, place the bread on a cookie sheet and bake at 275° for 15 minutes. Turn the slices over and bake for 15 minutes more. Set aside.

6. To serve, ladle the soup into individual bowls. Sprinkle with the parsley. Top each serving with a crouton and a teaspoon of Parmesan.

SERVES 4.

Preparation Time: 15 min.
Cooking Time: 1 ¼ hr.

CHEF'S NOTES

MICROWAVE OPTION:

Save time by doing step 1 in the microwave. Place the onions in a large glass casserole dish. Add the oil, mix well and cover the dish with a lid or vented plastic wrap. Cook on high for 3 minutes. Stir and cook another 3 minutes, until the onions are softened.

KITCHEN TRICKS:

Don't cry when chopping onions: Refrigerate onions for several hours before cutting, to minimize the pungent juices that cause tears. Or use a very sharp knife to avoid crushing the flesh and releasing the juices; dip the knife in ice water as you work to wash away any juices.

NUTRITION AT A GLANCE

PER SERVING:

Calories 205
Fat . . . . . . .5.7 g. (25% of cal.)
Sat. fat . . . . . .1 g. (4% of cal.)
Cholesterol . . . . .2 mg.
Sodium . . . . .137 mg.

HEARTY RED CABBAGE SOUP

Cabbage is one of the cancer-preventing cruciferous vegetables. Soup is an excellent way to get this super vegetable into your diet. And this particular soup is nice and hearty—just the thing for cold-weather lunches.

HEARTY RED CABBAGE SOUP

- **1 tablespoon olive oil**
- **1 large onion, thinly sliced**
- **4 cloves garlic, chopped**
- **1 pound red cabbage, thinly sliced**
- **4 stalks celery, thinly sliced**
- **¼ cup vinegar**
- **1 tablespoon caraway seeds**
- **6 cups defatted chicken stock**
- **½ cup tomato puree**
- **1 teaspoon ground black pepper**
- **½ teaspoon dried thyme**
- **1 bay leaf**
- **1½ cups cooked Great Northern beans**
- **¼ cup nonfat yogurt or low-fat sour cream**
- **½ cup thinly sliced scallions**

1. Warm the oil in a 4-quart pot over medium heat. Add the onions and garlic. Stir, cover the pot and cook for 10 minutes, stirring frequently.

2. Add the cabbage, celery, vinegar and caraway seeds. Cover and cook for 10 minutes, stirring frequently.

3. Add the stock, tomato puree, pepper, thyme and bay leaf. Cover and simmer for 20 minutes. Remove bay leaf. Stir in the beans and heat through. To serve, add a dollop of yogurt or sour cream and sprinkle with the scallions.

SERVES 6.

Preparation Time: 20 min.
Cooking Time: 40 min.

CHEF'S NOTES

■ ■ ■ ■ ■ ■ ■ ■ ■ ■

DO FIRST:
If using dried beans, soak them for several hours or overnight, then cook until tender; drain well. If using canned beans, rinse them well in a strainer to remove excess sodium.

■

ACCOMPANIMENTS:
Serve with corn bread and a green salad for a hearty lunch or light dinner.

■

NUTRI-NOTE:
To safeguard nutrients, don't wash the cabbage or remove the outer leaves until cooking time.

■

MAKE-AHEAD TIP:
This soup keeps well and can be stored in the refrigerator for five days.

NUTRITION AT A GLANCE ▬▬

PER SERVING:

Calories 165
Fat . . . . . . .4.5 g. (25% of cal.)
Sat. fat . . . . .0.6 g. (3% of cal.)
Cholesterol . . . . .0 mg.
Sodium . . . . .128 mg.

POTATO-PARSLEY SOUP

What more could you ask from such a simple soup? This low-cal dish supplies commendable amounts of blood-building iron and infection-fighting vitamin C. And studies have shown that clear, vegetable-based soups like this can help dieters lose weight.

POTATO-PARSLEY SOUP

- **1 leek**
- **2 teaspoons olive oil**
- **2 cloves garlic, minced**
- **4 cups defatted chicken stock**
- **3 cups diced red potato**
- **½–1 cup minced fresh parsley**
- **⅛ teaspoon grated nutmeg**
- **2 tablespoons snipped chives**

1. Remove and discard the tough green leaves and root end of the leek. Halve the leek lengthwise and wash it well to remove any dirt from between the layers. Shake dry and chop finely.

2. Heat a 3-quart saucepan on medium high and add the oil. Add the leeks and sauté for 1 minute. Add the garlic and continue to sauté until the leeks are tender and fragrant, about 2 minutes. Don't let the garlic brown.

3. Add the stock and potatoes. Bring to a boil. Reduce the heat to low and simmer the soup until the potatoes are tender, about 10 minutes. Stir in the parsley and nutmeg. Serve sprinkled with the chives.

SERVES 4.

Preparation Time: 15 min.
Cooking Time: 15 min.

CHEF'S NOTES

PRESENTATION:
If desired, serve the soup topped with herb- or garlic-flavored croutons.

ACCOMPANIMENT:
This soup makes a great first course. Try it as a prelude to roast chicken or grilled fish.

VARIATIONS:
Substitute watercress or shredded spinach for the parsley.

KITCHEN TRICK:
Another way to rid the leek of sand that often lurks between the layers is to mince it, then place the pieces in a strainer. Rinse well. Pat the pieces dry in a paper towel before sautéing.

NUTRITION AT A GLANCE

PER SERVING:
Calories 141
Fat . . . . . . .3.9 g. (19% of cal.)
Sat. fat . . . . .0.3 g. (2% of cal.)
Cholesterol . . . . .0 mg.
Sodium . . . . .96 mg.

CLEAR SPINACH AND TOMATO SOUP

This delicious Mediterranean soup is cholesterol-free and has only 116 calories per serving. Yet it's nice and filling, thanks to the pasta in it. The spinach and tomatoes contribute lots of immunity-building vitamin C.

CLEAR SPINACH AND TOMATO SOUP

- **1 onion, diced**
- **2 teaspoons minced garlic**
- **1 tablespoon olive oil**
- **4 cups defatted chicken stock**
- **½ cup orzo or other tiny pasta**
- **1 pound spinach, chopped into bite-size pieces**
- **3 tomatoes, peeled, seeded and diced**
- **1 tablespoon minced fresh basil or 1½ teaspoons dried**
- **½ teaspoon ground black pepper**
- **Grated Parmesan cheese (optional)**

1. In a 3-quart saucepan over medium heat, sauté the onions and garlic in the oil for 3 minutes, or until the onions look translucent.

2. Add the stock and bring to a boil. Reduce the heat to medium low, add the pasta and simmer for 10 minutes.

3. Stir in the spinach and tomatoes. Simmer for 5 minutes. Stir in the basil and pepper. Serve sprinkled with the Parmesan.

SERVES 6.

Preparation Time: 20 min.
Cooking Time: 20 min.

CHEF'S NOTES

DO FIRST:

Prepare the tomatoes: Drop ripe, room-temperature tomatoes into boiling water; let them stand about 30 seconds. (If the tomatoes are cold or not perfectly ripe, let them remain in the water longer.) Remove and rinse under cold water. Use a sharp knife to remove the peels. Cut each tomato in half crosswise and gently squeeze to remove the seeds and excess juice.

Prepare the spinach: In a large sink of cold water, wash spinach to remove any sand or other grit. Discard any large stems. Place in a wire basket or large towel and shake off most of the water. Tear into pieces or chop with a knife.

NUTRITION AT A GLANCE

PER SERVING:

Calories 116
Fat . . . . 3.8 g. (29% of cal.)
Sat. fat . . . . . 0.4 g. (3% of cal.)
Cholesterol . . . . 0 mg.
Sodium . . . . 119 mg.

WHITE BEAN AND CORN SOUP

A serving of this hearty, delicious soup has only 203 calories. And it's brimming with fiber: There's a hefty 5.4 grams in every bowlful—as much as in two bran muffins. That makes it an excellent choice for promoting good digestive health.

WHITE BEAN AND CORN SOUP

1 cup dried navy beans, soaked overnight
1 cup chopped onion
1 teaspoon oil
2 cloves garlic, minced
6 cups defatted chicken stock
½ cup minced carrot

1 bay leaf
1 cup corn
½ cup peeled, seeded and diced tomato
2 tablespoons chopped fresh basil or parsley
¼ teaspoon ground black pepper

1. Drain the beans and set aside.

2. In a 3-quart saucepan over low heat, sauté the onions in the oil, stirring often, until golden, about 10 minutes. Add the garlic; sauté for 1 minute.

3. Add the stock, carrots, bay leaf and beans. Bring to a boil. Reduce the heat and simmer for 2 to 2½ hours, or until the beans are tender.

4. Add the corn and tomatoes. Cook for 15 minutes.

5. Season with the basil or parsley and pepper. Discard the bay leaf.

SERVES 6.

Preparation Time: 15 min. + standing time
Cooking Time: 3 hr.

CHEF'S NOTES

DO FIRST:

Soak the beans. (Or use 3 cups rinsed and drained canned beans. Because these beans are already cooked, you should add them to the soup in step 4 along with the corn.)

INGREDIENTS NOTE:

In season, fresh corn is best. But you may also use frozen or canned kernels. You may also use canned tomatoes.

MICROWAVE OPTION:

To quick-soak dried beans: Place in a 1-quart casserole and cover with 2'' cold water. Microwave on high for 15 minutes, or until the beans have swelled. Drain; proceed with the recipe.

NUTRITION AT A GLANCE

PER SERVING:

Calories 203
Fat . . . . .3 g. (13% of cal.)
Sat. fat . . . . .0.2 g. (1% of cal.)
Cholesterol . . . . .0 mg.
Sodium . . . . .94 mg.

ORANGE-SCENTED BEET SOUP

This delicious soup is a variation on old-fashioned borscht. But it's much lower in fat, calories and cholesterol because there's no sour cream or beef. The beets, potatoes and cabbage contribute a good helping of dietary fiber—a definite boon to weight-watchers.

ORANGE-SCENTED BEET SOUP

1 large onion, diced
1 teaspoon minced garlic
2 teaspoons corn oil
1 strip orange rind (½" × 3")
½–2 teaspoons caraway seed or dried dill
4 cups defatted chicken or beef stock
1 bay leaf
1–3 cups very thinly shredded cabbage
2 cups diced cooked red beet
1 cup diced red potato
1 teaspoon honey
½ teaspoon ground black pepper
Nonfat yogurt
Julienned orange rind

1. In a 3-quart saucepan over medium heat, sauté the onions and garlic in the oil for 5 minutes, or until translucent. Add the strip of orange rind and caraway or dill. Sauté, stirring constantly, for 1 minute.

2. Add the stock and bay leaf. Cover and bring to a boil. Reduce the heat and simmer for 10 minutes.

3. Add the cabbage, beets, potatoes and honey. Simmer for 10 to 20 minutes, until the potatoes are tender. Stir in the pepper. Remove and discard the orange rind and bay leaf.

4. Serve topped with a dollop of yogurt and sprinkled with julienned orange rind.

SERVES 4.

Preparation Time: 20 min.
Cooking Time: 40 min.

CHEF'S NOTES

DO FIRST:
Cook the red beets: Start with about 1 pound of trimmed small to medium beets. Scrub well and leave about 1" of stem. Boil until tender, about 45 minutes. Drain, rinse with cold water and slip off the skins.

INGREDIENTS NOTE:
You may substitute canned beets (about 15 ounces) for fresh as long as they're not pickled or sweetened like Harvard-style.

NUTRI-NOTE:
Using canned stock rather than a low-sodium homemade broth could increase sodium to about 800 milligrams per serving.

NUTRITION AT A GLANCE

PER SERVING:
Calories 139
Fat . . . . .3 g. (19% of cal.)
Sat. fat . . . . .0.3 g. (2% of cal.)
Cholesterol . . . . .0 mg.
Sodium . . . . .134 mg.

SALADS AND DRESSINGS

SHRIMP PASTA SALAD WITH KALE

Kale is truly a green great! It's rich in vitamins A and C to help prevent both cancer and a variety of common infections. And unlike some other dark leafy greens, kale has plenty of bone-building calcium in a form the body can readily absorb.

SHRIMP PASTA SALAD WITH KALE

DRESSING
- ½ cup buttermilk
- 2 tablespoons wine vinegar
- 1-2 tablespoons olive oil or walnut oil
- 1 tablespoon Dijon mustard
- 1 teaspoon ground black pepper

SALAD
- 8 ounces small pasta shells
- 1½ cups broccoli florets
- ½ cup thinly sliced carrot
- 1 cup sliced (½") asparagus
- ¾ cup snow peas
- 12 ounces shrimp, peeled, deveined, cooked and sliced lengthwise
- ½ cup sliced black olives
- 3 tablespoons minced fresh dill or 1 teaspoon dried
- 1 scallion, minced
- 1 pound kale
- 1 large tomato, diced
- 1 tablespoon wine vinegar
- Ground black pepper (to taste)

1. *To make the dressing:* In a large bowl, whisk together the buttermilk, vinegar, oil, mustard and pepper. Set aside.

2. *To make the salad:* Bring a large pot of water to a boil. Add the pasta and cook until tender, about 12 minutes. Drain well and add to the bowl with the dressing. Toss well.

3. In the same pot, bring 4 cups of water to a boil. Add the broccoli and cook for 1 minute. Add the carrots; cook for 1 minute. Add the asparagus and peas; cook for 1 minute. Pour into a colander, rinse with cold water to stop the cooking process and drain well.

4. Add the vegetables to the pasta. Add the shrimp, olives, dill and scallions. Toss well. Cover and refrigerate until serving time.

5. Wash the kale in plenty of cold water to remove any grit. Drain well and pat the leaves dry. Remove any thick stems. Cut or tear the leaves into desired sizes. Place in a large bowl. Add the tomatoes, vinegar and pepper. Toss well.

6. Serve with the shrimp mixture.

SERVES 8.

Preparation Time: 25 min.
Cooking Time: 20 min.

CHEF'S NOTES
■ ■ ■ ■ ■ ■ ■ ■

PRESENTATION:
For an attractive presentation, arrange the kale mixture around the outside edge of a large platter or individual plates. Mound the shrimp salad in the middle.

■

VARIATIONS:
Substitute sliced grilled or poached chicken breast for the shrimp. Use other pasta, such as tricolor twists or two-color rosettes.

■

NUTRI-NOTE:
Black olives, also known as Mission olives, tend to be much lower in sodium than common green types.

NUTRITION AT A GLANCE

PER SERVING:
Calories 231
Fat . . . . .5 g. (19% of cal.)
Sat. fat . . . . .0.6 g. (2% of cal.)
Cholesterol . . . . .65 mg.
Sodium . . . . .234 mg.

GARDEN HARVEST SALAD WITH SEARED TUNA

This main-dish salad is a heart-healthy Mediterranean favorite. It has olive oil and fresh tuna, both of which can help reduce high cholesterol. In addition, there are plenty of vitamin-packed, fiber-rich fresh vegetables for immunity to infections.

GARDEN HARVEST SALAD WITH SEARED TUNA

TUNA
- 1 teaspoon olive oil
- 1 tablespoon minced fresh parsley
- 1 teaspoon lemon juice
- ½ teaspoon reduced-sodium soy sauce
- 1 clove garlic, minced
- ¼ teaspoon ground black pepper
- 12 ounces tuna steak

PICKLED RED ONIONS
- 1 red onion
- 2 tablespoons vinegar
- 1 tablespoon honey
- ½ teaspoon reduced-sodium soy sauce

DRESSING
- ¼ cup apple juice
- 2 tablespoons olive oil
- 2 tablespoons grated Parmesan cheese
- 1 tablespoon vinegar
- 1 tablespoon minced fresh parsley
- 1 clove garlic, minced
- 1 anchovy fillet (optional)
- 2 teaspoons Dijon mustard
- 1 teaspoon lemon juice
- 1 teaspoon minced fresh basil or ½ teaspoon dried
- ⅛ teaspoon ground black pepper

SALAD
- 4 large leaves romaine lettuce
- 1 cup green beans, lightly cooked
- 8 small red potatoes, cooked and sliced
- 4 radishes
- 1 sweet red pepper, roasted, seeded and sliced
- 12 cherry tomatoes
- 4 black olives
- 4 sprigs Italian parsley
- 1 hard-cooked egg, quartered

1. *To make the tuna:* In a shallow dish, combine the oil, parsley, lemon juice, soy sauce, garlic and pepper. Add the tuna and turn to coat both sides of each piece. Cover, refrigerate and marinate for 30 minutes.

2. *To make the pickled red onions:* Thinly slice the onion crosswise. Separate the slices into rings. In a medium bowl, combine the vinegar, honey and soy sauce. Add the onions, toss to coat and set aside.

3. *To make the dressing:* In a blender, combine the apple juice, oil, Parmesan, vinegar, parsley, garlic, anchovy, mustard, lemon juice, basil and pepper. Process until smooth. Refrigerate until needed.

4. *To make the salad:* Divide the romaine among 4 chilled plates. Add the beans, potatoes, radishes, peppers, tomatoes and onions. Heat a large, well-seasoned cast-iron frying pan over medium-high heat. Cut the tuna into 4 servings. Cook quickly (2 minutes per side). Add to the plates. Drizzle with the dressing and add the olives, parsley and eggs.

SERVES 4.

Preparation Time: 25 min. + standing time
Cooking Time: 5 min.

CHEF'S NOTES

■ ■ ■ ■ ■ ■ ■ ■ ■ ■

DO FIRST:
Steam the green beans and potatoes. Cook the eggs. Broil the pepper until charred on all sides; remove the peel and seeds.

■

VARIATIONS:
Replace the fresh tuna with albacore tuna packed in water. Drain, mix with the marinade and chill. Replace the red pepper with canned pimentos.

■

NUTRI-NOTE:
If you are cutting back on cholesterol, eliminate the eggs or discard the yolks. That will reduce the cholesterol to 38 milligrams per serving. A middle ground would be to use fresh quail eggs (they're smaller and have less cholesterol — 76 milligrams per egg).

NUTRITION AT A GLANCE ■■■

PER SERVING:
Calories 322
Fat . . . . . .12.1 g. (34% of cal.)
Sat. fat . . . . .2.7 g. (8% of cal.)
Cholesterol . . . . .73 mg.
Sodium . . . . .240 mg.

CRAB SALAD WITH AVOCADO AND MANGO

This light luncheon salad gets a health assist from two nutritious fruits: avocado and mango. The avocado is very high in heart-smart monounsaturated fat, and the mango is a treasure trove of immunity-bolstering vitamins A and C.

CRAB SALAD WITH AVOCADO AND MANGO

POPPY-SEED DRESSING
¼ cup orange juice
3 tablespoons honey
3 tablespoons lime juice
3 tablespoons nonfat yogurt
¼ teaspoon celery seed
¼ teaspoon poppy seed

CRAB SALAD
8 ounces lump crab meat
½ cup minced celery
¼ cup minced sweet red pepper
2 teaspoons minced scallions
4 teaspoons lime juice
3-4 teaspoons reduced-calorie mayonnaise
4 red lettuce leaves
6 cups mixed salad greens, torn into bite-size pieces
1 ripe avocado
1 ripe mango

1. *To make the poppy-seed dressing:* In a small bowl whisk together the orange juice, honey, lime juice, yogurt, celery seeds and poppy seeds. Cover and refrigerate for at least 20 minutes to allow flavors to blend.

2. *To make the crab salad:* In a medium bowl combine the crab, celery, red peppers, scallions, lime juice and mayonnaise.

3. Line 4 large salad plates with red lettuce. Divide mixed greens among plates. Top with the crab mixture.

4. Peel and slice both the avocado and the mango. Divide the slices among plates. Serve drizzled with the dressing.

SERVES 4.

Preparation Time: 20 min. + standing time

CHEF'S NOTES

DO FIRST:
Pick over the crab to remove bits of shell or white membrane.

INGREDIENTS NOTE:
You may use canned, frozen or fresh crab. For variety, use cantaloupe, honeydew, papaya, orange or peach slices in place of the mango and avocado.

NUTRI-NOTE:
Colorful greens, such as spinach, red leaf lettuce, kale and beet greens, have more vitamins than pale varieties.

KITCHEN TRICKS:
Avocados have a tendency to discolor when exposed to air. Either slice them at the last minute or squeeze lemon juice over cut surfaces.

NUTRITION AT A GLANCE

PER SERVING:
Calories 273
Fat . . . . 9 g. (30% of cal.)
Sat. fat . . . . . 1.8 g. (6% of cal.)
Cholesterol . . . . 51 mg.
Sodium . . . . 246 mg.

SALMON STARR SALAD

Here's a wonderful seafood salad that can be the centerpiece of your next get-together. You make it ahead, so there's no last-minute fuss. And it's just swimming with health-boosting nutrients—including vitamin B$_{12}$, which is so essential for steady nerves and strong blood.

SALMON STARR SALAD

- 3 cups defatted chicken stock
- 2 tablespoons lemon juice
- 1 tablespoon Dijon mustard
- 1 teaspoon white-wine Worcestershire sauce
- ¼–½ teaspoon hot-pepper sauce
- 1 pound skinless, boneless salmon fillet
- 4 ounces small shrimp, peeled and deveined
- 1 cup white rice
- ½ cup diced carrot
- ½ cucumber, peeled, seeded and thinly sliced
- ½ cup diced sweet red pepper
- ¼ cup orange juice
- 1–2 tablespoons lime juice
- 1–2 tablespoons minced fresh tarragon

1. In a large frying pan, combine the stock, lemon juice, mustard, Worcestershire and hot-pepper sauce. Bring to a boil.

2. Slice the salmon crosswise into 1″ cutlets. Add the salmon and the shrimp to the pan. Simmer over medium heat for 3 to 5 minutes, or until just cooked through.

3. Use a slotted spoon to carefully remove the salmon and shrimp from the liquid. Place both on a plate and refrigerate.

4. Add the rice and carrots to the liquid in the frying pan. Cover and cook over medium heat for 20 minutes, or until the rice is tender. A lot—but not all—of the liquid will be absorbed. Drain the rice through a strainer and reserve the excess liquid.

5. Place the rice in a large bowl. Add the cooked shrimp, cucumbers and peppers; toss lightly.

6. In a small bowl, combine the reserved liquid, orange juice, lime juice and tarragon. Pour over the rice salad. Toss well. Chill 1 hour and serve with salmon or lightly toss the salmon with the rice mixture and serve.

SERVES 6.

Preparation Time: 25 min. + standing time
Cooking Time: 25 min.

CHEF'S NOTES

DO FIRST:

Remove the skin and any bones from the salmon. Peel and devein the shrimp.

PRESENTATION:

If desired, arrange the salmon pieces around the edges of a serving platter. Spoon the rice salad onto the center of the plate.

VARIATION:

Replace the shrimp with mussels or clams that have been steamed, then removed from their shells. Add to the rice with the peppers.

KITCHEN TRICK:

Use tweezers or needle-nose pliers reserved for kitchen duty to remove the bones from fish.

NUTRITION AT A GLANCE

PER SERVING:

Calories 298
Fat . . . . 6.2 g. (18% of cal.)
Sat. fat . . . . . 0.9 g. (3% of cal.)
Cholesterol . . . . 70 mg.
Sodium . . . . 177 mg.

GRILLED PORK LOIN AND NECTARINE SALAD

You may think that pork has no place in a healthy diet. But the lean loin—trimmed of all visible fat—is on par with lean beef. This dish combines a small amount of meat with fiber-rich brown rice and vitamin-packed fruits and vegetables—a combination that can help prevent cancer and bolster your immunity.

GRILLED PORK LOIN AND NECTARINE SALAD

1 tablespoon reduced-sodium soy sauce
1 teaspoon grated fresh ginger
1 clove garlic, crushed
8 ounces well-trimmed boneless pork loin cutlets
2 cups cooked short-grain brown rice
1 cup diced nectarine
¼ cup thinly sliced scallions

1 tablespoon olive oil
1 tablespoon lime juice
½ teaspoon sesame oil
8 ounces green beans
4 cups torn mixed salad greens
12 thin diagonal slices peeled cucumber
8 paper-thin rounds yellow pepper
1 nectarine, sliced

1. In a small cup combine the soy sauce, ginger and garlic. Place the pork on a plate and spread the mixture over the meat; turn to coat evenly. Cover and refrigerate at least 30 minutes or up to 2 hours.

2. Just before serving combine the rice, diced nectarines, scallions, olive oil, lime juice and sesame oil; toss to blend. Set aside.

3. Steam the beans over boiling water for about 3 minutes or until crisp-tender; rinse with cold water to stop cooking. Set aside to cool.

4. Heat a no-stick frying pan over high heat. Add the pork and cook, brushing with any leftover liquid, about 3 minutes per side. Remove to a platter and let cool slightly.

5. To serve, divide greens among 4 dinner plates. Spoon the rice mixture in a mound in the center of each plate.

6. Cut the pork into thin crosswise slices. Divide evenly among the plates, making 2 bundles of meat on either side of the plates.

7. Arrange the beans, cucumber slices, peppers, and nectarine slices on the plates.

SERVES 4.

Preparation Time: 25 min. + standing time
Cooking Time: 10 min.

CHEF'S NOTES

DO FIRST:
Cook the rice: To get about 2 cups of cooked brown rice you'll need to start with ⅔ cup raw rice and 1½ cups of water. Cook for 45 minutes, or until tender. Chill or let cool to lukewarm before mixing with salad ingredients.

VARIATIONS:
Replace the nectarines with peeled peaches. Use snow peas or sugar snap peas in place of green beans. Broil or grill the pork instead of sautéing it. Or substitute turkey or chicken cutlets for the pork.

MAKE-AHEAD TIP:
Although this salad is best served at room temperature, you may prepare it ahead and refrigerate until serving time.

NUTRITION AT A GLANCE

PER SERVING:

Calories 297
Fat . . . . . . .9.4 g. (28% of cal.)
Sat. fat . . . . .2.1 g. (6% of cal.)
Cholesterol . . . . .31 mg.
Sodium . . . . .184 mg.

CHINESE CHICKEN SALAD WITH PEANUT DRESSING

The single carrot in this oriental-style salad provides almost twice the RDA of vitamin A per serving. And the sugar snap peas have large amounts of vitamin C. This vitamin duo makes up half the team (along with vitamin E and the mineral selenium) of "anti-aging nutrients," named because of their ability to help slow wear and tear on body cells.

CHINESE CHICKEN SALAD WITH PEANUT DRESSING

- **1** large carrot
- **1** red onion, thinly sliced
- **8** ounces sugar snap peas
- **1½** cups shredded or chopped cooked chicken breast
- **1½** cups sliced mushrooms
- **½** cup sliced water chestnuts
- **1** cup defatted chicken stock
- **1** tablespoon peanut butter
- **2** tablespoons reduced-sodium soy sauce
- **1** teaspoon sesame oil
- **1** tablespoon lemon juice
- **½** teaspoon hot-chili oil (optional)
- **2** tablespoons minced fresh parsley
- **1** tablespoon grated fresh ginger
- **1** clove garlic, minced
- **4** ounces alfalfa sprouts
- **8** red or yellow plum tomatoes

1. Cut the carrot into julienne pieces (¼″ × ¼″ × 2″). Place them in a steamer basket with the onions and peas. Steam the vegetables for 3 to 5 minutes, until crisp-tender.

2. Transfer to a large bowl. Add the chicken, mushrooms and water chestnuts. Toss lightly to combine.

3. In a 1-quart saucepan boil the stock uncovered for 5 minutes, or until reduced to ⅓ cup.

4. Place the peanut butter in a small bowl. Whisk in the hot stock until smooth. Whisk in the soy sauce, sesame oil, lemon juice and chili oil. Stir in the parsley, ginger and garlic.

5. Pour the dressing over the chicken mixture. Toss lightly. Cover and refrigerate until chilled.

6. To serve, place the alfalfa sprouts on a large platter. Top with the chicken salad and serve with the tomatoes.

SERVES 6.

Preparation Time: 25 min. + standing time
Cooking Time: 10 min.

CHEF'S NOTES

■ ■ ■ ■ ■ ■ ■ ■ ■ ■

DO FIRST:

Cook the chicken: Poach 1 pound of boneless, skinless chicken breast in water or stock until tender, about 15 to 20 minutes.

■

VARIATIONS:

Replace the chicken with cooked shrimp, turkey or very lean pork. Replace the peanut butter with tahini (sesame seed paste). Use other vegetables, including snow peas, bok choy, green beans or peppers.

■

NUTRI-NOTE:

Scrubbing the carrot rather than peeling it helps retain vitamins that are present just under the skin.

NUTRITION AT A GLANCE ▨

PER SERVING:

Calories 145
Fat . . . . 4.8 g. (30% of cal.)
Sat. fat . . . . . 1.1 g. (7% of cal.)
Cholesterol . . . . 26 mg.
Sodium . . . . 267 mg.

SAVORY CABBAGE SALADS

Cruciferous vegetables—including cabbage—may be your best line of defense against certain types of cancer. And because studies suggest they're even more effective when eaten raw, this pair of salads makes extra dietary sense.

SAVORY CABBAGE SALADS

CHINESE SESAME SLAW

5½ cups thinly sliced green cabbage	1 tablespoon sesame oil
1 large carrot, julienned	1 clove garlic, minced
3 scallions, julienned	½ teaspoon grated fresh ginger
¼ cup lemon juice	1 tablespoon sesame seeds

1. In a large bowl, combine the cabbage, carrots and scallions.

2. In a small bowl, whisk together the lemon juice, oil, garlic and ginger. Pour over the cabbage mixture and toss well to combine.

3. Place the sesame seeds in a dry no-stick frying pan. Stir over medium heat until lightly toasted, about a minute. Transfer to a mortar and pound lightly to break them up and release flavors. Don't crush into a paste. Sprinkle over the salad.

SERVES 6.

Preparation Time: 20 min.
Cooking Time: 1 min.

CREAMY MIXED CABBAGE SALAD

3 cups thinly sliced red cabbage	¼ cup nonfat mayonnaise
2½ cups thinly sliced green cabbage	1 clove garlic, minced
1 large carrot, julienned	½ teaspoon grated fresh ginger
3 scallions, julienned	2 tablespoons snipped chives
¼ cup lemon juice	

1. In a large bowl, combine the red cabbage, green cabbage, carrots and scallions.

2. In a small bowl, whisk together the lemon juice, mayonnaise, garlic and ginger. Pour over the cabbage mixture and toss well to combine. Sprinkle with the chives.

SERVES 6.

Preparation Time: 20 min.

CHEF'S NOTES

ACCOMPANIMENT:

Serve with poached chicken or Pepper-Marinated Flank Steak (page 123).

VARIATION:

To turn either salad into a vegetarian sandwich, add some shredded low-fat cheese and serve it stuffed into whole wheat pita bread.

NUTRITION AT A GLANCE

PER SERVING:

CHINESE SESAME SLAW

Calories	52
Fat	3.2 g. (55% of cal.)
Sat. fat	0.4 g. (7% of cal.)
Cholesterol	0 mg.
Sodium	16 mg.

CREAMY MIXED CABBAGE SALAD

Calories	42
Fat	0.2 g. (4% of cal.)
Sat. fat	0 g.
Cholesterol	3 mg.
Sodium	13 mg.

ORANGE-SCENTED CUCUMBER SALAD

This refreshing side salad is virtually fat free and incredibly low in calories. What's more, the addition of oranges gives you fully one-third of your daily requirement of vitamin C, which some studies show may help protect against cancer.

ORANGE-SCENTED CUCUMBER SALAD

1 cucumber
1 navel orange
2 tablespoons low-fat yogurt
2 teaspoons honey

2 teaspoons orange juice
1 teaspoon lemon juice
1 tablespoon thinly sliced mint leaves
4 lettuce leaves

1. If desired, peel the cucumber. Cut in half lengthwise, then thinly slice on diagonal.

2. Use a vegetable peeler to remove a few thin strips of rind from the orange. Remove only the colored part, not the underlying bitter white pith. Very finely slice the rind into shreds. Measure out 2 teaspoons.

3. Peel the orange, divide the flesh into sections, remove the membranes, if desired, and dice the sections.

4. In a medium bowl whisk together the yogurt, honey, orange juice and lemon juice. Mix in the cucumbers, oranges, mint leaves and orange rind.

5. Chill for 20 minutes.

6. To serve, place a lettuce leaf on each of 4 salad plates. Divide salad among leaves.

SERVES 4.

Preparation Time: 10 min. + standing time

CHEF'S NOTES

ACCOMPANIMENT:

Serve with a Middle Eastern dish, such as Lamb-Vegetable Kabobs (page 147) or chicken with couscous.

VARIATIONS:

Add very thinly sliced sweet onions, chopped scallions or snipped chives. If desired, double the oranges.

KITCHEN TRICK:

When choosing an orange, opt for one that feels heavy for its size — it will have plenty of juice inside.

NUTRITION AT A GLANCE

PER SERVING:

Calories 40
Fat . . . . .0.3 g. (7% of cal.)
Sat. fat . . . . .0.1 g. (2% of cal.)
Cholesterol . . . . .0 mg.
Sodium . . . . .8 mg.

PICNIC POTATO SALAD

Potato salad is an all-American favorite. Unfortunately, standard recipes are just loaded with fat and calories. We've slimmed our spuds considerably by using only a moderate amount of nonfat mayo.

Picnic potato salad

1½ pounds red potatoes
1 cup thinly sliced celery
2 scallions, minced
¼ cup thinly sliced red onion
1 hard-cooked egg, chopped (optional)
1 Italian tomato, diced
2 tablespoons minced fresh dill
½ cup nonfat mayonnaise
1 tablespoon coarse mustard

1 tablespoon lemon juice
1 tablespoon olive oil
1 tablespoon apple-cider vinegar
1 teaspoon reduced-sodium soy sauce (optional)
1 teaspoon honey
1 teaspoon minced fresh parsley
¼ teaspoon ground black pepper
⅛–¼ teaspoon celery seed

1. Scrub the potatoes and cut into 1″ cubes. Steam until tender, about 15 minutes. Place in a large bowl.

2. Add the celery, scallions, onions, eggs, tomatoes and dill. Toss well.

3. In a small bowl, whisk together the mayonnaise, mustard, lemon juice, oil, vinegar, soy sauce, honey, parsley, pepper and celery seed.

4. Pour over the potato mixture and combine well. Serve warm or chilled.

SERVES 6.

Preparation Time: 15 min.
Cooking Time: 15 min.

CHEF'S NOTES

■ ■ ■ ■ ■ ■ ■ ■ ■ ■

INGREDIENTS NOTE:

The best spuds for salads are boiling potatoes. They have waxy flesh that contains less starch than baking potatoes, so they're less likely to fall apart when boiled. Although this recipe calls for red potatoes, you may also use brown ones.

■

NUTRI-NOTE:

Using the optional egg will increase cholesterol to 36 milligrams per serving. The optional soy sauce will increase sodium to 202 milligrams.

■

CHEF'S SECRET:

Combining the potatoes with dressing while they're still warm allows them to absorb more flavor from the dressing.

NUTRITION AT A GLANCE ▬▬▬

PER SERVING:
Calories 136
Fat . . . . . . .2.6 g. (17% of cal.)
Sat. fat . . . . .0.3 g. (2% of cal.)
Cholesterol . . . . .0 mg.
Sodium . . . . .169 mg.

WILD RICE SALAD

Contrary to what you may think, wild rice is not a true rice at all. It's actually the seed of an aquatic grass that shares many of rice's characteristics. Among them are low calories, low fat, low sodium, high fiber and high complex carbohydrates—all the elements doctors recommend for both weight loss and maximum nutrition across the board.

WILD RICE SALAD

4 cups water
1 cup wild rice, rinsed
2 tablespoons pine nuts
1 sweet red pepper, thinly sliced
1 yellow pepper, thinly sliced
2 scallions, minced
1 clove garlic, minced
1 shallot, minced
1 tablespoon minced fresh basil or 1 teaspoon dried

1½ teaspoons fresh thyme or ½ teaspoon dried
2 tablespoons red-wine vinegar
1 tablespoon lemon juice
2 teaspoons olive oil
Pinch of dry mustard
Lettuce leaves
2 tablespoons crumbled feta cheese (optional)

1. Bring the water to a boil in a 2-quart saucepan. Add the rice and boil uncovered for 35 minutes, or until the rice is tender but still a bit chewy. Drain well and set aside.

2. Heat a no-stick frying pan over medium heat. Add the pine nuts and shake the pan over the heat for 2 to 3 minutes to toast the nuts. Take care that they don't burn.

3. In a large bowl combine the pine nuts with the rice, red peppers, yellow peppers, scallions, garlic, shallots, basil and thyme.

4. In a small bowl, whisk together the vinegar, lemon juice, oil and mustard. Pour over the rice mixture and toss well to combine. Serve warm or chilled over lettuce leaves. Sprinkle with feta cheese.

SERVES 4.

Preparation Time: 15 min.
Cooking Time: 35 min.

CHEF'S NOTES

ACCOMPANIMENTS:

Serve as a light luncheon dish with crusty bread and citrus sections. Or serve as a side dish to accompany roast chicken or lean pork.

VARIATION:

Use a mixture of rice. Choose from regular white or brown or more unusual varieties such as basmati, Wehani or Texas pecan rice. Because various types require different cooking times, cook each separately and combine later.

NUTRITION AT A GLANCE

PER SERVING:
Calories 164
Fat . . . . . . .5.6 g. (20% of cal.)
Sat. fat . . . . . .1 g. (5% of cal.)
Cholesterol . . . . .2 mg.
Sodium . . . . .31 mg.

ROSEMARY LENTIL SALAD

If you'd like to cut back on your meat consumption but worry about getting enough protein, we have just one word for you: lentils. In terms of total protein, lentils can hold their own against meat and dairy foods. But even though they have more protein than beef, lentils have virtually no fat. So make a point of featuring hearty vegetarian salads—like this one-dish meal—in your culinary repertoire.

ROSEMARY LENTIL SALAD

DRESSING
- 3 tablespoons olive oil
- 2 tablespoons apple-cider vinegar or red-wine vinegar
- 1 teaspoon Dijon mustard
- 1 teaspoon minced fresh rosemary or ¼ teaspoon dried
- ½ teaspoon ground coriander
- 1 clove garlic, minced

SALAD
- 3 cups defatted chicken stock
- 1 cup lentils
- ¼ cup diced onion
- 1 bay leaf
- ½ cup diced yellow pepper
- ¼ cup diced celery
- Green or red lettuce
- 1 cup shredded cooked beet
- 1 cup shredded carrot
- 1 cup shredded zucchini
- 1 cup shredded red radish

1. *To make the dressing:* In a small bowl combine the oil, vinegar, mustard, rosemary, coriander and garlic. Set aside.

2. *To make the salad:* In a 2-quart saucepan combine the stock, lentils, onions and bay leaf. Bring to a boil, then lower the heat and simmer for 20 minutes, or until the lentils are tender but not mushy. Discard the bay leaf.

3. Carefully strain the lentils, reserving any remaining stock for another use.

4. Transfer the lentils to a large bowl. Add the peppers and celery. Toss gently to combine.

5. Whisk the dressing to combine well, then pour over the lentils. Toss lightly. Chill, if desired.

6. Line 4 serving plates with the lettuce. Divide the lentils, beets, carrots, zucchini and radishes among the plates.

SERVES 6.

Preparation Time: 20 min.
Cooking Time: 20 min.

CHEF'S NOTES

DO FIRST:
Cook the red beets: Scrub them well, trim the stems to ½'' and cook in water to cover, until tender, about 40 minutes. Remove the tops with a paring knife and slip off the skins. Refrigerate whole and shred just before serving.

ACCOMPANIMENT:
Serve with Italian bread or Melba toast.

MICROWAVE OPTION:
Cook the lentils: In a 2-quart casserole dish combine the stock, lentils, onions and bay leaf. Cook uncovered on full power until the lentils are tender, 20 to 25 minutes, stirring occasionally. Remove the bay leaf.

NUTRITION AT A GLANCE

PER SERVING:
Calories 217
Fat . . . . . . .7.2 g. (30% of cal.)
Sat. fat . . . . . .1 g. (4% of cal.)
Cholesterol . . . . .0 mg.
Sodium . . . . .84 mg.

THREE-BEAN SALAD WITH MUSTARD DRESSING

You'll love the fresh flavors of this tangy salad. Beans are high in hunger-appeasing complex carbohydrates, so they help fill you up even though they're not that high in calories. One study found that beans can even help suppress the appetite for hours because they're digested very slowly.

THREE-BEAN SALAD WITH MUSTARD DRESSING

SALAD
- **2 cups halved young green beans**
- **1 cup cooked chick-peas**
- **1 cup cooked kidney beans**
- **1 large tomato, seeded and diced**

MUSTARD DRESSING
- **2 tablespoons olive oil**
- **2 tablespoons Dijon mustard**
- **2 tablespoons water**
- **1 tablespoon chopped fresh basil or 1½ teaspoons dried**
- **1 teaspoon honey**
- **¼ teaspoon ground black pepper**
- **¼ cup snipped chives**

1. *To make the salad:* Steam the green beans until crisp-tender, about 5 minutes. Place in a large bowl. Add the chick-peas, kidney beans and tomatoes. Mix well.

2. *To make the mustard dressing:* In a blender, combine the oil, mustard, water, basil, honey and pepper. Process on medium speed for 1 minute. Pour over the salad. Sprinkle with the chives. Toss well. Let stand for 20 minutes before serving.

SERVES 8.

Preparation Time: 10 min. + standing time
Cooking Time: 5 min.

CHEF'S NOTES

DO FIRST:

If using dried chick-peas and kidney beans, cook them (see page 354). If using canned beans, place them in a strainer and rinse with cold water to remove excess sodium.

PRESENTATION:

Serve in lettuce cups. For variety, use colorful greens such as radicchio, ornamental kale or Boston lettuce. Garnish with fresh basil.

VARIATION:

Use other beans. Try fresh limas or wax beans in place of the green beans. Replace the chick-peas or kidney beans with fava, pinto, cranberry beans, black or anasazi beans.

NUTRITION AT A GLANCE

PER SERVING:

Calories 112
Fat . . . . 4.1 g. (33% of cal.)
Sat. fat . . . . . 0.5 g. (4% of cal.)
Cholesterol . . . . 0 mg.
Sodium . . . . 55 mg.

SPINACH SALAD WITH STRAWBERRY MAYONNAISE

Mayonnaise is not taboo in a healthy diet—especially since nonfat brands are so readily available. This recipe gives commercial mayo a flavor boost by blending in fresh strawberries. The salad itself is a snap to toss together, requiring only spinach, onions, berries and canned oranges.

SPINACH SALAD WITH STRAWBERRY MAYONNAISE

½ **pound spinach leaves**
1 **red onion, thinly sliced crosswise**
20 **large strawberries, halved**
1 **can (11 ounces) mandarin oranges, drained**

½ **cup nonfat mayonnaise**
¼ **cup crushed strawberries**

1. Wash the spinach in lots of cold water to remove any grit. Remove thick stems and pat the leaves dry.

2. Separate the onion slices into individual rings.

3. Toss together the spinach, onions, halved strawberries and oranges.

4. In a small bowl, mix the mayonnaise and crushed strawberries. Drizzle over the salad.

SERVES 8.

Preparation Time: 15 min.

CHEF'S NOTES

ACCOMPANIMENTS:
Serve as a light lunch with low-fat cheese and warm sourdough bread or dinner rolls.

VARIATIONS:
Serve the strawberry mayonnaise as a dip with vegetables or fruit. Try carrot sticks, blanched broccoli spears, lightly cooked asparagus, whole strawberries, banana slices and pineapple chunks. For a bolder taste, add a little minced garlic to the mayonnaise. Serve the salad with a vinaigrette dressing, such as the one used on Rosemary Lentil Salad (page 83).

NUTRITION AT A GLANCE

PER SERVING:
Calories 65
Fat . . . . .0.3 g. (4% of cal.)
Sat. fat . . . . .0 g.
Cholesterol . . . . .0 mg.
Sodium . . . . .136 mg.

FESTIVE FRUIT SALAD

Fruit salad is rich in potassium, the mineral linked to reducing blood pressure and preventing strokes. This version is extra-refreshing, with a honey-lime dressing and the ripest summer fruits. To enjoy it other times of the year, just substitute seasonal fruits.

FESTIVE FRUIT SALAD

HONEY-LIME DRESSING
- **1** cup nonfat yogurt
- **½** cup red raspberries
- **2–4** tablespoons honey or other sweetener
- **¼** cup lime juice
- **1** teaspoon vanilla

FRUIT SALAD
- **2** peaches or nectarines, sliced
- **1** cup red or black raspberries
- **1** cup pineapple chunks
- **1** cup honeydew chunks
- **1** cup red or green grapes
- **4** fresh figs, quartered
  Red and green leaf lettuce
- **1** tablespoon shredded fresh mint

1. *To make the honey-lime dressing:* Place the yogurt, raspberries, honey or other sweetener, lime juice and vanilla in a blender. Process until smooth.

2. *To make the fruit salad:* In a large bowl, combine the peaches or nectarines, raspberries, pineapple, honeydew, grapes and figs. Add the dressing and toss well. Allow to marinate for 30 minutes at room temperature.

3. Place the lettuce on a serving platter. Top with the salad. Sprinkle with the mint.

SERVES 6.

Preparation Time: 15 min. + standing time

CHEF'S NOTES

ACCOMPANIMENTS:
Serve as a light lunch with low-fat cottage cheese and date-nut bread or Filled Pineapple Muffins (page 293).

VARIATIONS:
Substitute other fruit. Try strawberries, blueberries, kiwifruit, cantaloupe, watermelon, papaya or apricots. Sprinkle the salad with whole-grain granola or a high-fiber cereal.

NUTRI-NOTE:
Most fresh fruits are good sources of vitamin C. And those with a deep orange color tend to be brimming with cancer-fighting beta-carotene.

NUTRITION AT A GLANCE

PER SERVING:
Calories 143
Fat . . . . .0.7 g. (4% of cal.)
Sat. fat . . . . .0.1 g. (1% of cal.)
Cholesterol . . . . .0 mg.
Sodium . . . . .35 mg.

PASTA DISHES

TWO-COLOR STUFFED SHELLS

Between the squash and the spinach, this dish is overflowing with vitamin A, which doctors say helps the body ward off various types of cancer. And as if that weren't enough to earn these vegetables a prominent place in your diet, their A content helps guard against night blindness and maybe even glaucoma.

TWO-COLOR STUFFED SHELLS

SQUASH FILLING

12 ounces frozen squash

6 ounces low-fat cottage cheese

2 tablespoons dry bread crumbs

1 tablespoon grated Parmesan cheese

1 egg white

1 tablespoon minced fresh parsley

¼ teaspoon grated nutmeg

¼ teaspoon ground black pepper

SPINACH FILLING

10 ounces frozen chopped spinach

6 ounces low-fat cottage cheese

2 tablespoons dry bread crumbs

1 tablespoon grated Parmesan cheese

1 egg white

½ teaspoon dried dill

¼ teaspoon ground black pepper

SHELLS

30 jumbo pasta shells

3 cups chunky tomato sauce

1. *To make the squash filling:* Thaw the squash and drain in a fine strainer for 15 minutes. Place in a food processor with the cottage cheese, bread crumbs, Parmesan, egg white, parsley, nutmeg and pepper. Process until pureed. Transfer to a bowl.

2. *To make the spinach filling:* Thaw the spinach and squeeze out excess moisture. Place in the food processor with the cottage cheese, bread crumbs, Parmesan, egg white, dill and pepper. Process for 15 seconds, until well-mixed.

3. *To make the shells:* Cook the shells in a large pot of boiling water for 10 to 12 minutes, or until tender. Carefully drain and let cool for 5 minutes.

4. Using a spoon or a pastry bag fitted with a large plain or star tube, fill the shells halfway with the squash mixture. Finish with the spinach.

5. Coat a 9″ × 13″ baking dish with no-stick spray. Spread 1 cup of tomato sauce in the dish. Arrange the shells in a single layer. Cover with foil and bake at 350° for 20 minutes. Remove the foil and bake 5 minutes.

6. Heat the remaining tomato sauce and serve with the shells.

MAKES 30.

Preparation Time: 35 min.
Cooking Time: 35 min.

CHEF'S NOTES

VARIATIONS:

Fill 15 of the shells with squash and the remainder with spinach. In place of frozen squash use a fresh winter variety such as buttercup or acorn. Steam or cook the squash in water until tender, mash and measure out 1 cup.

MICROWAVE OPTIONS:

Thaw the frozen squash and spinach in the microwave. Remove the vegetables from their cartons and place each in a glass pie plate. Microwave separately on low power for about 2 minutes. Use a fork to break up the blocks as they thaw. Microwave in 2-minute intervals until thawed.

MAKE-AHEAD TIPS:

Prepare both fillings and refrigerate until needed. Or stuff the shells, cover and refrigerate until baking time.

NUTRITION AT A GLANCE

PER 3 SHELLS:

Calories 261
Fat . . . . .2 g. (7% of cal.)
Sat. fat . . . . .0.9 g. (3% of cal.)
Cholesterol . . . . .2 mg.
Sodium . . . . .231 mg.

BROCCOLI AND PEPPER STRATA

This easy casserole has flavors reminiscent of stroganoff dishes—but it's much lower in fat! The broccoli, red peppers and spinach contribute lots of vitamin C, a nutrient that helps heal wounds and form the collagen so necessary for healthy bones, teeth and skin.

BROCCOLI AND PEPPER STRATA

9 lasagna noodles
3 tablespoons cornstarch
1½ cups defatted chicken stock
15 ounces part-skim or nonfat ricotta cheese
2 egg whites, lightly beaten
1 jar (15 ounces) roasted red peppers, drained well
1 teaspoon olive oil
1 pound mushrooms, thinly sliced
2 tablespoons minced fresh parsley

1 clove garlic, minced
1 teaspoon dried thyme
½ teaspoon dried sage
½ teaspoon dried rosemary
10 ounces frozen chopped spinach, thawed and squeezed dry
2 cups steamed chopped broccoli
2–3 tablespoons grated Parmesan cheese

1. In a large pot of boiling water, cook the lasagna noodles until just tender, about 12 minutes. Drain, rinse with cold water and set aside in a single layer on trays lined with paper towels.

2. In a small bowl, whisk together the cornstarch and about ¼ cup of the stock until the cornstarch is dissolved. Stir in the remaining stock.

3. In a small bowl, stir together the ricotta and egg whites. Set aside.

4. Pat the peppers dry with paper towels and cut into strips.

5. Warm the oil in a large frying pan over medium heat. Add the mushrooms and sauté until they release their moisture, about 5 minutes. Add the parsley, garlic, thyme, sage and rosemary. Stir until the mushrooms have shrunk and are thoroughly dry, about 5 minutes.

6. Give the cornstarch mixture a quick stir, then add to the frying pan. Cook, stirring constantly, until the liquid turns clear and thickens. Remove from the heat and stir in the ricotta mixture and the spinach.

7. Coat a 9″ × 13″ baking dish with no-stick spray. Place 3 of the lasagna noodles in a single layer in the dish. Spread with one-third of the mushroom sauce. Sprinkle with half of the peppers and half of the broccoli.

8. Repeat with another layer of noodles and mushroom sauce. Top with the remaining peppers and broccoli. Finish with a layer of noodles and sauce. Sprinkle with the Parmesan.

9. Bake at 350° for 25 minutes. Let stand for 15 minutes before cutting.

SERVES 6.

Preparation Time: 40 min. + standing time
Cooking Time: 40 min.

CHEF'S NOTES

DO FIRST:
Cook the broccoli. Thaw the spinach.

ACCOMPANIMENT:
Serve with tomato sauce or a low-fat white sauce.

MICROWAVE OPTION:
Microwave the casserole on high for 12 to 15 minutes, turning the dish twice, until the cheese sets.

VARIATION:
Replace the lasagna noodles with fettuccine. Toss with the mushroom sauce (omit the egg whites) and sprinkle with the peppers. Serve the broccoli as a side dish.

NUTRITION AT A GLANCE

PER SERVING:

Calories 355
Fat . . . . .9 g. (23% of cal.)
Sat. fat . . . . .4 g. (10% of cal.)
Cholesterol . . . . .24 mg.
Sodium . . . . .215 mg.

LINGUINE WITH ITALIAN CONFETTI SAUCE

Do you still think pasta's fattening? It's not! As a low-fat complex carbohydrate, it is filling and satisfying. But beware of high-fat sauces, which turn this healthy food into heavy fare. Instead, try a light sauce of fresh tomatoes, red peppers and basil, such as this one.

LINGUINE WITH ITALIAN CONFETTI SAUCE

CONFETTI SAUCE
- **1** cup peeled, seeded and chopped tomato
- **½** cup chopped roasted sweet red pepper (or 4 ounces pimentos, drained)
- **½** cup chopped fresh basil
- **¼** cup defatted chicken stock
- **1** tablespoon olive oil
- **⅓** cup grated Parmesan cheese

PASTA
- **8** ounces linguine
- **1** teaspoon olive oil
- **1** teaspoon minced garlic
- **2** tablespoons defatted chicken stock
- **1** tablespoon minced sun-dried tomato
- **1** tablespoon minced Kalamata olive or other black olive
- **¼** cup peeled, seeded and chopped tomato

1. *To make the confetti sauce:* In a blender or food processor combine the tomatoes, peppers, basil, stock and oil. Using on/off turns, lightly chop until the sauce is colorful and resembles confetti. Do not puree or over-process. Stir in the Parmesan. Set aside.

2. *To make the pasta:* Bring a large pot of water to a boil. Add the linguine and cook according to package directions. Drain and keep warm.

3. While the linguine is cooking, heat the oil over medium heat in a large no-stick frying pan. Add the garlic and sauté for a few minutes, until fragrant but not browned. Add the stock, dried tomatoes and olives. Heat through. Add the confetti sauce and heat briefly. Remove from the heat.

4. Divide the linguine among 4 dinner plates. Top with sauce and chopped tomatoes.

SERVES 4.

Preparation Time: 15 min.
Cooking Time: 10 min.

CHEF'S NOTES

■ ■ ■ ■ ■ ■ ■ ■

DO FIRST:
Prepare the tomatoes: Dip tomato into a pan of boiling water for about 1 minute. Remove and run under cold water. With a paring knife, remove core and skin. Slice in half crosswise and gently squeeze to remove seeds and excess liquid. Chop.

Prepare the peppers: Broil 1 large red pepper close to the heat until charred on all sides. Place in a paper bag for 10 minutes or until cool enough to handle. Use a sharp knife to remove loosened skin.

■

ACCOMPANIMENT:
Serve with regular Italian bread or Italian Flat Bread with Fresh Herbs (page 279).

NUTRITION AT A GLANCE ■■■

PER SERVING:
Calories 300
Fat . . . . . . 8.4 g. (24% of cal.)
Sat. fat . . . . . 2.3 g. (7% of cal.)
Cholesterol . . . . 7 mg.
Sodium . . . . 175 mg.

SPINACH GNOCCHI

These tasty little Italian dumplings get lots of health appeal from two terrific vegetables: potatoes and spinach. Despite their fattening reputation, potatoes are actually a low-cal, low-fat, low-sodium source of filling complex carbohydrates—just what a prudent diet needs. Plus potatoes are a rich source of potassium, a nutrient believed to be beneficial to blood pressure and a protector against stroke.

SPINACH GNOCCHI

GNOCCHI
- **1 pound baking potatoes**
- **10 ounces frozen chopped spinach**
- **2 tablespoons grated Parmesan cheese**
- **1 cup unbleached flour**

TOMATO SAUCE
- **1 teaspoon olive oil**
- **1 tablespoon minced onion**
- **½ clove garlic, minced**
- **1 can (14 ounces) plum tomatoes**
- **½ cup low-fat milk**
- **Grated Parmesan cheese (optional)**

1. *To make the gnocchi:* Cook the whole, unpeeled potatoes in boiling water until tender, about 30 to 40 minutes. When cool enough to handle, discard skins and cut the potatoes into cubes. Press through a sieve or run through a food mill placed over a large bowl. Cool completely.

2. Cook the spinach according to package directions. Drain in a sieve until cool. Press with the back of a spoon to extract as much water as possible. Spoon onto a triple thickness of paper towels and blot dry. Set aside.

3. Stir the spinach and Parmesan into the potatoes. Using a fork, gradually stir in only enough flour to form a ball. Try not to add more than necessary and do not overwork the dough or the gnocchi will be tough.

4. Divide the dough into 6 equal portions. With floured hands form each portion into a rope about ¾'' in diameter. Cut into ½'' lengths.

5. To form the gnocchi, place a piece of dough on the tines of a fork near the handle. Press the gnocchi against the fork to form a ridged crescent. Keep your hands and fork lightly dusted with flour.

6. *To make the tomato sauce:* Heat the oil in a large no-stick frying pan. Sauté the onions until tender. Stir in the garlic.

7. Add the tomatoes (with juice). Cook over medium heat, stirring and breaking up the tomatoes with a spoon, until the mixture thickens, about 10 to 15 minutes. Gradually stir in the milk. Simmer, stirring, until the sauce thickens, about 5 minutes. Set aside.

8. Bring a large pot of water to a boil. Cook the gnocchi until they float to the top, about 1 minute. Drain. Transfer to a lightly oiled platter; toss to coat with the oil. Top with the tomato sauce and sprinkle with Parmesan. Cover with foil and reheat briefly in an oven set at the lowest setting.

SERVES 6.

Preparation Time: 1 hr.
Cooking Time: 20 min.

CHEF'S NOTES

ACCOMPANIMENTS:
Serve with antipasto and a loaf of warm Italian or French bread.

MICROWAVE OPTION:
Gnocchi are best served immediately, but you may reheat them briefly in the microwave.

KITCHEN TRICKS:
For best results when making gnocchi, use a light hand and don't incorporate any more flour than necessary (which will make the gnocchi heavy). Idaho baking potatoes are lighter and fluffier than waxy varieties and give the best results.

NUTRITION AT A GLANCE

PER SERVING:
Calories 186
Fat . . . . . . .2.2 g. (11% of cal.)
Sat. fat . . . . .0.7 g. (3% of cal.)
Cholesterol . . . . .3 mg.
Sodium . . . . .97 mg.

PUMPKIN WONTONS WITH GREENS

Bitter greens, such as spinach, kale, collards and chard, are amazing—and often overlooked—storehouses of nutrients. They provide abundant cancer-fighting vitamin A, lots of antistress vitamin C and cholesterol-lowering fiber. The greens that these pumpkin-stuffed wontons are served on give you more than three times the RDA of vitamin A, a full day's supply of C and about one-third of a day's healthy dose of fiber.

Pumpkin wontons with greens

SAUCE

- 1 tablespoon minced onion
- 1 teaspoon minced garlic
- 2 teaspoons light margarine
- 1 tablespoon flour
- ⅔ cup low-fat milk
- ¼ cup defatted chicken stock
- ¼ cup pureed cooked pumpkin
- 1 teaspoon lemon juice
- 1 teaspoon minced fresh parsley
- ½ teaspoon vinegar
- ¼ teaspoon dried sage
- ⅛ teaspoon ground black pepper

PUMPKIN WONTONS

- ¼ cup minced onion
- 2 teaspoons minced garlic
- 1 tablespoon water
- ¾ cup pureed cooked pumpkin
- ⅓ cup bread crumbs
- 1 teaspoon lemon juice
- 3 tablespoons grated Parmesan cheese
- 2 teaspoons minced fresh parsley
- ⅛ teaspoon ground black pepper
- 20 square wonton skins

GREENS

- 8 cups coarsely chopped bitter greens
- 1 teaspoon vinegar
- 1 teaspoon minced garlic
- 2 tablespoons chopped toasted walnuts
- 1 tablespoon grated Parmesan cheese

1. *To make the sauce:* In a 1-quart saucepan over medium heat, sauté the onions and garlic in the margarine. Stir in the flour. Whisk in the milk and stock. Cook over low heat, stirring often, until thickened. Add the pumpkin, lemon juice, parsley, vinegar, sage and pepper.

2. *To make the pumpkin wontons:* In a large no-stick frying pan over medium heat, cook the onions and garlic in the water until soft. Stir in the pumpkin, bread crumbs and lemon juice. Cook for 1 minute. Add the Parmesan, parsley and pepper.

3. Place a teaspoon of filling in the center of a wonton skin. Lightly wet the edges, then fold the wonton in half to make a triangle. Seal well. Moisten 2 opposite corners at the base of the triangle and overlap them; pinch to seal. Transfer to a tray and cover with plastic wrap. Repeat with remaining wontons and filling. Cook in boiling water for 4 to 5 minutes. Drain.

4. *To make the greens:* Place the greens in a large no-stick frying pan. Sprinkle with the vinegar and garlic. Cover and cook over medium-high heat until wilted. Serve with the wontons, sauce, walnuts and Parmesan.

SERVES 4.

Preparation Time: 45 min.
Cooking Time: 15 min.

CHEF'S NOTES

DO FIRST:

If using fresh pumpkin, scoop out the seeds. Cut the flesh into large sections. Bake at 350° for 40 minutes, or until tender. Or cook in boiling water, about 25 minutes. Drain well, remove the skin and mash the flesh. Place in a saucepan and cook over medium heat, stirring constantly, to evaporate excess moisture that would dilute your filling and sauce.

VARIATION:

Substitute mashed winter squash, such as acorn, butternut or buttercup, for the pumpkin.

MAKE-AHEAD TIPS:

Prepare the sauce and filling ahead. But don't fill the wontons until just before cooking or they'll become soggy.

NUTRITION AT A GLANCE

PER SERVING:

Calories 300
Fat . . . . . . 8.2 g. (25% of cal.)
Sat. fat . . . . . 2.3 g. (7% of cal.)
Cholesterol . . . . 8 mg.
Sodium . . . . 379 mg.

CORN PASTA WITH FIESTA SALSA

For less than 300 calories you get a large portion of corn noodles—a delicious change of pace from regular pasta—plus a festive tomato-corn-avocado salsa with garden-fresh flavors. Although avocados are higher in fat than most other fruit and vegetables, their fat is mostly the healthy monounsaturated type that helps control cholesterol. And here's a surprise: The avocado contributes a nice dose of disease-fighting vitamins A and C.

CORN PASTA WITH FIESTA SALSA

FIESTA SALSA

- **1 jalapeño pepper**
- **¾ cup diced tomato**
- **½ cup cooked corn**
- **1 avocado, diced**
- **¼ cup minced fresh coriander**
- **1 clove garlic, minced**
- **4 teaspoons lime juice**
- **1 tablespoon minced onion**
- **½ teaspoon reduced-sodium soy sauce**

SAUCE

- **3 large dried ancho or poblano chili peppers**
- **¼ cup tomato sauce**
- **¼ cup defatted chicken stock**
- **2 cloves garlic**
- **1 tablespoon chopped onion**
- **1 teaspoon lime juice**
- **1 teaspoon dried oregano**
- **½ teaspoon reduced-sodium soy sauce**
- **¼ teaspoon ground cumin**
- **¼ cup chopped fresh coriander**

PASTA

- **12 ounces corn ribbons or spaghetti**

1. *To make the fiesta salsa:* Fresh jalapeño peppers and other chili peppers can be fiery hot, so wear rubber gloves when handling them and don't rub your eyes or face until you've removed the gloves and washed your hands.

2. Mince the pepper. In a medium bowl combine it with the tomatoes, corn, avocados, coriander, garlic, lime juice, onions and soy sauce.

3. *To make the sauce:* Discard the stems and seeds from the chili peppers. Place the chili peppers in a medium bowl and cover with boiling water. Let stand for 10 minutes. Drain, reserving ½ cup of the liquid.

4. Place the chili peppers, reserved liquid, tomato sauce, stock, garlic, onions, lime juice, oregano, soy sauce and cumin in a blender. Blend until smooth. Transfer to a medium bowl. Stir in the coriander.

5. *To make the pasta:* Cook the corn ribbons or spaghetti according to the package directions. Be very careful not to overcook.

6. Drain the pasta, then return it to the pot. Add the pureed sauce and toss to combine. Serve topped with the salsa.

SERVES 6.

Preparation Time: 25 min.
Cooking Time: 5 min.

CHEF'S NOTES

ACCOMPANIMENTS:

Serve with dollops of yogurt and a sprinkling of cheese (such as Monterey Jack). Also good with Chili Corn Bread (page 283).

VARIATION:

Serve the salsa with steamed corn tortillas.

NUTRITION AT A GLANCE

PER SERVING:

Calories 283
Fat . . . . 5.2 g. (17% of cal.)
Sat. fat . . . . . 0.9 g. (3% of cal.)
Cholesterol . . . . 0 mg.
Sodium . . . . 98 mg.

SPINACH AND CHEESE MANICOTTI

Many Italian dishes present a good way to get extra bone-strengthening calcium into your diet, thanks to their emphasis on dairy products. To keep levels of fat low in our manicotti, we used part-skim mozzarella and ricotta bound together with fat-free egg whites.

SPINACH AND CHEESE MANICOTTI

10 manicotti tubes
2½ cups finely chopped mushrooms
½ cup finely chopped onion
10 ounces frozen chopped spinach, thawed and squeezed dry
¼ teaspoon grated nutmeg
¼ teaspoon ground black pepper

3 egg whites
4–6 ounces part-skim mozzarella cheese, shredded
½–¾ cup part-skim ricotta cheese
2 tablespoons minced fresh parsley
1 cup tomato sauce

1. Cook the manicotti in a large pot of boiling water until just tender, about 10 minutes. Drain and rinse under cold water. Set on a tea towel or paper towels to soak up any remaining water.

2. Coat a no-stick frying pan with no-stick spray. Place over medium heat. Add the mushrooms and onions. Cook until almost tender, about 3 minutes. Add the spinach, nutmeg and pepper. Simmer a few additional minutes. Set aside to cool.

3. In a medium bowl, beat the egg whites with a fork until light and fluffy but not stiff. Stir into the cooled spinach mixture. Add the mozzarella, ricotta and parsley.

4. Stuff the tubes with the filling.

5. Pour ½ cup of the tomato sauce into the bottom of a 9″ × 13″ baking dish. Arrange the stuffed manicotti tubes in the pan. Pour the remaining sauce over the tubes. Cover and bake at 350° until heated through, about 25 minutes.

SERVES 5.

Preparation Time: 40 min.
Cooking Time: 35 min.

CHEF'S NOTES

DO FIRST:

Thaw the spinach (try microwaving it on low power for a few minutes). Squeeze out all excess moisture so you don't dilute the filling.

NUTRI-NOTE:

Drop fat and cholesterol levels even further by using the new nonfat ricotta or dry-curd cottage cheese.

KITCHEN TRICKS:

Don't overcook the pasta; they're easier to handle if still a bit stiff. Use a teaspoon or a pastry bag fitted with a large tube to add the filling. Fill the pasta halfway from one end, then turn it around.

NUTRITION AT A GLANCE

PER SERVING:
Calories 404
Fat . . . . . . 12.6 g. (28% of cal.)
Sat. fat . . . . . 3.8 g. (9% of cal.)
Cholesterol . . . . 20 mg.
Sodium . . . . 426 mg.

VEGETABLE LO MEIN

Lo mein is an easy Chinese stir-fry made with noodles. This version is very low in calories and fat but exceptionally high in vitamin A for healthy eyes, skin and even bones. Just one serving delivers over 2½ times your daily need for the vitamin.

VEGETABLE LO MEIN

- **4 ounces vermicelli or thin spaghetti**
- **¼ cup stock**
- **2 tablespoons oyster sauce**
- **1 tablespoon mirin or other vinegar**
- **1 tablespoon cornstarch**
- **1 clove garlic, minced**
- **4 teaspoons peanut oil**
- **1 large red onion, cut into thin wedges**
- **2 carrots, julienned**
- **1 sweet red pepper, julienned**
- **1 cup broccoli florets**
- **¼ teaspoon sesame oil**

1. Cook the pasta in a large pot of boiling water until just tender, about 5 minutes. Do not overcook. Pour into a colander, rinse with cold water and drain well. Coat a large platter with no-stick spray. Add the pasta and spread out in a thin layer to cool. Refrigerate at least 20 minutes.

2. In a small bowl, whisk together the stock, oyster sauce, vinegar, cornstarch and garlic. Set aside.

3. Heat a wok or large frying pan on medium high. Add 1 teaspoon of the peanut oil. Add the vermicelli and sauté for several minutes to lightly brown. Remove from the pan and set aside.

4. Add the remaining 1 tablespoon peanut oil to the pan and allow to warm for 1 minute. Add the onions and stir-fry until slightly tender and just beginning to brown, about 2 minutes.

5. Add the carrots, peppers and broccoli. Stir-fry for 2 minutes, until crisp-tender. Pour the sauce over the vegetables and stir until thickened and shiny, about 4 minutes.

6. Add the noodles and sesame oil. Toss to combine. Serve immediately.

SERVES 4.

Preparation Time: 30 min.
Cooking Time: 15 min.

CHEF'S NOTES

DO FIRST:
Cut all the vegetables and have them next to the stove before starting to stir-fry.

VARIATION:
Replace the pasta with bean thread noodles. Cook in boiling water for 2 minutes. Pour into a sieve, rinse with cold water and drain well. Transfer to a platter in a very thin layer to minimize clumping. Use scissors to cut into 2" lengths for easier handling when stir-frying. Let cool.

NUTRITION AT A GLANCE

PER SERVING:
Calories 194
Fat . . . . . . .5.7 g. (26% of cal.)
Sat. fat . . . . .0.8 g. (4% of cal.)
Cholesterol . . . . .0 mg.
Sodium . . . . .371 mg.

ROTELLE GIOVANNA

Cauliflower is the secret ingredient in this savory, low-fat white sauce. When properly cooked, it has a wonderful mild flavor. From a nutrition standpoint, it's a surprising vegetable: Ounce for ounce, cauliflower has more vitamin C than oranges.

ROTELLE GIOVANNA

- **12 ounces cauliflower florets**
- **1 large onion, sliced into thin wedges**
- **1 teaspoon olive oil**
- **3 ounces roasted turkey breast, cut into strips**
- **6 sun-dried tomatoes, thinly sliced**
- **1 cup sliced pimentos**
- **1⅓ cups low-fat milk**
- **1 tablespoon lemon juice**
- **¼ teaspoon dried thyme**
- **¼ teaspoon ground black pepper**
- **⅓ cup grated Parmesan cheese**
- **8 ounces tri-color rotelle or other shaped pasta**

1. Steam the cauliflower until very tender, 15 to 18 minutes.

2. While the cauliflower is cooking, combine the onions and oil in a large no-stick frying pan. Sauté over medium-high heat for 5 minutes. Add the turkey and tomatoes; cook for 5 minutes, until lightly browned. Stir in the pimentos. Cover and keep warm over low heat.

3. Place the cauliflower in a blender. Add the milk, lemon juice, thyme and pepper. Blend until smooth. Transfer to a 2-quart saucepan and warm over medium heat. Stir in the Parmesan. Cover and keep warm over low heat.

4. In a pot of boiling water, cook the rotelle according to package directions until tender. Drain. Serve topped with the sauce and the turkey mixture.

SERVES 4.

Preparation Time: 15 min.
Cooking Time: 25 min.

CHEF'S NOTES

DO FIRST:

If the dried tomatoes are packed in oil, pat them dry. If they are totally dehydrated, soak them in hot water until pliable, about 15 minutes; drain. Drain the pimentos on paper towels.

ACCOMPANIMENTS:

Serve with a tossed salad and warm bread, such as Braided French Bread with Herb Spread (page 275).

KITCHEN TRICK:

Colored pasta retains more of its color if cooked in less water than usual (about 3 cups for 8 ounces). Drain as soon as it is tender.

NUTRITION AT A GLANCE

PER SERVING:

Calories 377
Fat . . . . . . .6.7 g. (16% of cal.)
Sat. fat . . . . .2.5 g. (6% of cal.)
Cholesterol . . . . .25 mg.
Sodium . . . . .226 mg.

RUFFLED PASTA WITH FOUR CHEESES

Here's an exciting update on old-fashioned macaroni and cheese. This dish has only 300 calories per serving, compared with nearly 550 in some standard recipes. And it's much lower in fat, thanks to light cheeses and fresh vegetables that extend the pasta.

RUFFLED PASTA WITH FOUR CHEESES

- **1 tablespoon light margarine**
- **3 tablespoons unbleached flour**
- **¼ teaspoon dry mustard**
- **2 cups low-fat milk**
- **½ cup defatted chicken stock**
- **1 teaspoon minced garlic**
- **1 teaspoon reduced-sodium soy sauce**
- **½ teaspoon Worcestershire sauce**
- **⅛ teaspoon ground black pepper**
- **Dash of hot-pepper sauce**
- **½ cup coarsely chopped mushrooms**
- **¼ cup minced onion**
- **¼ cup minced sweet red pepper**
- **¼ cup minced green pepper**
- **1 tablespoon water**
- **8 ounces ruffled pasta, elbow macaroni or other medium pasta**
- **½ cup nonfat or part-skim ricotta cheese**
- **¼ cup diced reduced-fat Cheddar cheese**
- **¼ cup diced reduced-fat Monterey Jack cheese**
- **2 tablespoons grated Parmesan cheese**
- **2 teaspoons minced fresh basil**
- **2 teaspoons minced fresh parsley**
- **1–4 teaspoons minced pickled jalapeño pepper (optional)**
- **1½ cups seasoned fresh bread crumbs (see Chef's Notes)**

1. In a 3-quart saucepan over medium heat, melt the margarine. Stir in the flour and mustard. Cook, stirring constantly, for 1 minute. Slowly whisk in the milk and stock to make a smooth liquid. Stir in the garlic, soy sauce, Worcestershire, black pepper and hot-pepper sauce. Cook, whisking often, until the sauce thickens. Remove from the heat and set aside.

2. In a large no-stick frying pan over medium-high heat, cook the mushrooms, onions, red peppers and green peppers in the water until limp, about 5 minutes. Fold into the sauce.

3. In a large pot of boiling water, cook the pasta until just tender, 8 to 10 minutes. Drain and add to the sauce. Stir in the ricotta, Cheddar, Monterey Jack, Parmesan, basil, parsley and jalapeño peppers.

4. Coat a 9″ × 9″ baking dish with no-stick spray. Add the pasta mixture. Top with the bread crumbs. Bake at 400° for 20 minutes, or until heated through and golden on top.

SERVES 6.

Preparation Time: 30 min.
Cooking Time: 40 min.

CHEF'S NOTES

■ ■ ■ ■ ■ ■ ■ ■

DO FIRST:

Make the bread crumbs: In a food processor, combine 1 cup bread cubes, 1 tablespoon Parmesan cheese, 2 teaspoons light margarine, 1 teaspoon minced parsley, 1 teaspoon minced basil and some hot-pepper sauce. Process with on/off turns until finely chopped. Makes 1½ cups.

■

NUTRI-NOTE:

If you're on a low-salt diet, reduce the sodium in this dish by choosing low-sodium cheeses, omitting the soy sauce and replacing part of the milk with water. Be aware that bread can be a significant source of sodium; check labels carefully.

NUTRITION AT A GLANCE

PER SERVING:

Calories	300
Fat	8.5 g. (26% of cal.)
Sat. fat	3.1 g. (9% of cal.)
Cholesterol	20 mg.
Sodium	302 mg.

LIGHT
PASTA PRIMAVERA

Pasta primavera is an excellent way to include a wide array of vegetables in your diet. And you can vary the recipe according to what's in season. This version has an added health bonus: It's much lower in fat than standard recipes, which lean heavily on saturated cream, butter and cheese.

LIGHT PASTA PRIMAVERA

- **1 jar (6 ounces) artichoke hearts packed in oil**
- **1 clove garlic, minced**
- **1 sweet red pepper, thinly sliced**
- **4 radishes, thinly sliced**
- **1 small zucchini, julienned**
- **3 scallions, cut into 1" pieces**
- **1 package (10 ounces) frozen peas, thawed**
- **8 ounces cherry tomatoes**
- **3 tablespoons minced fresh basil or 1 table-spoon dried**
- **2 tablespoons minced fresh parsley, chopped**
- **2 tablespoons defatted chicken stock**
- **8 ounces penne, fettuccine or fusille**
- **⅓ cup grated Parmesan cheese**
- **¼ teaspoon ground black pepper**
- **Pinch of red-pepper flakes (optional)**

1. Place the artichokes in a strainer set over a bowl and drain well; reserve 2 tablespoons of the oil. Cut the larger artichokes in half. Place on a large plate lined with paper towels and allow to drain further.

2. Place the reserved oil in a large no-stick frying pan. Add the garlic. Sauté over medium-high heat for 1 minute.

3. Add the peppers and radishes; sauté for 2 minutes. Add the zucchini and scallions; sauté for 2 minutes. Add the peas, tomatoes, basil, parsley, stock and artichokes; sauté for 2 minutes.

4. Meanwhile, cook the pasta in a large pot of boiling water until just tender, about 8 minutes. Drain and place in a large serving bowl. Top with the vegetables. Sprinkle with the Parmesan, black pepper and pepper flakes. Toss lightly.

SERVES 6.

Preparation Time: 15 min.
Cooking Time: 15 min.

CHEF'S NOTES

INGREDIENTS NOTE:
You may use fresh peas instead of frozen. Buy 1 pound of podded peas, shell and cook in a little water until tender, about 4 minutes. Drain.

VARIATIONS:
Use other vegetables, such as sliced sun-dried tomatoes, green beans, cauliflower florets, broccoli florets or sliced asparagus. You may also add some cooked shrimp, chicken or turkey in step 3 along with the zucchini.

NUTRITION AT A GLANCE

PER SERVING:

Calories 269
Fat . . . . 7.3 g. (24% of cal.)
Sat. fat . . . . . 1.8 g. (6% of cal.)
Cholesterol . . . . 4 mg.
Sodium . . . . 176 mg.

SPINACH FETTUCCINE WITH SHRIMP

Shrimp has long been considered a dietary no-no for the cholesterol conscious. But newer measuring techniques show that cholesterol levels in most shellfish are lower than originally believed. More to the point, shrimp and other shellfish are very low in saturated fat. So even though they do contain cholesterol, in moderation they're acceptable parts of the heart-healthy diet.

SPINACH FETTUCCINE WITH SHRIMP

SAUCE

- **2 tablespoons minced fresh parsley**
- **2 tablespoons minced fresh basil or 1 teaspoon dried**
- **1 tablespoon minced fresh oregano or ½ teaspoon dried**
- **½ teaspoon ground black pepper**
- **¼ teaspoon red-pepper flakes (or to taste)**
- **⅓ cup unbleached flour or whole wheat pastry flour**
- **2½ cups low-fat milk**
- **½ cup defatted chicken stock**
- **¼ cup grated Parmesan cheese**

PASTA

- **8 ounces spinach fettuccine**

SHRIMP

- **8 ounces sugar snap peas**
- **1 tablespoon olive oil**
- **8 ounces large shrimp, peeled, deveined and halved lengthwise**
- **1 clove garlic, minced**
- **1 pint cherry tomatoes, halved or quartered**

1. *To make the sauce:* In a small bowl mix the parsley, basil, oregano, black pepper and red-pepper flakes. Set aside.

2. Place the flour in a 2-quart saucepan. Whisk in about ½ cup of milk until smooth. Gradually whisk in the remaining milk and stock. Cook over medium heat, whisking constantly, until thickened, about 5 minutes. Stir in the Parmesan and half of the herb mixture. Set aside and keep warm.

3. *To make the pasta:* Bring a large pot of water to a boil. Add the fettuccine and cook according to package directions until *al dente,* just tender to the bite. Do not overcook. Drain and keep warm.

4. *To make the shrimp:* While the pasta is cooking, steam the peas for about 5 minutes, or until crisp-tender. Do not overcook. Set aside.

5. Heat a large no-stick frying pan over medium-high heat until hot. Add the oil and swirl the pan to evenly coat the bottom. Add the shrimp and stir-fry for 1 minute. Add the garlic and stir-fry for 1 minute.

6. Add the peas and tomatoes to the pan. Stir-fry for 1 minute, until the shrimp are opaque and the tomatoes are warmed through. Do not overcook or the shrimp will become tough and the tomatoes will turn mushy. Stir in the remaining herb mixture. Remove from the heat.

7. Place the fettuccine on a serving platter. Top with the sauce and shrimp mixture.

SERVES 4.

Preparation Time: 25 min.
Cooking Time: 15 min.

CHEF'S NOTES

DO FIRST:

Peel and devein the shrimp. Remove strings from the peas.

ACCOMPANIMENTS:

Serve with warm whole wheat bread and a tossed salad with creamy reduced-calorie Italian dressing.

VARIATIONS:

Replace the shrimp with scallops. Replace the snap peas with snow peas, sliced peppers or sliced zucchini.

KITCHEN TRICK:

Slicing the shrimp in half lengthwise gives the appearance of more shrimp per serving — saving you money.

NUTRITION AT A GLANCE

PER SERVING:

Calories 471
Fat . . . . 9.1 g. (17% of cal.)
Sat. fat . . . . . 2.9 g. (6% of cal.)
Cholesterol . . . . 97 mg.
Sodium . . . . 297 mg.

PASTA WITH ROASTED FISH AND CABBAGE

This is a new twist on cabbage noodles. And it's so easy to make that you can enjoy it often with different types of fish. The fish adds extra protein to the noodles and contributes a nice helping of heart-healthy omega-3's.

PASTA WITH ROASTED FISH AND CABBAGE

- **6 ounces broad noodles or ruffled noodles**
- **1 cup thinly sliced onion**
- **1 teaspoon canola oil**
- **3 cups thinly sliced cabbage**
- **½ teaspoon caraway seed**
- **1 pound mackerel (skin on) or other fish fillet**
- **½ cup sliced scallions**
- **¼ cup bread crumbs**
- **2 tablespoons Dijon mustard**

1. Cook the noodles in a large pot of boiling water until just tender, 5 to 8 minutes. Drain and set aside.

2. In a large no-stick frying pan over medium-high heat, sauté the onions in the oil for 1 minute. Add the cabbage and caraway seeds. Stir and sauté for 5 minutes.

3. Cover the pan, reduce the heat to low and cook for 5 minutes.

4. Add the noodles and toss to combine. Spoon into a shallow 2-quart casserole or oval gratin dish.

5. Place the fish, skin side down, on top of the noodles.

6. In a cup, mix the scallions, bread crumbs and mustard. Spread evenly over the fish.

7. Bake at 400° for 17 to 20 minutes, or until the fish is cooked through and the crumbs are golden brown.

SERVES 4.

Preparation Time: 15 min.
Cooking Time: 40 min.

CHEF'S NOTES

INGREDIENTS NOTE:

Choose fillets that are at least ½'' thick. Choose the type of cabbage you like best: green, savoy, Chinese or red.

NUTRI-NOTE:

If you're concerned about your cholesterol, mackerel is the best fish choice. Of all fish, it's the highest in omega-3's. Nutrient information below is for mackerel.

MICROWAVE OPTION:

Place the onions, cabbage, oil and caraway seeds in the casserole. Cover with a lid. Microwave on high for 4 minutes, or until the cabbage is wilted.

NUTRITION AT A GLANCE

PER SERVING:

Calories 450
Fat . . . . . . .19 g. (38% of cal.)
Sat. fat . . . . .3.8 g. (7% of cal.)
Cholesterol . . . . .117 mg.
Sodium . . . . .258 mg.

CHICKEN BOW TIES

One serving of this delicious stir-fry gives you almost three-quarters of the RDA for niacin, a B vitamin. Originally noted for its ability to prevent pellagra (a now rare vitamin-deficiency disease), niacin is also valued for other properties. One of them is its soothing effect upon the nervous system. You might almost consider it a natural tranquilizer because it helps muscles to relax and even helps relieve insomnia.

Chicken bow ties

1 **pound boneless skinless chicken breast**

8 **ounces bow-tie noodles**

2 **teaspoons oil (optional)**

1 **tablespoon sesame or peanut oil**

8 **scallions, cut into 1" pieces**

1 **sweet red pepper, cut into 1" pieces**

1 **green pepper, cut into 1" pieces**

1 **celery stalk, thinly cut on the diagonal**

1 **pound sugar snap peas or snow peas, cut into 1" pieces**

½ **cup sliced water chestnuts**

1 **tablespoon grated fresh ginger**

1 **clove garlic, minced**

1 **cup water**

2 **tablespoons cornstarch**

2 **tablespoons low-sodium soy sauce**

¼ **cup minced fresh coriander**

1. Place the chicken between sheets of waxed paper. Use a mallet to lightly pound them to a uniform thickness, about ½". Cut into bite-size pieces.

2. Cook the noodles in boiling water until tender, about 18 minutes. Do not overcook. Drain. If desired, heat 2 teaspoons of the oil in a large no-stick frying pan or wok over medium heat. Add the noodles and cook for a few minutes to lightly brown. Transfer to a platter and keep warm.

3. Heat half of the sesame or peanut oil in the same pan over medium heat. Add the chicken and stir-fry for 4 minutes, or until opaque. Remove with a slotted spoon and keep warm.

4. Add the remaining oil to the pan. Stir-fry the scallions, red peppers, green peppers, celery, peas, water chestnuts, ginger and garlic for about 4 minutes, or until crisp-tender.

5. Return the chicken to the pan and stir-fry for 1 minute.

6. In a cup combine the water, cornstarch and soy sauce until smooth. Add to the pan. Cook for 2 minutes, or until the sauce thickens. Stir in the coriander. Serve over the warm noodles.

SERVES 6.

Preparation Time: 25 min.
Cooking Time: 30 min.

CHEF'S NOTES

VARIATIONS:
Replace the chicken with thin strips of round steak, lean pork or whole shrimp. Use other vegetables, such as yellow squash, mushrooms, cucumbers, carrots or baby corn.

KITCHEN TRICK:
As with all stir-fries, this recipe will proceed most smoothly if you have all the ingredients chopped, measured and lined up next to your stove before you begin cooking. The beauty of stir-fries is that, although they require some extra prep time, they proceed quickly at the stove.

NUTRITION AT A GLANCE

PER SERVING:
Calories 298
Fat . . . . . . .4.8 g. (14% of cal.)
Sat. fat . . . . .0.6 g. (2% of cal.)
Cholesterol . . . . .77 mg.
Sodium . . . . .264 mg.

MEAT ENTRÉES

PEPPER-MARINATED FLANK STEAK

Meat is an excellent source of vitamin B_{12}, which is essential to the regeneration and production of red blood cells. Just make sure that while you're safeguarding your supply of B_{12}, you're not also upping your intake of cholesterol and fat. Do that by choosing cuts that have very little fat showing and then trimming all of it away.

PEPPER-MARINATED FLANK STEAK

2 teaspoons dried thyme
2 cloves garlic, minced
½ teaspoon crushed black pepper
2 tablespoons olive oil
1 pound flank steak, trimmed of all visible fat

1 pound sweet potatoes, peeled
4 small yellow squash, halved lengthwise

1. In a cup mix the thyme, garlic and pepper with 1 teaspoon of the oil.

2. Rub ¾ of the mixture over the steak. Cover and let stand for 30 minutes. (Or refrigerate up to 1 day.)

3. Add the remaining oil to the rest of the herb mixture.

4. Cut the sweet potatoes in half lengthwise. Then cut each half lengthwise to make 4 long spears from each potato.

5. Brush the sweet potatoes and squash halves with some of the herb mixture.

6. Place the vegetables on a broiler pan, leaving room for the steak. Broil the vegetables 6″ from the heat for about 10 minutes total. Turn and rearrange them as needed to cook evenly.

7. Add the steak to the broiler pan. Cook for 6 to 8 minutes per side for medium rare to medium. As the meat cooks, continue to turn the vegetables until the sweet potatoes can be easily pierced with a fork. (The vegetables will take about 20 minutes total and the meat 12 to 18 minutes.)

8. To serve, cut the meat thinly across the grain on the diagonal. Arrange on a large platter with the vegetables.

SERVES 4.

Preparation Time: 10 min. + standing time
Cooking Time: 20 min.

CHEF'S NOTES

VARIATION:

Cook the meat and vegetables on a grill. Start the sweet potatoes first because they tend to take longer on a grill. Let them cook about 10 minutes before adding the squash. Then follow the time-table in the recipe. Be sure to move the vegetables and turn them frequently to compensate for the uneven heat of most grills.

NUTRI-NOTE:

All sweet potatoes are an excellent source of anticancer beta-carotene, but gardeners can reap even more by planting a variety called Jewell. These sweet potatoes develop 10 percent to 50 percent more beta-carotene than other varieties.

MICROWAVE OPTION:

To shorten cooking time of the sweet potatoes, microwave them for about 5 minutes first.

NUTRITION AT A GLANCE

PER SERVING:

Calories 359
Fat . . . . . . 18 g. (45% of cal.)
Sat. fat . . . . . 1 g. (3% of cal.)
Cholesterol . . . . 57 mg.
Sodium . . . . 96 mg.

LIGHT AND LEAN MEAT-LOAF DINNER

An old-fashioned meat-loaf dinner would cost you a whopping amount of fat, calories and cholesterol. This version gives you all the taste of the original without the health traps. How? In part by using low-fat turkey, lean sirloin and cholesterol-stomping oats to replace fatty ground beef.

LIGHT AND LEAN MEAT-LOAF DINNER

MEAT LOAF

- ¾ **cup diced carrot**
- ¾ **cup diced onion**
- ½ **cup diced sweet red pepper**
- ½ **pound extra-lean ground sirloin**
- ½ **pound ground turkey breast**
- ¾ **cup rolled oats**
- ½ **cup cooked rice**
- ¾ **cup tomato juice**
- ¼ **cup fat-free egg substitute**
- ½ **teaspoon dried oregano**
- ½ **teaspoon dried thyme**
- ½ **teaspoon hot-pepper sauce (optional)**
- ½ **teaspoon ground black pepper**
- 2 **tablespoons ketchup**
- 2 **tablespoons water**

POTATOES

- 1 **pound potatoes**
- 1 **teaspoon margarine**
- 1 **cup buttermilk**

GRAVY

- 2 **teaspoons cornstarch**
- 1½ **cups defatted beef stock**

1. *To make the meat loaf:* Coat a large no-stick frying pan with no-stick spray. Add the carrots, onions and red peppers. Sauté for 5 to 10 minutes.

2. Crumble the sirloin and turkey into a large bowl. Lightly toss with the cooked vegetables, oats and rice.

3. In a small bowl combine the tomato juice, egg, oregano, thyme, hot-pepper sauce and black pepper. Drizzle over the meat and mix well.

4. Coat an 8½″ × 4½″ loaf pan with no-stick spray. Add the meat. Mix the ketchup and water; brush over the meat.

5. Preheat the oven to 450°. Place the meat in the oven and reduce the temperature to 350°. Bake for 45 to 50 minutes, or until cooked through. If the top begins to brown too much, cover with a piece of foil.

6. *To make the potatoes:* If desired, peel the potatoes. Cut into 1″ cubes. Place in a 3-quart saucepan and cover with cold water. Bring to a boil and cook until tender, about 15 minutes.

7. Drain, then mash the potatoes. Beat in the margarine and enough buttermilk to make the potatoes creamy.

8. *To make the gravy:* In a 1-quart saucepan combine the cornstarch with about ¼ cup of the stock. Stir to dissolve completely. Whisk in the remaining stock. Cook over medium heat, stirring constantly, until gravy comes to a boil and thickens, about 5 minutes.

SERVES 4.

Preparation Time: 30 min.
Cooking Time: 50 min.

CHEF'S NOTES

DO FIRST:

Cook the rice. Let cool before adding to other ingredients.

MICROWAVE OPTION:

Microwave the carrots, onions and peppers in a glass measuring cup for 5 minutes, or until tender.

KITCHEN TRICK:

For the leanest ground turkey breast, grind your own. Remove skin, visible fat and thick white tendons running through each breast. Cut meat into 1″ cubes and finely chop in the food processor with a few on/off turns.

NUTRITION AT A GLANCE

PER SERVING:

Calories 433
Fat . . . . .7 g. (15% of cal.)
Sat. fat . . . . .2.6 g. (5% of cal.)
Cholesterol . . . . .74 mg.
Sodium . . . . .235 mg.

GREEK ZUCCHINI AND BEEF

Take advantage of beef's muscle-building protein—without getting too much cholesterol or fat—by using just a small amount of extra-lean ground meat per serving and cooking it right. Brown the beef in a skillet, then drain it well on paper towels.

GREEK ZUCCHINI AND BEEF

ZUCCHINI

- **2 pounds thin zucchini (1" diameter)**
- **2–3 teaspoons olive oil**

MEAT SAUCE

- **8 ounces extra-lean ground beef**
- **1 large onion, minced**
- **2 tablespoons water**
- **1 tablespoon unbleached flour**
- **1 teaspoon dried oregano**
- **½ teaspoon ground cinnamon**
- **¼ teaspoon grated nutmeg**
- **1 cup tomato sauce**
- **1 cup cooked orzo or other tiny pasta**
- **½ cup minced fresh parsley**

CHEESE SAUCE

- **⅓ cup unbleached flour**
- **1½ cups skim milk**
- **½ cup fat-free egg substitute**
- **2 tablespoons grated Parmesan cheese**
- **¼ cup shredded low-fat Cheddar cheese**

1. *To make the zucchini:* Trim the ends and cut each zucchini into 4 lengthwise spears or 3 lengthwise flat pieces. Divide each piece in half crosswise.

2. Coat a jelly-roll pan with no-stick spray. Add the zucchini and only enough oil to lightly coat all the pieces. Arrange in a single layer. Bake at 500° for 10 minutes, flipping the pieces once. Drain on paper towels.

3. *To make the meat sauce:* Coat a large no-stick frying pan with no-stick spray. Place over medium heat for 2 minutes. Crumble in the beef and brown well. Transfer to a platter lined with a triple thickness of paper towels to drain any excess fat.

4. Wipe out the frying pan. Add the onions and water. Sauté for 5 minutes. Add the browned meat, flour, oregano, cinnamon and nutmeg. Stir well. Add the tomato sauce. Cover and simmer for 5 minutes. Remove the lid and cook until very thick. Stir in the orzo and parsley. Set aside.

5. *To make the cheese sauce:* In a 2-quart saucepan, whisk the flour and about ¼ cup of the milk until smooth. Gradually whisk in the remaining milk. Cook over medium heat, whisking constantly, until thickened and bubbling. Whisk in the egg. Cook, stirring, for 1 minute. Remove from the heat. Stir half of the sauce into the meat mixture. Add the Parmesan to the remaining sauce. Set aside.

6. Coat a 9" × 9" baking dish with no-stick spray. Place half the zucchini in the dish in a single layer. Spread with half the meat mixture. Repeat to use all the zucchini and meat. Top with the remaining cheese sauce. Sprinkle with the Cheddar. Bake at 350° for 20 minutes.

SERVES 6.

Preparation Time: 40 min.
Cooking Time: 30 min.

CHEF'S NOTES

DO FIRST:

Cook the orzo or other pasta. Start with about ½ cup and cook until just tender.

MICROWAVE OPTION:

Brown the meat in a micro-safe colander placed over a bowl. Stir often to break up the pieces and move the cooked portion to the middle.

MAKE-AHEAD TIP:

Assemble the casserole and refrigerate uncovered for about 30 minutes so the sauce congeals. Wrap with foil or plastic. To serve, uncover and bake.

NUTRITION AT A GLANCE

PER SERVING:

Calories 239
Fat . . . . .7 g. (26% of cal.)
Sat. fat . . . . . .2 g. (8% of cal.)
Cholesterol . . . . .30 mg.
Sodium . . . . .150 mg.

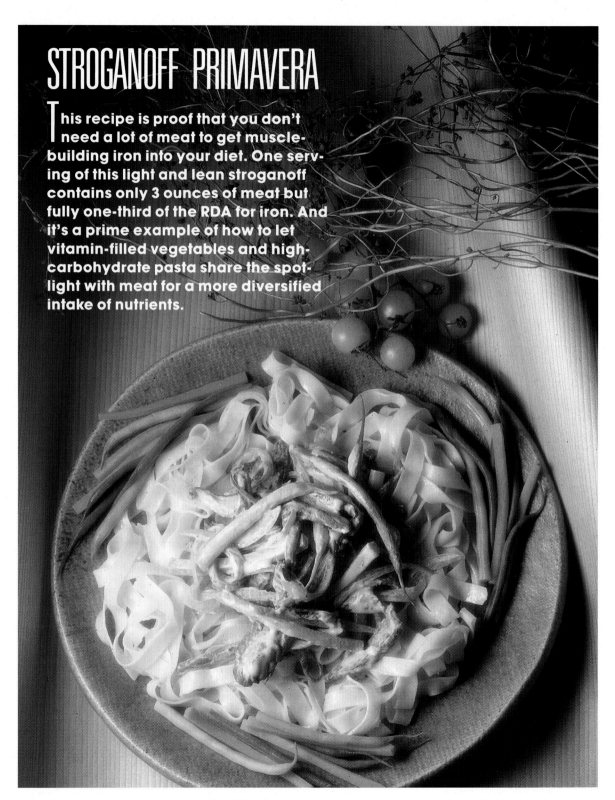

STROGANOFF PRIMAVERA

This recipe is proof that you don't need a lot of meat to get muscle-building iron into your diet. One serving of this light and lean stroganoff contains only 3 ounces of meat but fully one-third of the RDA for iron. And it's a prime example of how to let vitamin-filled vegetables and high-carbohydrate pasta share the spotlight with meat for a more diversified intake of nutrients.

Meat Entrées

STROGANOFF PRIMAVERA

4 ounces green beans
4 ounces yellow beans
2 carrots
12 ounces well-trimmed round steak
2 teaspoons olive oil
1 cup thinly sliced mushrooms
½ cup thinly sliced onion
1 clove garlic, minced
1 cup defatted beef stock

2 tablespoons tomato paste
2 teaspoons cornstarch
2 tablespoons nonfat yogurt
2 tablespoons sour cream
1 tablespoon flour
8 ounces fettuccine, cooked and drained

1. If possible, use whole green and yellow beans, trimmed to equal lengths. Cut the carrots into julienne pieces the same length as the beans. Steam the vegetables until crisp-tender, about 5 minutes.

2. Cut the meat across the grain into very thin slices (⅛'' to ¼'').

3. Coat a no-stick frying pan with no-stick spray. Place over medium-high heat until hot. Add a few slices of the beef and brown them quickly on both sides. Transfer to a plate and repeat until all the beef has been browned.

4. Drizzle the oil into the pan. Add the mushrooms and onions; sauté just until the edges begin to brown. Add the garlic, cover and reduce the heat to low. Cook for 5 minutes, or until the mushrooms have released some of their liquid and the onions are tender.

5. In a small bowl combine the stock, tomato paste and cornstarch. Stir into the mushrooms and cook over low heat until the sauce boils and thickens slightly. Stir in half of the vegetables and all of the beef. Heat briefly.

6. In a cup combine the yogurt, sour cream and flour. Remove the frying pan from the heat. Stir in the yogurt mixture. Return the pan to the heat for a minute just to heat the sauce.

7. Place the fettuccine on a serving platter. Spoon the stroganoff in the center and arrange the remaining vegetables around the edges.

SERVES 4.

Preparation Time: 15 min.
Cooking Time: 20 min.

CHEF'S NOTES

■ ■ ■ ■ ■ ■ ■ ■ ■

ACCOMPANIMENTS:
Serve with Spinach Salad with Strawberry Mayonnaise (page 87) and Fruit Ices (page 305).

■

VARIATIONS:
Replace the onions with scallions cut into 2'' lengths. Replace the beans and carrots with other vegetables, such as peppers, zucchini and yellow squash.

■

KITCHEN TRICK:
It's easier to cut the meat into very thin slices if it's partially frozen. Place it in the freezer for about 20 minutes, then use a very sharp knife to make thin cuts across the grain.

NUTRITION AT A GLANCE

PER SERVING:
Calories 497
Fat . . . . . . .11 g. (20% of cal.)
Sat. fat . . . . .3.2 g. (6% of cal.)
Cholesterol . . . . .72 mg.
Sodium . . . . .92 mg.

NOUVELLE BEEF STEW

This recipe updates classic beef stew in some important ways: It removes a lot of the fat—thanks to a sauce thickened with onions and tomatoes rather than butter and flour. And it retains more vitamins because the other vegetables in it are steamed separately and, therefore, not overcooked.

Nouvelle beef stew

- 8 ounces extra-lean beef cubes
- ½ cup finely chopped onion
- 2 cloves garlic, minced
- 1 cup finely chopped tomato
- 1½ cups defatted beef stock
- ½ cup nonalcoholic white wine or defatted beef stock
- 1 tablespoon minced fresh parsley
- ½ bay leaf
- ¼ teaspoon ground black pepper
- Pinch of ground cloves
- 3 small red potatoes, halved or quartered
- 2 large carrots, cut into chunks
- 2 stalks celery, cut into chunks
- 4 small turnips, cut into wedges
- ¼ cup peas

1. Coat a 3-quart saucepan with no-stick spray. Place over medium-high heat until hot. Add the beef and cook until brown. Add the onions and garlic. Sauté until the onions are lightly browned.

2. Stir in the tomatoes, stock, wine or stock, parsley, bay leaf, pepper and cloves. Bring to a boil. Cover, reduce the heat and simmer until the meat is tender, 1 to 1½ hours. Skim off any fat.

3. While the meat is cooking, place the potatoes, carrots, celery and turnips in a steamer basket. Steam for about 7 minutes, or until just barely tender. Set aside.

4. When the meat is tender, add the steamed vegetables and simmer for 10 minutes. Remove bay leaf.

5. Just before serving, cook the peas in a small amount of water until tender. Add to the stew.

SERVES 4.

Preparation Time: 20 min.
Cooking Time: 2 hr.

CHEF'S NOTES

DO FIRST:
Trim all visible fat from the beef.

ACCOMPANIMENT:
Serve over broad noodles.

VARIATION:
Replace the beef with lean lamb or veal.

NUTRI-NOTE:
Be aware that if you use standard canned stock rather than a low-salt variety, sodium could rise as high as 500 milligrams per serving.

NUTRITION AT A GLANCE

PER SERVING:
Calories 162
Fat . . . . 3 g. (17% of cal.)
Sat. fat . . . . . . 1 g. (5% of cal.)
Cholesterol . . . . 33 mg.
Sodium . . . . 77 mg.

SAVORY BEEF KABOBS

These kabobs illustrate several ways to eat beef without going overboard on fat. First, start with lean meat, such as ground sirloin. Then extend it with ground turkey breast and bread crumbs. Finally, bind the mixture together with egg substitute. The result: kabobs sure to gratify even the staunchest beef-lovers.

SAVORY BEEF KABOBS

8 ounces extra-lean ground sirloin

8 ounces ground turkey breast

½ cup dry bread crumbs

¼ cup fat-free egg substitute

3 tablespoons minced fresh coriander or parsley

3 tablespoons minced fresh mint or 1 tablespoon dried

1 tablespoon ground cumin

1 tablespoon lemon juice

1 teaspoon powdered ginger

1. In a large bowl, combine the sirloin, turkey, bread crumbs, egg, coriander or parsley, mint, cumin, lemon juice and ginger. Work lightly with your hands until well-mixed.

2. Form the mixture into small logs about 4″ × ½″.

3. Warm a large no-stick frying pan over medium heat. Add half of the kabobs. Brown on all sides. Transfer to a platter and keep warm. Repeat with the remaining kabobs.

SERVES 6.

Preparation Time: 20 min.
Cooking Time: 20 min.

CHEF'S NOTES

INGREDIENTS NOTE:

Ground turkey breast is not readily available in many supermarkets. To make your own, buy a piece of boneless, skinless turkey breast. Cut it into cubes and mince with on/off turns in a food processor.

ACCOMPANIMENTS:

Serve with chopped tomatoes, green beans, a yogurt sauce (combine nonfat yogurt with hot-pepper sauce and ground cumin to taste) and cooked bulgur, rice or couscous. You may also serve these kabobs in pita pockets with lettuce, tomatoes, cucumbers and yogurt sauce.

VARIATION:

Replace the beef with all turkey or ground chicken breast.

NUTRITION AT A GLANCE

PER SERVING:

Calories 158
Fat . . . . .6 g. (34% of cal.)
Sat. fat . . . . .2 g. (11% of cal.)
Cholesterol . . . . .47 mg.
Sodium . . . . .125 mg.

VEAL ROULADES WITH RICE STUFFING

Veal is a low-fat meat that is a nice alternative to chicken for special occasions. And it's higher in blood-strengthening iron than poultry, so it's a good hedge against anemia. This recipe has a Middle Eastern flair to it, pairing rice, currants and almonds with the meat.

VEAL ROULADES WITH RICE STUFFING

RICE STUFFING
- **1 cup long-grain white rice**
- **2–4 tablespoons currants or chopped raisins**
- **1 clove garlic, minced**
- **1 tablespoon oil**
- **2 cups defatted chicken stock**
- **¼ cup toasted sliced almonds**
- **1 teaspoon grated lemon rind**
- **2 tablespoons minced fresh parsley**
- **1 tablespoon minced fresh thyme or 1 teaspoon dried**

VEAL ROULADES
- **12 ounces veal scaloppine (4 scallops)**
- **3 tablespoons lemon juice**
- **1 tablespoon unbleached flour**
- **¼ teaspoon ground black pepper**
- **2 teaspoons olive oil**
- **¼ cup water or defatted chicken stock**

1. *To make the rice stuffing:* In a 2-quart saucepan over low heat, sauté the rice, currants and garlic in the oil for 2 minutes, or until the rice turns milky white. Add the stock and bring to a boil over high heat. Stir, cover and reduce the heat to medium low. Cook for 20 minutes.

2. Take the pan off the heat and remove the lid. Let stand for 10 minutes. Fluff with a fork; mix in the almonds, lemon rind, parsley and thyme. Reserve ½ cup of the rice for the roulades. Place the remaining rice on a large heat-proof platter. Cover with foil and keep warm.

3. *To make the veal roulades:* Place the veal between sheets of plastic wrap. Using a mallet, pound to ⅛″. Remove the top piece of plastic. Sprinkle the veal with 1 tablespoon of the lemon juice.

4. Divide the reserved rice among the veal, placing a thin strip of filling down the center of each. Carefully roll up the meat to enclose the rice; discard the plastic. Skewer the rolls shut with sturdy wooden picks or tie with kitchen string. On a piece of wax paper, combine the flour and pepper. Dredge the rolls lightly in the flour.

5. In a large no-stick frying pan over medium heat, heat the oil until sizzling. Add the roulades and brown on all sides, about 10 minutes. Reduce the heat to low. Cover the pan and cook for 10 minutes. Transfer the roulades to the rice platter. Remove the picks or string.

6. Add the water or stock and the remaining 2 tablespoons lemon juice to the frying pan. Stir over medium-high heat for 1 minute, scraping up any browned bits from the bottom of the pan. Drizzle over the roulades.

SERVES 4.

Preparation Time: 20 min.
Cooking Time: 30 min.

CHEF'S NOTES

INGREDIENTS NOTE:
When buying the veal, ask for top round from the leg.

ACCOMPANIMENTS:
Serve with braised spinach, kale or other greens and cooked carrots — try Carrots with Garlic and Basil (page 249).

VARIATIONS:
Replace the veal with chicken or turkey cutlets. Substitute wild rice for part of the white rice. Use other herbs such as sage, basil, oregano or marjoram.

NUTRITION AT A GLANCE

PER SERVING:

Calories 391
Fat . . . . . . 14.7 g. (34% of cal.)
Sat. fat . . . . . 2.9 g. (7% of cal.)
Cholesterol . . . . 69 mg.
Sodium . . . . 99 mg.

LEAN VEAL PICCATA

Traditional recipes for this Italian favorite sometimes use ½ cup of butter. That's a lot of fat, which doctors say is more likely than protein and carbohydrates to make you fat. By considerably cutting the fat (and the calories attached to it) in this recipe, you're helping to control more than just your profile. Studies show that excess weight can lead to osteoarthritis, a degenerative joint disease.

LEAN VEAL PICCATA

6 ounces veal scallops, cut into ½″ strips
2 teaspoons cornstarch
2 teaspoons olive oil
1 clove garlic, minced
16 ounces potatoes, sliced and steamed
2 roasted sweet red peppers, cut into ½″ strips
1 tablespoon minced fresh parsley
1 tablespoon snipped chives
Juice of 1 lemon

1. Sprinkle the veal with the cornstarch and toss to lightly dust all the pieces.

2. Heat the oil over medium-high heat in a large no-stick frying pan. Add the veal and garlic. Sauté for about 1 minute.

3. Add the potatoes. Continue to sauté until the veal is cooked through, about 1 minute more. Add the peppers and cook for another 30 seconds. Remove the veal and vegetables from the pan.

4. Add the parsley, chives and lemon juice to the pan. Raise the heat to high. Stir with a plastic-coated spatula, scraping up browned bits from the bottom of the pan, until the juice is reduced by half, about 1 minute. Pour over the veal and toss well.

SERVES 4.

Preparation Time: 20 min.
Cooking Time: 5 min.

CHEF'S NOTES

DO FIRST:

Prepare the potatoes: Cut the potatoes into ¼″ slices. Steam until tender, about 10 to 15 minutes. Pat dry on paper towels.

Prepare the peppers: Broil the peppers 4″ from the heat until charred on all sides, about 15 minutes. Remove from the oven, wrap in a paper bag and let stand 5 minutes. Peel off the skins and discard the seeds.

ACCOMPANIMENT:

Serve with herb-flavored rice or orzo, a rice-shaped pasta.

NUTRI-NOTE:

Although lemons contain almost no sodium, they seem to satisfy the taste buds in the same way as salt and make an excellent flavor substitute for it.

NUTRITION AT A GLANCE

PER SERVING:
Calories 146
Fat . . . . . . .5.8 g. (36% of cal.)
Sat. fat . . . . .0.4 g. (3% of cal.)
Cholesterol . . . . .39 mg.
Sodium . . . . .53 mg.

BRAISED VEAL WITH ESCAROLE

Veal is the leanest form of beef you can buy. It has lots of protein, iron and niacin, a vitamin known to calm nerves. Combining the veal with carrots and escarole, as we do in this dish, adds considerable amounts of disease-fighting vitamins A and C.

Meat Entrées

BRAISED VEAL WITH ESCAROLE

- **1 teaspoon oil**
- **1 pound veal stew meat, trimmed of any visible fat and cut into 1″ chunks**
- **2 cups plus 2 table- spoons beef stock**
- **1½ cups sliced carrot**
- **1½ cups thinly sliced (on the diagonal) celery**
- **1 cup chopped onion**
- **1 clove garlic, minced**
- **½ teaspoon dried basil**
- **½ teaspoon dried thyme**
- **¼ teaspoon ground black pepper**
- **1 bay leaf**
- **1 pound escarole, coarsely chopped**
- **1 tablespoon cornstarch**
- **¼ cup cold water**

1. In a 6-quart pot or Dutch oven over medium-high heat, warm the oil. Add the veal and 2 tablespoons of the stock. Brown the meat on all sides, then remove it from the pan with a slotted spoon.

2. In the same pan, stir-fry the carrots, celery, onions and garlic for 3 minutes.

3. Return the meat to the pan. Add 2 cups of stock, basil, thyme, pepper and bay leaf. Cover and simmer for 45 minutes to 1 hour, or until the meat is tender.

4. Add the escarole to the pan. Cook, stirring occasionally, for 6 to 7 minutes, or until wilted.

5. In a cup, dissolve the cornstarch in the water. Add to the stew. Simmer for 1 minute, or until slightly thickened. Discard the bay leaf.

SERVES 4.

Preparation Time: 20 min.
Cooking Time: 1¼ hr.

CHEF'S NOTES

ACCOMPANIMENTS:

Serve over brown rice or couscous. If using brown rice, start it cooking just after the veal begins simmering (step 3). If using couscous, prepare it at the last minute. See page 147 for quanti- ties and directions.

VARIATIONS:

Replace the veal with very lean beef or lamb. Replace the escarole with other dark leafy greens, such as chicory, kale, collards or mus- tard greens.

NUTRITION AT A GLANCE

PER SERVING:

- Calories 221
- Fat . . . . . . .7.8 g. (32% of cal.)
- Sat. fat . . . .2.8 g (11% of cal.)
- Cholesterol . . . . .117 mg.
- Sodium . . . . .180 mg.

LIGHT-STYLE OSSO BUCO

You might call veal shanks forgotten pieces of meat, since they've been largely forsaken in favor of chops and steaks. But when slowly braised, they produce a wonderfully rich and flavorful dish that's low in fat.

LIGHT-STYLE OSSO BUCO

Ingredients

- **1** teaspoon oil
- **1** veal shank, about 2½ pounds (see Chef's Notes)
- **½** cup nonalcoholic red wine
- **½** cup diced onion
- **½** cup diced carrot
- **½** cup diced celery
- **½** cup diced parsnip
- **¼** teaspoon ground black pepper
- **2** cloves garlic, minced
- **2** cups defatted chicken or beef stock
- **2** tablespoons tomato paste
- **3** boiling potatoes, quartered
- **8** ounces green beans, cut into 1″ lengths
- **2** small yellow squash, cut diagonally into ¼″ slices
- **⅓** cup packed fresh parsley
- **1** teaspoon grated lemon rind

1. Coat the bottom of a Dutch oven with the oil. Over medium heat, brown the veal for about 5 minutes per side. Transfer the veal to a plate and set it aside.

2. Add the wine to the pan. Bring to a boil and use a wooden spoon to scrape up any browned bits from the bottom of the pan.

3. Add the onions, carrots, celery and parsnips. Boil gently until the wine is reduced by half, about 5 minutes. Stir in the pepper and half of the garlic. Return the veal and any juices on the plate to the saucepan. Arrange the veal in a single layer.

4. In a medium bowl, whisk together the stock and tomato paste. Pour over the veal. Cover and simmer until very tender, about 1¼ hours.

5. Transfer the veal to a serving platter, cover with foil and keep warm.

6. Set a strainer over a large bowl. Pour the cooked vegetables into it, reserving the liquid. Transfer the vegetables to a blender. Measure out 1½ cups of the liquid and add to the blender. (Save any remaining liquid for another use.) Puree, transfer to a 1-quart saucepan and keep warm over low heat.

7. Steam the potatoes, green beans and squash until crisp-tender, about 5 minutes.

8. Place the parsley, lemon rind and remaining garlic on a cutting board and chop finely.

9. To serve, arrange the steamed vegetables around the veal shanks. Pour the sauce over the veal. Sprinkle the meat and vegetables with the parsley mixture.

SERVES 6.

Preparation Time: 20 min.
Cooking Time: 1 ½ hr.

CHEF'S NOTES

■ ■ ■ ■ ■ ■ ■ ■

INGREDIENTS NOTE:

Look for veal shanks in ethnic markets and large supermarkets, where they are sometimes labeled osso buco. Have the butcher cut 6 equal pieces. You may replace the red wine with stock.

■

VARIATION:

Serve with other vegetables, including carrots, snap peas, broccoli or cauliflower.

■

MAKE-AHEAD TIP:

You may prepare the veal and sauce ahead. While you're reheating them, steam the vegetables.

NUTRITION AT A GLANCE

PER SERVING:

Calories 232
Fat . . . . . . .6.2 g. (24% of cal.)
Sat. fat . . . . .2.3 g. (9% of cal.)
Cholesterol . . . . .74 mg.
Sodium . . . . .112 mg.

STUFFED PORK LOIN

Pork tends to have a bad dietary reputation because bacon and luncheon meats have so much fat. But many cuts of fresh pork are acceptably lean. One serving of this stuffed loin, for instance, has only 8 grams of fat—less than a tablespoon of mayonnaise.

STUFFED PORK LOIN

STUFFING
- **1 cup cooked brown rice**
- **½ cup corn**
- **¼ cup diced onion**
- **¼ cup diced sweet red pepper**
- **2 cloves garlic, minced**
- **¼ cup fat-free egg substitute or 1 egg**

PORK
- **2 pounds pork tenderloin**
- **2 cloves garlic, minced**
- **2 small chili peppers, seeded and minced**

- **2 tablespoons lime juice**
- **1 tablespoon minced fresh oregano or 1 teaspoon dried**
- **½ teaspoon ground cumin**
- **½ teaspoon honey Pinch of ground cinnamon**
- **1 tablespoon flour**
- **½ cup defatted chicken stock**

1. *To make the stuffing:* In a medium bowl combine the rice, corn, onions, peppers, garlic and egg. Cover and refrigerate.

2. *To make the pork:* Remove and discard all visible fat from the pork. You'll have about 1¾ pounds of meat left. Make a lengthwise slit in the meat as a pocket for the stuffing.

3. In a small bowl combine the garlic, peppers, lime juice, oregano, cumin, honey and cinnamon. Rub over the meat, inside and out. Cover and refrigerate overnight.

4. Preheat the oven to 450°. Pack the stuffing into the slit area. Tie the roast with kitchen string to contain the stuffing. Set the meat on a roasting rack.

5. Place the flour in an oven cooking bag and shake to coat the interior of the bag. Place the roast and rack in the bag. Add the stock. Tie the bag shut and follow the bag package directions for making slits for the steam to escape. Place in a shallow roasting pan.

6. Place the roast in the oven and reduce the temperature to 350°. Bake for 50 minutes, or until an internal temperature of 160° to 165° is reached. Remove from the oven and let stand for 15 minutes for easier carving.

SERVES 8.

Preparation Time: 25 min. + standing time
Cooking Time: 50 min.

CHEF'S NOTES

DO FIRST:

Cook the rice: Use ½ cup of brown rice and cook according to package directions. Chill, if desired, for easier handling.

ACCOMPANIMENTS:

Serve with baked potatoes, steamed broccoli and a fruit salad of apple and orange slices.

VARIATION:

Replace the rice stuffing with a bread stuffing flavored with chopped apples and prunes.

NUTRITION AT A GLANCE

PER SERVING:

Calories	215
Fat	8 g. (33% of cal.)
Sat. fat	2.6 g. (11% of cal.)
Cholesterol	55 mg.
Sodium	63 mg.

PORK CUTLETS WITH APPLE SLICES

If you're watching your cholesterol, you might consider pork forbidden meat. But each serving of this lean tenderloin dish has only 46 milligrams of cholesterol. And the apples that accompany it add soluble fiber, which can help keep cholesterol levels down.

PORK CUTLETS WITH APPLE SLICES

1 teaspoon grated lemon rind

1 teaspoon fresh thyme or ¼ teaspoon dried

1 clove garlic, minced

1 teaspoon olive oil

10 ounces pork tenderloin, trimmed of all visible fat and cut into 8 equal slices

2–3 tart baking apples, cut into ½″ wedges

2 tablespoons lemon juice

1. On a plate, combine the lemon rind, thyme and garlic.

2. Lightly rub the pork slices with the herb mixture.

3. Warm the oil in a large no-stick frying pan over medium heat. Add the pork and sauté for 3 minutes per side to brown.

4. Push the pork to one side of the pan. Add the apples and 1 tablespoon of the lemon juice. Sauté, turning the apples as they brown, for about 5 minutes.

5. Rearrange the pork so that the slices are in a single layer under the apples. Cover and cook until the apples and pork are tender, about 5 minutes.

6. Transfer to a platter. Add the remaining 1 tablespoon lemon juice to the pan and scrape up the browned bits. Drizzle the juices over the pork and apples.

SERVES 4.

Preparation Time: 10 min.
Cooking Time: 20 min.

CHEF'S NOTES

DO FIRST:

Using a sharp knife, remove all visible fat from the outside of the tenderloin.

INGREDIENTS NOTE:

You may use any type of tart baking apple, such as Granny Smith, Northern Spy or Jonathan. Baking apples hold their shape better than cooking varieties such as McIntosh. If you leave the skin on, the finished dish will be more colorful and have more fiber.

VARIATION:

You may use other boneless cutlets, such as chicken, turkey or veal.

NUTRITION AT A GLANCE

PER SERVING:

Calories 133
Fat . . . . 3.1 g. (21% of cal.)
Sat. fat . . . . . 0.8 g. (5% of cal.)
Cholesterol . . . . 46 mg.
Sodium . . . . 36 mg.

LAMB-VEGETABLE KABOBS

Even lamb—often considered a high-fat meat—can star in a disease-fighter's diet. The secret? Choose the leanest cut you can find, then trim off every bit of visible fat. For extra measure, serve just a modest amount of meat with an array of nutrient-packed vegetables.

LAMB-VEGETABLE KABOBS

MARINADE

- ¼ **cup chopped fresh coriander**
- ¼ **cup chopped fresh mint**
- 1 **green chili pepper, seeded and chopped**
- 3 **cloves garlic, sliced**
- 2 **tablespoons grated fresh ginger**
- ½ **cup nonfat yogurt**
- 1 **teaspoon ground cumin**
- 1 **teaspoon ground coriander**
- ½ **teaspoon ground cinnamon**
- **Pinch of ground cloves**

- 12 **ounces lean lamb from leg, cut into 1″ cubes**

KABOBS

- 1 **large onion**
- 1 **sweet red pepper, cut into 1″ cubes**
- 1 **yellow pepper, cut into 1″ cubes**
- 1 **zucchini, cut into 1″ cubes**
- 1 **yellow squash, cut into 1″ cubes**

COUSCOUS

- 2 **cups defatted stock**
- 2 **cups couscous**

1. *To make the marinade:* In a food processor grind together the fresh coriander, mint, chili pepper, garlic and ginger (or finely chop by hand). Place in a mixing bowl with the yogurt, cumin, ground coriander, cinnamon and cloves. Add the lamb and mix well. Allow to marinate for at least 2 to 3 hours in the refrigerator.

2. *To make the kabobs:* Peel the onion and trim off the root hairs, leaving the root stem attached. Cut into 1″ wedges, leaving the root on each section so wedges don't separate. Add the onions, red peppers, yellow peppers, zucchini and squash to marinade mixture. Mix to coat well.

3. Preheat the broiler or light a charcoal or gas grill, allowing it to get very hot. Thread meat and vegetables onto metal or bamboo skewers. Grill over high heat for 15 to 20 minutes, turning skewers to cook all sides, until meat is cooked as desired.

4. *To make the couscous:* While the lamb is cooking, bring the stock to a boil in a 1-quart saucepan. Add the couscous. Cover the pan and remove it from the heat. Let stand for 3 to 4 minutes, or until all the liquid has been absorbed. Fluff with a fork. Serve hot with the lamb.

SERVES 4.

Preparation Time: 20 min. + standing time
Cooking Time: 20 min.

CHEF'S NOTES

ACCOMPANIMENTS:

Serve with Orange-Scented Cucumber Salad (page 77), pita bread and mango chutney.

VARIATIONS:

You may substitute small mushrooms, cherry tomatoes or cubes of eggplant for any of the other vegetables. You may also substitute cubes of lean beef for the lamb. Try cooked bulgur or rice in place of the couscous.

MAKE-AHEAD TIP:

Prepare the yogurt marinade early in the day or even the night before. Add the lamb and refrigerate until ready to cook.

NUTRITION AT A GLANCE

PER SERVING:

Calories 281
Fat . . . . . . .5.7 g. (18% of cal.)
Sat. fat . . . . .1.7 g. (5% of cal.)
Cholesterol . . . . .56 mg.
Sodium . . . . .111 mg.

LAMB CUTLETS WITH ROSEMARY POTATOES

Lamb is an excellent source of blood-building iron. And it has lots of zinc, a mineral needed for proper wound healing and the ability to fight off infections. This recipe combines lean lamb with a wide array of healthy vegetables for a nutrient-dense meal.

LAMB CUTLETS WITH ROSEMARY POTATOES

- ½ **cup defatted chicken stock**
- 2 **tablespoons red-wine vinegar**
- 1½ **tablespoons fresh rosemary**
- 4 **teaspoons olive oil**
- ½ **large eggplant, cubed**
- 8 **cherry tomatoes**
- 1 **zucchini, cubed**
- 8 **small mushrooms**
- 1 **small onion, quartered**
- 1 **pound new potatoes, quartered**
- 1 **whole garlic bulb**
- 1 **pound lamb cutlets**
- ¼ **teaspoon ground black pepper**

1. In a large bowl, combine the stock and vinegar. Add ½ tablespoon of the rosemary and 1 teaspoon of the oil. Mix well. Add the eggplant, tomatoes, zucchini, mushrooms and onions. Set aside to marinate.

2. In a 7″ × 11″ baking dish, toss together the potatoes, the remaining 1 tablespoon rosemary and 1 teaspoon of the remaining oil. Make sure the potatoes are coated with oil. Bake at 400° for 15 minutes.

3. While the potatoes are baking, divide the marinating vegetables among 4 metal skewers; reserve the marinade. Place the skewers on a cookie sheet; baste with marinade.

4. Cut the top quarter off the bulb of garlic and discard it. Place the remaining bulb on a square of foil. Drizzle with 1 teaspoon of the remaining oil and wrap tightly. Add to the pan with the potatoes. Place the cookie sheet with the kabobs in the oven.

5. Bake the potatoes and vegetables for 15 minutes, or until all are tender. Baste the kabobs with some of the reserved marinade. Remove from the oven and keep warm.

6. Season the lamb on both sides with the pepper and the remaining 1 teaspoon oil. Place on a broiler rack and broil about 3″ from the heat for 2 minutes per side, or until cooked as desired.

7. To serve, remove the garlic from the foil. Using several thicknesses of paper towels to protect your hands from the heat, squeeze the softened garlic from its peel into a small bowl; mash with a fork. Serve as a condiment to spread on the meat. Serve the meat with the potatoes and kabobs. Use any remaining marinade as a dipping sauce for the vegetables.

SERVES 4.

Preparation Time: 20 min.
Cooking Time: 35 min.

CHEF'S NOTES

INGREDIENTS NOTE:
For the cutlets, use either thinly sliced leg of lamb or boned shoulder lamb chops pounded to ¼″ thick.

VARIATION:
You may prepare the meat and kabobs on a backyard grill: Grill the kabobs for 10 to 20 minutes, basting often, until tender. Grill the meat for 2 to 5 minutes per side.

CHEF'S SECRET:
If using bamboo skewers, soak them in cold water for 15 minutes so they won't burn.

NUTRITION AT A GLANCE

PER SERVING:

Calories 328
Fat . . . . . . 10.8 g. (30% of cal.)
Sat. fat . . . . 3.7 g. (10% of cal.)
Cholesterol . . . . 76 mg.
Sodium . . . . 104 mg.

TUSCAN-STYLE RABBIT

Rabbit is an oft-overlooked meat that's ideal for anyone concerned with weight loss or high blood pressure. It's lower in fat than most red meats. And it has more potassium and less sodium than more common meats, which is important for lowering blood pressure. Further, it's a super source of both vitamin B_{12} and niacin.

Meat Entrées

TUSCAN-STYLE RABBIT

1 lemon
1 tablespoon olive oil
2 cloves garlic, minced
1 teaspoon fresh rosemary or ½ teaspoon dried

¼ teaspoon ground black pepper
2 pounds rabbit pieces

1. Grate the rind from the lemon. Place in a 9″ × 13″ baking dish with the juice from the lemon, oil, garlic, rosemary and pepper.

2. Add the rabbit and turn the pieces to coat all sides. Cover and refrigerate for several hours or overnight. Turn the pieces occasionally.

3. Bake the rabbit uncovered at 400° for about 25 minutes. Turn the pieces frequently and baste with pan juices until the rabbit is tender and the juices run clear when you pierce the meat with a fork.

4. If desired, broil the meat for a few minutes to achieve a light brown color.

SERVES 4.

Preparation Time: 5 min. + standing time
Cooking Time: 25 min.

CHEF'S NOTES

■ ■ ■ ■ ■ ■ ■ ■

ACCOMPANIMENTS:
Serve with Maple-Glazed Radishes and Carrots (page 257) and Barley with Toasted Pecans (page 265).

■

KITCHEN TRICKS:
If buying a whole rabbit, choose one that weighs 2 pounds or less to ensure tenderness. Look for smooth, pale flesh. For easier handling ask your butcher to cut the rabbit into pieces for you. Once home, tightly wrap your purchase in plastic and store it in the coldest part of the refrigerator for no more than two days.

NUTRITION AT A GLANCE

PER SERVING:
Calories 238
Fat . . . . . . .9.5 g. (36% of cal.)
Sat. fat . . . .2.8 g. (11% of cal.)
Cholesterol . . . . .96 mg.
Sodium . . . . .71 mg.

POULTRY MAIN DISHES

■■■■■■■■■■■

JAMAICAN CHICKEN

Chili peppers, featured in this delicious Caribbean entrée, have great healing potential. They've been shown to help relieve congestion from colds and allergies. And they may even protect against heart disease by increasing the body's ability to break up potentially dangerous clots.

JAMAICAN CHICKEN

½ cup water

5-6 thin slices fresh ginger

2 dried chili peppers, crumbled

½ onion, chopped

¼ cup white-wine vinegar

1 tablespoon pepper sauce (see Chef's Notes)

1 teaspoon dried thyme

½ teaspoon ground allspice

½ teaspoon ground black pepper

1¼ pounds boneless skinless chicken breasts, cubed

1. In a blender, combine the water, ginger, chili peppers, onions, vinegar, pepper sauce, thyme, allspice and black pepper. Puree until fairly smooth.

2. Pour the marinade into a large bowl. Add the chicken and stir to coat well. Cover and refrigerate for 4 to 5 hours, stirring occasionally.

3. Thread the meat onto metal skewers. Reserve the marinade, transfer to a saucepan and bring to a full boil. Keep warm over low heat.

4. Grill or broil the chicken, until cooked through, about 5 minutes per side. Serve the boiled marinade as a sauce.

SERVES 4.

Preparation Time: 10 min. + standing time
Cooking Time: 10 min.

CHEF'S NOTES

INGREDIENTS NOTE:

For authentic Jamaican flavor, choose a pepper sauce that contains tamarind and hot peppers, such as Pickapeppa. It is sold in large supermarkets and specialty stores. You may replace it with Worcestershire sauce and a splash of hot-pepper sauce.

ACCOMPANIMENTS:

Serve with black beans, yellow rice and corn bread. For a real tropical flair, garnish with pineapple, mango or papaya slices.

VARIATION:

You may replace the chicken with cubes or strips of turkey breast, pork tenderloin or flank steak, or use bone-in chicken pieces. Adjust the cooking time accordingly.

NUTRITION AT A GLANCE

PER SERVING:

Calories 171
Fat . . . . 1.9 g. (10% of cal.)
Sat. fat . . . . . 0.5 g. (3% of cal.)
Cholesterol . . . . 82 mg.
Sodium . . . . 132 mg.

MUSHROOM-STUFFED CHICKEN BREASTS

Chicken breast is a health-lover's favorite. Besides being low in calories and fat (if you discard the skin), it's a wonderful source of B complex vitamins. This particular dish is high in thiamine, riboflavin and niacin—all of which help the body metabolize food and promote a healthy nervous system.

MUSHROOM-STUFFED CHICKEN BREASTS

4 teaspoons olive oil
½ cup minced shallot
1 tablespoon minced garlic
12 ounces mushrooms, sliced
¼ cup sliced scallions
1 tablespoon minced fresh parsley
2 slices rye bread
6 tablespoons defatted chicken stock
1 teaspoon dried thyme
½ teaspoon ground black pepper
4 boneless skinless chicken breasts (5 ounces each)
½ cup low-fat yogurt
1 tablespoon cornstarch

1. Heat 3 teaspoons of the oil in a large no-stick frying pan over medium-high heat. Add the shallots and garlic. Sauté for 1 minute, stirring constantly. Add the mushrooms; sauté for 3 to 4 minutes, tossing frequently until crisp-tender.

2. Transfer half of the mushrooms to a small bowl. Add half of the scallions and the parsley. Set aside.

3. Lightly toast the bread and cut it into ¼″ cubes. Add to the mushrooms in the frying pan along with 2 tablespoons stock, remaining scallions, ½ teaspoon thyme and ¼ teaspoon pepper. Mix well.

4. Place the chicken between pieces of foil. Pound with the smooth side of a meat mallet until ⅛″ to ¼″ thick. Remove the foil. Divide the bread mixture among the cutlets. Roll up the pieces to enclose the filling. Secure the bundles with toothpicks.

5. Coat a 9″ × 13″ baking dish with no-stick spray. Add the chicken, seam side down. Brush with the remaining oil. Sprinkle with the remaining thyme and pepper. Add the remaining stock to the pan.

6. Cover the pan with foil. Bake at 425° for 20 to 25 minutes, or until the chicken is cooked through. Discard the toothpicks.

7. Pour the pan juices into a small saucepan. Whisk in the yogurt and cornstarch. Cook over low heat, stirring constantly, until the sauce just begins to thicken. Do not let it boil or the mixture will curdle. Remove from the heat and stir in the reserved mushroom mixture. Serve with the chicken.

SERVES 4.

Preparation Time: 20 min.
Cooking Time: 30 min.

CHEF'S NOTES

ACCOMPANIMENTS:
Serve with steamed green beans and boiled new potatoes drizzled with lemon juice. Add a crisp green salad and sweet ripe pears or dried apricots.

VARIATIONS:
Substitute turkey cutlets. You may also use thin fish fillets, such as flounder, but be extra careful not to overcook them.

KITCHEN TRICK:
Large shallots are easier to mince than smaller ones. Cut them in half through the root end. Make small vertical cuts up to but not through the root. Then slice the shallot crosswise.

NUTRITION AT A GLANCE

PER SERVING:
Calories 291
Fat . . . . . . .8.2 g. (25% of cal.)
Sat. fat . . . . .1.8 g. (6% of cal.)
Cholesterol . . . . .86 mg.
Sodium . . . . .270 mg.

CHICKEN FAJITAS

With a little advance preparation, fajitas are a quick-and-easy dinner dish. They're also another tasty way to work low-fat, high-protein chicken breast into your menus. And the avocado in the filling adds a nice complement of cholesterol-lowering monounsaturates.

CHICKEN FAJITAS

2½ tablespoons lime juice
2 cloves garlic, minced
2 teaspoons olive oil
½ teaspoon crushed red-pepper flakes
12 ounces boneless skinless chicken breast, cut into ½" strips
4 large flour tortillas
½ cup mashed avocado
½ teaspoon minced chili pepper
1 cup salsa
1 cup nonfat yogurt
¼ cup minced fresh coriander

1. In a cup, combine 2 tablespoons of the lime juice with the garlic, oil and red-pepper flakes.

2. Place the chicken in a large bowl. Add the garlic mixture, combine well and refrigerate, covered, for at least 2 hours.

3. About 10 minutes before serving, wrap the tortillas in aluminum foil and place in a 350° oven to warm while the chicken is cooking.

4. In a small bowl, combine the avocado and chili peppers with the remaining ½ tablespoon lime juice.

5. Heat a large no-stick frying pan or a grill on medium high until very hot. Add the chicken strips a few at a time and cook until browned and cooked through, about 5 to 7 minutes.

6. To serve, divide the chicken among the tortillas. Top with a spoonful each of the avocado mixture, salsa and yogurt. Sprinkle with some of the coriander. Roll up to enclose the filling. Serve topped with the remaining salsa, yogurt and coriander.

SERVES 4.

Preparation Time: 20 min. + standing time
Cooking Time: 10 min.

CHEF'S NOTES

INGREDIENTS NOTE:
Prepare the avocado just before serving. Cut it in half; the pit will remain in one half. Brush the exposed flesh of that half with lime or lemon juice, wrap well in plastic, refrigerate and reserve for another use. Scoop out the flesh of the remaining half and mash with a fork.

ACCOMPANIMENTS:
Serve with cooked rice and sautéed onions.

NUTRITION AT A GLANCE

PER SERVING:
Calories 281
Fat . . . . . .10.2 g. (33% of cal.)
Sat. fat . . . . .1.4 g. (4% of cal.)
Cholesterol . . . . .50 mg.
Sodium . . . . .89 mg.

MEDITERRANEAN CHICKEN THIGHS

This French-style dish gives you good amounts of vitamin C and niacin. Both strengthen your immune system, so you're less likely to come down with pesky infections. By the way, although thighs aren't as lean as breast meat, you can easily pare out much of their excess fat with a knife.

Mediterranean chicken thighs

1 teaspoon olive oil
1½ cups sliced onion
1 tablespoon minced garlic
1 green pepper, thinly sliced
1 yellow pepper, thinly sliced
10 whole Niçoise olives or 5 pitted black olives, chopped
¼ teaspoon fennel seed

⅛ teaspoon dried thyme
⅛ teaspoon dried rosemary
Pinch of red-pepper flakes
1¼ pounds boneless skinless chicken thighs, trimmed of all visible fat
2 teaspoons red-wine vinegar
⅛ teaspoon ground black pepper

1. Heat the oil in a large no-stick frying pan over medium heat. Add the onions and garlic. Sauté for 4 to 5 minutes, stirring frequently, until the onions are nearly tender.

2. Add the green and yellow peppers. Sauté for 5 to 6 minutes, stirring frequently, until tender. Add the olives, fennel seeds, thyme, rosemary and red-pepper flakes. Sauté for 1 minute, stirring frequently.

3. Arrange the chicken in a single layer in a shallow baking dish. Drizzle with the vinegar and sprinkle with the black pepper. Spoon the vegetables over the chicken.

4. Bake at 425° for 25 to 30 minutes, or until the chicken is cooked through and the juices run clear when you pierce the thighs with a fork.

SERVES 4.

Preparation Time: 15 min.
Cooking Time: 45 min.

CHEF'S NOTES

ACCOMPANIMENTS:
Serve with steamed asparagus and cooked pasta tossed with a splash of extra-virgin olive oil and chopped fresh basil or parsley.

VARIATIONS:
Use chicken cutlets instead of thighs. They may cook a little faster than the thighs so check for doneness after 15 minutes. If yellow peppers are not available, use all red or a mixture of red and green.

MICROWAVE OPTION:
To cook the vegetables, place the onions, peppers and oil in a 2-quart glass bowl. Cover with plastic and microwave for 3 to 5 minutes, stirring twice, until tender. Add the spices and micro-wave for 1 minute.

NUTRITION AT A GLANCE

PER SERVING:
Calories 218
Fat . . . . .8 g. (33% of cal.)
Sat. fat . . . .2.2 g. (8% of cal.)
Cholesterol . . . . .117 mg.
Sodium . . . . .149 mg.

CORNISH HENS WITH ORANGES AND RICE

Serving fruit with poultry is very popular among many cultures. We like this orange-accented version because it adds the vitamin C that poultry lacks. And the fruit provides a sweet counterpoint to the Mediterranean spices that take the place of salt. It's a tasty way to help boost immunity.

Poultry Main Dishes

CORNISH HENS WITH ORANGES AND RICE

⅔ cup apple-cider vinegar	1 dried red chili pepper
1 tablespoon Worcestershire sauce	1 jalapeño pepper
½ teaspoon paprika	2 cloves garlic, minced
¼ teaspoon Angostura bitters	2 Cornish hens, split in half
Dash of hot-pepper sauce	2 cups hot cooked rice
	1½ cups orange sections

1. In a large glass baking dish, combine the vinegar, Worcestershire sauce, paprika, bitters and hot-pepper sauce.

2. Wearing rubber gloves to protect your hands, split both the dried chili pepper and the jalapeño pepper in half and remove the seeds. Finely chop both, then transfer to a mortar and pestle. Mash the peppers and garlic into a paste. Add to the vinegar mixture and combine.

3. Remove any visible fat from the hens, especially the cavity area. Place in the dish, turning pieces several times to coat with marinade. Cover and refrigerate overnight or up to 24 hours.

4. To cook, remove the hens from marinade and place on a broiler pan. Broil 4″ from the heat for 10 to 15 minutes per side, or until juices run clear when a fork is inserted in thickest part of the thigh. Baste occasionally with remaining marinade. (If hens seem to darken too fast, move them farther from the heat source.)

5. Serve with the rice and orange sections.

SERVES 4.

Preparation Time: 15 min. + standing time
Cooking Time: 30 min.

CHEF'S NOTES

DO FIRST:
Cook the rice: Start cooking brown rice about 45 to 60 minutes before serving. If using white rice, start it 20 to 30 minutes before serving.

ACCOMPANIMENT:
Serve with a bright green vegetable such as broccoli, sugar snap peas or brussels sprouts.

NUTRI-NOTE:
Poultry skin is quite high in fat. Remove it before eating the cooked meat.

MICROWAVE OPTION:
If you precook the rice, you may reheat it in the microwave. Place it in a casserole or pie plate, sprinkle with water, cover and heat for about 2 minutes.

NUTRITION AT A GLANCE

PER SERVING:
Calories 300
Fat . . . . 4.5 g. (14% of cal.)
Sat. fat . . . . . 2.5 g. (8% of cal.)
Cholesterol . . . . 98 mg.
Sodium . . . . 123 mg.

CHICKEN WITH CHICK-PEAS AND ALMONDS

Here's an easy way to prepare chicken. Just combine it with almonds, onions, chick-peas and spices, then bake until tender. Nothing could be simpler. The chick-peas deliver a bonus amount of vitamin B_{12}, a nutrient that helps steady nerves and build strong blood.

CHICKEN WITH CHICK-PEAS AND ALMONDS

CHICKEN

- **1 chicken (about 3 pounds)**
- **1 cup diced onion**
- **2 teaspoons olive oil**
- **¼ cup unblanched almonds**
- **1 clove garlic, minced**
- **½ teaspoon powdered ginger**
- **¼ teaspoon ground cinnamon**
- **¼ teaspoon ground black pepper**
- **⅛ teaspoon turmeric**
- **1 cup thinly sliced onion**
- **1 cup defatted chicken stock**
- **¼ cup lemon juice**
- **⅛ teaspoon paprika**
- **1 can (19 ounces) chick-peas**

BULGUR

- **1½ cups defatted chicken stock**
- **1½ cups bulgur**

1. *To make the chicken:* Using kitchen shears or a cleaver, split the chicken in half lengthwise along the breast and down the backbone. Remove and discard the backbone and all visible fat. Trim off any excess skin. Rinse the chicken with cold water and pat dry with paper towels. Set aside.

2. In a 5-quart casserole or Dutch oven over medium heat, sauté the diced onions in the oil for 5 minutes, or until wilted. Stir in the almonds, garlic, ginger, cinnamon, pepper and turmeric. Sauté for about 3 minutes.

3. Top with the sliced onions. Pour on the stock and lemon juice. Bring to a simmer without stirring.

4. Lay the chicken pieces on top of the onions. Sprinkle with the paprika.

5. Cover the pan with a lid or heavy foil. Bake at 350° for 1 hour.

6. Drain the chick-peas and rinse with cold water to remove excess sodium. Add the chick-peas to the casserole, distributing them around the chicken. Cover and bake for 15 minutes, or until the juices run clear when a fork is inserted into the thickest part of the thigh.

7. *To make the bulgur:* About 20 minutes before serving, bring the stock to a boil in a 2-quart saucepan. Stir in the bulgur, cover the pan and remove it from the heat. Let stand for about 15 minutes, or until all the liquid has been absorbed and the bulgur is soft. Fluff with a fork and transfer to a serving platter.

8. Transfer the chicken to a large plate. Using a slotted spoon, cover the bulgur with the chick-pea and almond mixture. Moisten with stock from the casserole. Lay the chicken over the top. Remove the skin before eating.

SERVES 6.

Preparation Time: 20 min.
Cooking Time: 1¼ hr.

CHEF'S NOTES

■ ■ ■ ■ ■ ■ ■ ■

ACCOMPANIMENT:
Serve with a citrus salad such as Orange-Scented Cucumber Salad (page 77).

■

VARIATIONS:
Instead of a whole chicken, use just breasts or legs. You may serve the chicken over couscous, noodles or rice instead of bulgur. You may add about 1 cup sliced red or green peppers in step 3.

NUTRITION AT A GLANCE ■■■

PER SERVING:

Calories 438
Fat . . . . . .11.2 g. (23% of cal.)
Sat. fat . . . . .1.7 g. (3% of cal.)
Cholesterol . . . . .83 mg.
Sodium . . . . .141 mg.

ROAST CHICKEN LEGS WITH BASIL AND GARLIC

These succulent chicken legs are incredibly easy to prepare: Just season them with fresh herbs, then pop them into the oven with garlic and potatoes. The whole dish is quite low in sodium, so anyone with high blood pressure can enjoy it often.

ROAST CHICKEN LEGS WITH BASIL AND GARLIC

4 chicken legs
8 large basil leaves
1 whole garlic bulb
1 lemon, halved
4 baking potatoes

2 teaspoons olive oil
¼ teaspoon ground black pepper
¼ teaspoon paprika

1. Remove all visible fat from the chicken and trim excess skin, leaving just enough to cover the pieces. Carefully lift the skin on each piece and slide 2 basil leaves under it. Replace the skin.

2. Separate the garlic bulb into individual cloves. Trim the hard end off each clove and remove the peel. Trim any bruises and discard any cloves that are soft or dark. There should be about 12 to 15 whole cloves.

3. Place the garlic in a 9″ × 13″ baking dish. Top with the chicken.

4. Squeeze the juice from half of the lemon over the chicken. Remove the seeds from the remaining lemon half and cut into 4 pieces. Add these to the baking dish.

5. Cut the potatoes lengthwise into spears. Add to the dish. Drizzle the chicken and potatoes with the oil. Sprinkle with the pepper and paprika.

6. Bake at 350° for 45 to 50 minutes, or until the chicken is tender. Remove the skin before eating.

SERVES 4.

Preparation Time: 15 min.
Cooking Time: 50 min.

CHEF'S NOTES

ACCOMPANIMENT:
Serve with cole slaw, such as Creamy Mixed Cabbage Salad (page 75) or mixed steamed vegetables.

VARIATIONS:
Replace the chicken legs with breasts (or use a combination of the two). Use other herbs, including fresh parsley, sage, thyme or tarragon. Replace the white potatoes with sweet potatoes.

NUTRITION AT A GLANCE

PER SERVING:
Calories 439
Fat . . . . . .10.5 g. (22% of cal.)
Sat. fat . . . . .2.6 g. (5% of cal.)
Cholesterol . . . . .89 mg.
Sodium . . . . .106 mg.

ROAST TURKEY BREAST WITH ORANGE DRESSING

Try a different approach to turkey for festive family gatherings. This recipe serves a succulent roast breast with moist, orange-flavored stuffing. The oranges add extra cholesterol-lowering fiber and infection-fighting vitamin C to a low-fat entrée.

ROAST TURKEY BREAST WITH ORANGE DRESSING

TURKEY

- **1 boneless half turkey breast (about 2 pounds)**
- **1 teaspoon poultry seasoning**
- **1 teaspoon ground black pepper**
- **½ teaspoon olive oil**

1. Loosen the skin from the breast. In a cup, mix the poultry seasoning, pepper and oil. Rub the meat with the mixture. Put the skin back in place.

2. Coat a small roasting pan or 7″ × 11″ baking dish with no-stick spray. Add the turkey, skin side up. Bake at 400° for 20 minutes. (At this point, add the orange dressing to the oven.) Cover the turkey with foil and bake for 30 minutes, or until the turkey reaches an internal temperature of 165°.

3. To serve, remove the skin. Slice the meat and serve with the stuffing.

Preparation Time: 5 min.
Cooking Time: 50 min.

ORANGE DRESSING

- **2 cups diced onion**
- **4 teaspoons olive oil or peanut oil**
- **1 cup diced celery**
- **8 cups dry bread cubes**
- **4 teaspoons fresh thyme**
- **4 teaspoons grated fresh ginger**
- **2 teaspoons grated orange rind**
- **2 teaspoons grated lemon rind**
- **2 cups defatted chicken stock**
- **2–3 navel oranges, sectioned and coarsely chopped (see Chef's Notes)**
- **¼ cup chopped toasted walnuts**
- **1 teaspoon ground black pepper**
- **2 teaspoons margarine**

1. In a 4-quart pot or Dutch oven over medium heat, sauté the onions in the oil for 5 minutes. Add the celery and sauté for 5 minutes.

2. Reduce the heat to low, add the bread and sauté for 5 minutes. Stir in the thyme, ginger, orange rind and lemon rind. Sauté for 1 minute. Add the stock, oranges, walnuts and pepper. Mix well.

3. Coat a 9″ × 9″ baking dish or a medium ovenproof serving dish with no-stick spray. Add the stuffing. Dot the top with small pieces of the margarine. Bake for 30 minutes, or until nicely browned on top.

Preparation Time: 20 min.
Cooking Time: 45 min.

SERVES 8.

CHEF'S NOTES

DO FIRST:

Prepare the oranges: Use a serrated knife to remove the peel and underlying white pith. Free the segments from their surrounding membranes with a sharp paring knife. Discard the membranes; coarsely chop the oranges. Toast walnut halves at 350° for 10 minutes. Let cool, then chop.

INGREDIENTS NOTE:

To make dry bread cubes, cut bread into ½″ pieces. Place on baking sheets. Bake at 150° for 1 hour, stirring often.

ACCOMPANIMENTS:

Serve with cranberry sauce, mixed vegetables and low-fat gravy (see page 125; use chicken or turkey stock).

NUTRITION AT A GLANCE

PER SERVING:

Calories 297
Fat . . . . . . .8.4 g. (25% of cal.)
Sat. fat . . . . .1.4 g. (4% of cal.)
Cholesterol . . . . .66 mg.
Sodium . . . . .248 mg.

SPICY TURKEY BREAST WITH CRANBERRIES

There's no need to be concerned about fat and calories when you opt for roasting a lean turkey breast instead of the whole bird. And the sweet-tart cranberry sauce adds a sunny amount of vitamin C for protection against colds and many other infections.

SPICY TURKEY BREAST WITH CRANBERRIES

TURKEY

- **1 boneless skinless half turkey breast (about 2¼ pounds)**
- **¾ cup nonfat yogurt**
- **2 cloves garlic, minced**
- **1 tablespoon apple-cider vinegar**
- **1 teaspoon black peppercorns, crushed**
- **1 teaspoon cumin seed, crushed**
- **1 teaspoon dried rosemary, crushed**
- **1 teaspoon grated fresh ginger**
- **½ teaspoon ground cinnamon**

CRANBERRY SAUCE

- **2 cups cranberries**
- **½ cup dried apple slices**
- **1 cup orange juice**
- **½ cup all-fruit apple butter**
- **3 tablespoons maple syrup**

1. *To prepare the turkey:* Rinse the turkey with cold water and pat dry with paper towels. Set aside.

2. In a large, nonmetallic bowl, combine the yogurt, garlic, vinegar, pepper, cumin, rosemary, ginger and cinnamon. Add the turkey and turn to coat all over. Cover and refrigerate overnight, turning the meat occasionally.

3. *To make the cranberry sauce:* While the turkey is marinating, in a food processor or blender, process the cranberries, apples and juice until finely chopped but not pureed. Transfer to a 2-quart saucepan. Add the apple butter and maple syrup. Bring to a boil, then reduce the heat and simmer uncovered for about 10 minutes. Transfer to a serving bowl, let cool, cover and refrigerate until serving time.

4. To roast the turkey, lift it out of the marinade and set in a clay cooker. (If you don't have a clay cooker, see Chef's Notes.) Cover and bake at 350° for 1 to 1½ hours, or until cooked through and an internal temperature of 170° is reached.

5. Remove the turkey from the cooker and let it stand for about 10 minutes before slicing and serving. Serve with the cranberry sauce.

SERVES 8.

Preparation Time: 25 min.
Cooking Time: 1 ½ hr.

CHEF'S NOTES

ACCOMPANIMENTS:
Serve with roasted potatoes and a green or yellow vegetable.

VARIATION:
If you don't have a clay cooker, roast the turkey in an oven cooking bag, following the manufacturer's directions. Start checking the internal temperature after 1 hour.

MICROWAVE OPTIONS:
Place the cranberry sauce ingredients in a 1-quart casserole dish and cover with wax paper. Microwave on full power until bright in color and shiny, about 4 minutes.

NUTRITION AT A GLANCE

PER SERVING:

Calories 259
Fat . . . . 2.5 g. (9% of cal.)
Sat. fat . . . . 0.7 g. (2% of cal.)
Cholesterol . . . . 77 mg.
Sodium . . . . 104 mg.

BASIL AND LEMON TURKEY BREAST

Turkey breast meat is the leanest poultry there is, making it a perfect diet food. And this very simple method of roasting keeps it juicy despite its low fat content. Part of the trick is to roast it at a high temperature for a relatively short period of time, which seals in the juices. And keeping the skin on also acts as a protective coating. But don't eat the skin—it does contain fat.

BASIL AND LEMON TURKEY BREAST

1 **boneless half turkey breast with skin (about 2 pounds)**
1 **tablespoon olive oil**
1 **lemon, halved**
1 **clove garlic, halved**

8 **basil leaves**
3 **thin zucchini**
1 **small carrot, julienned**
½ **onion, thinly sliced**

1. Place the turkey breast in a 13″ × 9″ baking dish. Drizzle with the oil and turn to coat evenly. Squeeze the juice from 1 lemon half over the turkey.

2. Cut the remaining lemon half into 3 or 4 slices.

3. With your fingers, separate the turkey skin from the breast meat. Slide the garlic halves and 4 basil leaves between the skin and meat, distributing them evenly. Replace the skin and lay the lemon slices on top of it.

4. Bake at 400° for 40 minutes, basting occasionally with the pan juices.

5. Cut the remaining basil leaves into thin strips.

6. Cut the zucchini in half lengthwise. Scoop out and discard the center portion containing the seeds. Cut the rest of the zucchini into julienne pieces. Mix with the basil, carrots and onions; set aside.

7. Remove the baking dish from the oven. Discard the turkey skin and lemon slices. Carefully spoon some pan juices into the zucchini mixture and toss to blend. Spoon the vegetables over the turkey.

8. Bake another 15 minutes, or until the meat is cooked and the vegetables are tender. Remove from the oven and let stand 5 minutes. Transfer the vegetables to a serving platter. Cut the meat across grain into thin diagonal slices. Serve with the vegetables on the side and the pan juices spooned over the turkey.

SERVES 8.

Preparation Time: 10 min.
Cooking Time: 1 hr.

CHEF'S NOTES

ACCOMPANIMENTS:
Serve with baked potatoes or rice. If you have leftover turkey, it will make fine sandwiches or turkey salad.

VARIATION:
Do not substitute dried basil for fresh. Instead use about ⅛ teaspoon dried thyme rubbed into the turkey flesh and another ⅛ teaspoon added to the vegetables.

TECHNIQUE:
To make julienne pieces, cut zucchini into ¼″ × ¼″ × 2″ pieces. Because the carrot is a harder vegetable and takes longer to cook, you may cut those julienne pieces thinner (⅛″ × ⅛″ × 2″).

NUTRITION AT A GLANCE

PER SERVING:
Calories 152
Fat . . . . . . .4.7 g. (28% of cal.)
Sat. fat . . . . .1.2 g. (7% of cal.)
Cholesterol . . . . .67 mg.
Sodium . . . . .77 mg.

TURKEY SLOPPY JOES

Here's a down-home favorite with a difference. By using ground turkey breast instead of ground beef, we've slashed fat and calories enormously. As a health bonus, we've added lots of onions, peppers and tomatoes to what is often an all-meat dish. That greatly increases the amount of both dietary fiber and vitamin C in this lunch staple.

TURKEY SLOPPY JOES

- **4 teaspoons olive oil**
- **2 cups chopped onion**
- **1½ cups diced green pepper**
- **12 ounces ground turkey breast**
- **1 can (16 ounces) whole tomatoes**
- **1 can (8 ounces) tomato sauce**
- **3 tablespoons chili sauce**
- **½ teaspoon ground black pepper**
- **Pinch ground red pepper**

1. Heat the oil in a large pot or Dutch oven over high heat. Add the onions and green peppers. Sauté for 7 to 8 minutes, stirring frequently, until the peppers are tender and the onions begin to brown.

2. Add the ground turkey in batches. The pan will be very dry, so watch carefully to prevent scorching. Turn the meat and vegetables with a spatula a few times after each addition, until the turkey loses its pink color. Too much stirring will lower the temperature of the pan and cause the meat to exude juices.

3. Chop the tomatoes and add them (with juice) to the pot. Stir in the tomato sauce, chili sauce, black pepper and red pepper.

4. Reduce the heat to low and simmer the mixture for 15 minutes.

SERVES 4.

Preparation Time: 10 min.
Cooking Time: 30 min.

CHEF'S NOTES

ACCOMPANIMENTS:

Serve on toasted whole-grain buns or in pita pockets. Or spoon over baked potatoes. Add crisp radishes and low-sodium pickles or cucumber spears.

NUTRI-NOTE:

Sloppy joes are traditionally made from ground beef. If you would like to use beef instead of turkey, buy the extra-lean variety. To reduce fat content even further, brown it in a teaspoon of oil in a hot no-stick frying pan. Then spoon the meat into a fine sieve so any remaining fat can drain away. For extra measure, pat the meat dry with paper towels.

NUTRITION AT A GLANCE

PER SERVING:

Calories 231
Fat . . . . . . .6.5 g. (25% of cal.)
Sat. fat . . . . .1.1 g. (4% of cal.)
Cholesterol . . . . .51 mg.
Sodium . . . . .409 mg.

TURKEY AND MUSHROOM TETRAZZINI

Tetrazzini recipes normally feature a calorie-laden cream sauce. This casserole delivers all the old-fashioned flavor with just a fraction of the fat, cholesterol and calories. How? By replacing the fatty sauce with a low-fat buttermilk-based version.

TURKEY AND MUSHROOM TETRAZZINI

2 cups defatted chicken stock

1¾ cups low-fat buttermilk

2 tablespoons cornstarch

½ teaspoon dried thyme

½ teaspoon ground black pepper

2 cups small mushrooms, quartered

2 tablespoons water

2 cloves garlic, minced

2 cups small pearl onions, cooked

2 cups chopped cooked turkey breast

¾ cup orzo or other small pasta, cooked

½ cup minced fresh parsley

½ cup fresh bread crumbs

1 tablespoon olive oil

1. In a 3-quart saucepan, combine the stock, buttermilk, cornstarch and thyme. Stir well to dissolve the cornstarch. Bring to a boil, whisking constantly. Reduce the heat and simmer, whisking occasionally, for 10 minutes, until slightly thickened. Stir in the pepper. Remove from the heat and set aside.

2. In a large no-stick frying pan over medium-high heat, cook the mushrooms, water and garlic for 8 minutes, or until tender and all the liquid has evaporated. Add to the saucepan.

3. Stir in the onions, turkey, pasta and parsley.

4. Coat a 2½-quart casserole dish with no-stick spray. Add the turkey mixture.

5. In a cup, mix the bread crumbs and oil. Sprinkle over the turkey mixture. Bake at 375° for 30 to 45 minutes.

SERVES 4.

Preparation Time: 20 min.
Cooking Time: 55 min.

CHEF'S NOTES

DO FIRST:

Cook the turkey: Simmer about 1 pound of boneless turkey breast in water until tender, about 25 minutes. Let cool, then chop.

Cook the onions: Blanch them first in boiling water so the skins will slip off easily. Then simmer until just tender, about 5 minutes.

Cook the orzo: Boil in water for about 10 minutes. Drain well.

NUTRI-NOTE:

Some brands of buttermilk are much lower in fat than others; check the labels.

NUTRITION AT A GLANCE

PER SERVING:

Calories 371
Fat . . . . .8 g. (19% of cal.)
Sat. fat . . . .1.9 g. (5% of cal.)
Cholesterol . . . . .53 mg.
Sodium . . . . .200 mg.

HONEY-GLAZED DUCK BREAST

For very special dinners, serve duck breast. It's an excellent source of iron and even contains some vitamin A for healthy skin and good vision. This recipe pairs skinned duck with rice and vegetables for a complete, well-balanced meal.

HONEY-GLAZED DUCK BREAST

- **2 whole skinless, boneless duck breasts (about 12 ounces each)**
- **¼ cup orange juice**
- **1 tablespoon honey**
- **1 teaspoon grated orange rind**
- **1 teaspoon reduced-sodium soy sauce**
- **1 clove garlic, minced**
- **2½ cups defatted chicken stock**
- **1 cup short- or medium-grain brown rice**
- **6 ounces slender green beans**
- **2 carrots, julienned to the same length as the beans**
- **1 teaspoon minced fresh ginger**
- **1 teaspoon peanut oil**
- **1 sweet red pepper, julienned**
- **1 tablespoon thinly sliced scallion greens**

1. Trim any visible fat from the duck. Halve the pieces to make 4 individual breasts. Pierce all over with a fork or sharp knife. Place on a large plate.

2. In a cup, combine the orange juice, honey, orange rind, soy sauce and garlic. Pour over the duck breasts. Cover and refrigerate for at least 1 hour, turning once.

3. About 45 minutes before serving, combine the stock and rice in a 2-quart saucepan. Bring to a boil, cover and cook until the rice is tender and the water has been absorbed. Set aside and keep warm.

4. While the rice is cooking, blanch or steam the green beans and carrots for 2 minutes, or until almost crisp-tender. Rinse with cold water and set on a tray covered with several thicknesses of paper towels.

5. Over medium-high heat, heat a large, well-seasoned cast-iron frying pan until droplets of water sprinkled on it evaporate on contact. Coat the duck breasts evenly with the marinade. Place in the pan and sear for 3 to 4 minutes per side, or until cooked as desired. Transfer to a cutting board and let stand for at least 3 minutes before cutting across the grain into thin slices.

6. In the same frying pan over medium-high heat, stir-fry the ginger in the oil for 10 seconds. Add the beans, carrots and peppers. Stir-fry for 3 minutes, or until tender. Remove from the heat.

7. Fluff the rice with a fork. Top with the vegetables, scallions and duck. If any meat juices have accumulated on the cutting board, spoon them over the duck.

SERVES 4.

Preparation Time: 30 min. + standing time
Cooking Time: 45 min.

CHEF'S NOTES

INGREDIENTS NOTE:

You may substitute London broil, veal cutlets, turkey cutlets or boneless chicken breast for the duck.

PRESENTATION:

One attractive way to serve this meal is to mound the rice in the center of a large platter. Sprinkle with the scallions. Arrange the vegetables around the edges, leaving space for overlapping slices of duck.

NUTRITION AT A GLANCE

PER SERVING:

Calories 371
Fat . . . . . .12.8 g. (31% of cal.)
Sat. fat . . . .4.3 g. (10% of cal.)
Cholesterol . . . . .131 mg.
Sodium . . . . .243 mg.

FISH AND SHELLFISH

GRILLED TUNA

Tuna is an oil-rich, deep-water fish that's a good source of omega-3 fatty acids. Those are the heart-smart fats that help lower triglycerides and may reduce the risk of blood clots that could lead to heart attacks or strokes. As a bonus, studies have shown omega-3's can help reduce the painful inflammation associated with arthritis.

GRILLED TUNA

TUNA

- **1 pound tuna steak**
- **2 tablespoons lemon juice**
- **1 tablespoon olive oil**
- **½ teaspoon ground black pepper**

COUSCOUS SALAD

- **1¼ cups defatted chicken stock**
- **1 cup couscous**
- **2 teaspoons olive oil**
- **½ cup diced yellow pepper**
- **¼ cup thinly sliced scallions**
- **2 cloves garlic, minced**

- **1 pint cherry tomatoes, halved or quartered**
- **1½ tablespoons lemon juice**
- **¼ teaspoon grated lemon rind**
- **⅓ cup defatted chicken stock**
- **1½ cups shredded spinach**
- **2 tablespoons minced fresh parsley**
- **2 tablespoons minced fresh basil**
- **1 tablespoon grated Parmesan cheese**

1. *To make the tuna:* Trim the skin from the tuna and discard. Cut the flesh into chunks or thin ribbons.

2. In a glass baking dish combine the lemon juice, oil and pepper. Add the tuna and turn to coat. Refrigerate for 4 hours or overnight, turning occasionally.

3. Thread the tuna onto skewers. Grill over hot coals for 3 to 5 minutes, or until the tuna is opaque and cooked through. (Or broil 4″ from the heat for 3 to 5 minutes per side.)

4. *To make the couscous salad:* About 20 minutes before serving, boil 1¼ cups stock in a 1-quart saucepan. Stir in the couscous. Cover the pan and remove it from the heat. Let stand for 5 minutes.

5. In a large no-stick frying pan heat the oil over medium heat. Add the peppers and sauté until tender, about 3 minutes. Add the scallions and garlic; cook for 1 minute.

6. Add the tomatoes, lemon juice, lemon rind and 3 tablespoons of stock. Heat for 1 minute.

7. Fluff the couscous with a fork. Add to the vegetables. Mix well. Stir in the spinach. Warm through for 2 minutes. If the mixture seems dry, add the remaining stock. Stir in the parsley, basil and Parmesan.

8. Serve on a platter with the tuna.

SERVES 4.

Preparation Time: 35 min. + standing time
Cooking Time: 10 min.

CHEF'S NOTES

VARIATION:

Replace the tuna with salmon or swordfish steaks.

NUTRI-NOTE:

Although tomatoes in general contain a lot of vitamin C, certain varieties are even richer. If you're a gardener, try planting 'Sweet 100' cherry tomatoes, which have about twice the C of most other tomatoes.

KITCHEN TRICKS:

To get the most juice from your lemons, roll them on a countertop (exerting pressure) before juicing. Or microwave them for 20 to 30 seconds.

NUTRITION AT A GLANCE

PER SERVING:

Calories 264
Fat . . . . . . .7.9 g. (27% of cal.)
Sat. fat . . . . .1.4 g. (5% of cal.)
Cholesterol . . . . .44 mg.
Sodium . . . . .123 mg.

STEAMED COD WITH DILL SAUCE

Fish is a proven heart protector—as long as you don't sink it in a sea of fat by deep-frying it or burying it under a heavy sauce. Like most other fish, cod is low in calories and saturated fat, and it's a fine source of heart-healthy omega-3 fatty acids. Teaming fish with vegetables like carrots and red peppers adds cancer-fighting vitamin A and immunity-boosting vitamin C.

STEAMED COD WITH DILL SAUCE

DILL SAUCE

- ¼ **cup low-fat cottage cheese**
- ¼ **cup nonfat yogurt**
- 2 **teaspoons Dijon mustard**
- 1 **teaspoon lemon juice**
- 1 **teaspoon minced shallot**
- ⅛ **teaspoon reduced-sodium soy sauce (optional)**
- 1 **tablespoon minced fresh dill or ½ teaspoon dried**

FISH

- 1 **pound cod fillet, cut into 4 pieces**

- 1 **sweet red pepper, thinly sliced**
- 1 **celery stalk, thinly cut on the diagonal**
- 1 **carrot, halved lengthwise and thinly sliced on the diagonal**
- ¾ **cup green beans, split lengthwise and halved**
- 1 **tablespoon lemon juice**
- 2 **teaspoons olive oil**
- 2 **teaspoons minced fresh dill or ½ teaspoon dried**
- 1 **teaspoon minced onion**
- ⅛ **teaspoon reduced-sodium soy sauce**

1. *To make the dill sauce:* Using a blender or food processor, puree the cottage cheese, yogurt, mustard, lemon juice, shallots and soy sauce until smooth. Transfer to a small bowl and stir in the dill. Cover and refrigerate until serving time.

2. *To make the fish:* Bring about 1″ of water to a boil in a large saucepan. Place the cod in a steamer basket and add to the pot. Cover and steam for 3 to 4 minutes.

3. Add the peppers, celery, carrots and beans to the steamer basket. Cover and steam for another 3 to 5 minutes, or until the vegetables are tender. Remove from the heat and set aside.

4. In a large bowl mix the lemon juice, oil, dill, onions and soy sauce. Using a spoon or metal spatula, transfer the cooked vegetables to the bowl. Toss to coat well.

5. Divide the vegetables among 4 dinner plates, forming them into little nests. Nestle a piece of fish in each nest. Top each piece with dill sauce.

SERVES 4.

Preparation Time: 15 min.
Cooking Time: 10 min.

CHEF'S NOTES

ACCOMPANIMENTS:
Serve with brown rice or tricolor pasta.

VARIATION:
Use sole or other white-fleshed fish.

KITCHEN TRICKS:
If desired, place a few dill sprigs in the steaming water to flavor the fish as it cooks. To make removal of vegetables from the steamer basket easier, position fish to one side of the basket, leaving room for the vegetables.

MAKE-AHEAD TIP:
The sauce will keep well for a day if covered and refrigerated.

NUTRITION AT A GLANCE

PER SERVING:
Calories 160
Fat . . . . . . .3.5 g. (20% of cal.)
Sat. fat . . . . .0.7 g. (4% of cal.)
Cholesterol . . . . .50 mg.
Sodium . . . . .203 mg.

CARIBBEAN FISH EN PAPILLOTE

If you always thought of fish as brain food, you were right. The protein in fish can boost your brainpower, making you more alert. In fact, just 3 ounces of fish protein are enough to stimulate chemicals in the brain that sharpen brain function, say researchers. As a bonus, this recipe contains red peppers—a source of the trace mineral boron. Studies suggest that it too may contribute to mental alertness—and help prevent osteoporosis.

Fish and Shellfish

CARIBBEAN FISH EN PAPILLOTE

FISH

- **2 tablespoons lime juice**
- **2 teaspoons honey**
- **1 teaspoon olive oil**
- **½ teaspoon chili powder**
- **½ teaspoon ground cumin**
- **¼ teaspoon ground red pepper**
- **4 orange roughy fillets (4 to 6 ounces each)**

VEGETABLES

- **2 cups thinly sliced onion**
- **1 cup thinly sliced sweet red or yellow pepper**
- **2 teaspoons olive oil**
- **¼ cup lime juice**
- **¼ cup apple-juice concentrate**
- **3 tablespoons currants**
- **1 clove garlic, minced**
- **1 teaspoon grated fresh ginger**
- **¼ teaspoon saffron threads, crushed**
- **2 cups cooked rice**
- **½ cup diced mango**
- **3 tablespoons minced fresh coriander**
- **3 tablespoons grated coconut**

1. *To make the fish:* In a 9″ × 13″ baking dish combine the lime juice, honey, oil, chili powder, cumin and pepper. Add the fish and turn to coat.

2. Cut 4 squares of parchment (about 15″ × 15″ each). Fold each in half, then trim into a large heart. Open and coat the inside with no-stick spray.

3. *To make the vegetables:* In a large no-stick frying pan over medium-high heat, sauté the onions and peppers in the oil for 3 to 5 minutes, until crisp-tender. Add the lime juice, apple-juice concentrate, currants, garlic, ginger and saffron. Cook for 2 to 3 minutes. Remove about half of the vegetables and set aside. Stir the rice and mangoes into the pan.

4. Divide the rice mixture among the parchment hearts, about 1″ from the fold and at least 3″ from the outer edges. Top with the fish, reserved vegetables, coriander and coconut.

5. Fold the paper over the fish and align the edges. Make a small fold at the top edge, crease and repeat to make a double seal. Work your way around the edges. When you reach the pointed end, twist the parchment to hold the folds in place. Make sure the edges are tightly sealed.

6. Place the packets on a large cookie sheet. Bake at 400° for 20 minutes, until the paper is browned and puffed.

SERVES 4.

Preparation Time: 30 min.
Cooking Time: 30 min.

CHEF'S NOTES

■ ■ ■ ■ ■ ■ ■ ■ ■ ■

DO FIRST:
Cook the rice according to package directions. Start with ¾ to 1 cup of raw rice.

■

VARIATIONS:
Use other fish fillets, such as flounder. Or substitute boneless, skinless chicken breast, pounded to an even thickness.

■

NUTRI-NOTE:
If you like the convenience of white rice but prefer the nutritional merits of brown, be on the lookout for quick-cooking brown rice. It takes only 20 minutes to cook and has just about the same nutrient profile as regular brown rice.

NUTRITION AT A GLANCE

PER SERVING:

Calories 416
Fat . . . . . .13.5 g. (29% of cal.)
Sat. fat . . . . . .2 g. (4% of cal.)
Cholesterol . . . . .23 mg.
Sodium . . . . .99 mg.

RED SNAPPER WITH SALSA

Our spicy black-bean salsa gives this fish meal an exotic Caribbean flair. But it does more down-to-earth things for your diet. Studies show that eating beans can suppress your appetite for hours. And researchers suspect that this hunger-chasing ability may be linked with how slowly beans are digested. That's just one more reason to give legumes a prominent place in your diet.

RED SNAPPER WITH SALSA

SALSA
- **1½ cups cooked black beans**
- **½ green pepper, diced**
- **½ sweet red pepper, diced**
- **½ cup diced pineapple**
- **¼ cup diced red onion**
- **2 tablespoons lime juice**
- **2 tablespoons orange juice**
- **1 jalapeño pepper, minced**
- **1 clove garlic, minced**
- **1 tablespoon olive oil**
- **½ teaspoon ground coriander**
- **⅛ teaspoon ground black pepper**

RED SNAPPER
- **1 pound red snapper fillets**
- **⅓ cup orange juice**
- **¼ cup grapefruit juice**
- **4 scallions, minced**
- **1 teaspoon grated orange rind**
- **1 teaspoon grated grapefruit rind**
- **1 clove garlic, minced**
- **⅛ teaspoon dried thyme**
- **Pinch of ground red pepper**

1. *To make the salsa:* In a medium bowl combine the beans, green peppers, red peppers, pineapples, onions, lime juice, orange juice, jalapeño peppers, garlic, oil, coriander and black pepper. Cover and set aside.

2. *To make the red snapper:* Place the fish in a baking dish. In a small bowl combine the orange juice, grapefruit juice, scallions, orange rind, grapefruit rind, garlic, thyme and pepper. Pour over the fish and turn to coat. Cover and refrigerate for 2 hours.

3. Coat a broiler rack or grill rack with no-stick spray. Remove the fish from the marinade and place it, skin side down, on the rack. Reserve the marinade.

4. Broil or grill the fish about 4″ from the heat for 4 to 7 minutes. Carefully flip the fish. Brush with marinade and cook another 4 to 7 minutes, or until cooked through. Serve with the salsa.

SERVES 4.

Preparation Time: 15 min. + standing time
Cooking Time: 15 min.

CHEF'S NOTES

DO FIRST:
Cook the beans: Start with about ¾ cup of dried beans. Cook them until they're tender but still hold their shape, 45 to 60 minutes.

KITCHEN TRICK:
Grate the rind from the orange and grapefruit before extracting the juice.

MAKE-AHEAD TIP:
You may prepare the salsa a day ahead. Cover and refrigerate it until needed. To take the chill off, microwave it for about 30 seconds before serving.

NUTRITION AT A GLANCE

PER SERVING:

Calories	258
Fat	5.4 g. (19% of cal.)
Sat. fat	0.9 g. (3% of cal.)
Cholesterol	35 mg.
Sodium	64 mg.

HERBED MONKFISH
WITH FRESH TOMATO SALSA

Monkfish has earned the nickname "poor-man's lobster" because of its firm-textured meat. But you don't need to dip it in butter to enjoy its marvelous flavor. Try marinating it in a rich mixture of herbs, then quickly bake it for a lean main course.

HERBED MONKFISH WITH FRESH TOMATO SALSA

MONKFISH

- **6 cloves garlic, minced**
- **1 tablespoon dried basil**
- **1 tablespoon dried thyme**
- **2 teaspoons ground fennel**
- **2 teaspoons dried savory**
- **1 teaspoon dried lavender flowers (optional)**
- **½ teaspoon ground black pepper**
- **1 tablespoon olive oil**
- **2 teaspoons Dijon mustard**

- **1½ pounds monkfish fillet, cut into 6 equal pieces**

SALSA

- **2 large tomatoes, seeded and diced**
- **¼ cup diced black olives**
- **2 tablespoons minced fresh parsley**
- **2 tablespoons vinegar**
- **1 tablespoon minced fresh basil**
- **½ teaspoon ground black pepper**

1. *To make the monkfish:* In a cup, mix the garlic, basil, thyme, fennel, savory, lavender and pepper. Stir in the oil and mustard.

2. Rub all sides of each piece of monkfish with the herb mixture.

3. Place the fish on a large dish. Cover, refrigerate and allow to marinate 2 hours or overnight.

4. Coat a broiler rack with no-stick spray. Place over a drip pan. Place the fish on the rack in a single layer with space between the pieces.

5. Bake at 400° for 15 to 25 minutes, or until the fish is opaque all the way through.

6. *To make the salsa:* While the fish is marinating, combine the tomatoes, olives, parsley, vinegar, basil and pepper in a medium bowl. Cover and set aside.

7. To serve, divide the fish among serving plates and top with the salsa.

SERVES 6.

Preparation Time: 15 min. + standing time
Cooking Time: 25 min.

CHEF'S NOTES

■ ■ ■ ■ ■ ■ ■ ■

DO FIRST:
Monkfish often comes with a tough, inedible, blue-gray membrane covering the flesh. Have your fish dealer remove it or do it yourself with a sharp knife.

■

ACCOMPANIMENT:
Serve with small new potatoes: Scrub and cut into quarters. Roast with the monkfish until tender.

■

VARIATION:
The combination of basil, thyme, fennel, savory and lavender used here is a close approximation of Herbes de Provence, a commercial herb mixture. Use 3 tablespoons to replace the dried herbs.

NUTRITION AT A GLANCE

PER SERVING:

Calories 132
Fat . . . . . . 4.8 g. (33% of cal.)
Sat. fat . . . . . 0.4 g. (3% of cal.)
Cholesterol . . . . 28 mg.
Sodium . . . . 61 mg.

FISH IN FLAMING RED PEPPERS

If you like sardines—and are looking for new ways to prepare them—you'll love this unusual Tex-Mex entrée. With plenty of rice, fish and vegetables stuffed into each crimson pepper, this is a perfect low-fat, one-dish meal.

FISH IN FLAMING RED PEPPERS

- ½ **cup sliced celery**
- ½ **cup diced green pepper**
- ¾ **cup sliced scallions**
- 2 **teaspoons olive oil**
- 1 **clove garlic, minced**
- ¼ **teaspoon ground cumin**
- ¼ **teaspoon chili powder**

- 1–2 **cans (6½ ounces each) sardines in tomato sauce**
- 2 **cups cooked Basmati or other aromatic rice**
- 2 **cups chunky salsa**
- 4 **large sweet red peppers**
- 4 **black olives, sliced**

1. In a large no-stick frying pan over medium-high heat, sauté the celery, green peppers and ½ cup of the scallions in the oil for 3 minutes. Add the garlic, cumin and chili powder. Stir and cook for 3 minutes.

2. If desired, cut the sardines into bite-size pieces. Add to the vegetables (along with the tomato sauce in which the sardines are packed). Carefully stir in the rice and 1 cup of the salsa; take care not to mash the sardines. Remove from the heat and set aside.

3. Slice off the tops of the red peppers. Remove and discard the seeds and inner membranes. Blanch the peppers in boiling water for 4 minutes. Drain and let stand a few minutes until cool enough to handle.

4. Stuff the peppers with the sardine mixture. Stand them upright in a deep casserole. Spoon the remaining 1 cup salsa over them. Sprinkle with the olives and the remaining ¼ cup scallions. Bake at 400° for 20 minutes.

SERVES 4.

Preparation Time: 20 min.
Cooking Time: 35 min.

CHEF'S NOTES

DO FIRST:

Cook the rice. Let it cool before adding to the other ingredients.

NUTRI-NOTE:

Sardines can be quite high in sodium. If you're on a reduced-salt diet and can't find low-sodium sardines, you may replace them with cooked white fish, shrimp, scallops or crab.

MICROWAVE OPTION:

To blanch the peppers, wrap each in wax paper. Arrange in a square in the microwave. Cook on full power for 3 minutes, or until just tender.

NUTRITION AT A GLANCE

PER SERVING:

Calories 300
Fat . . . . 12 g. (36% of cal.)
Sat. fat . . . . 1.9 g. (5% of cal.)
Cholesterol . . . . 28 mg.
Sodium . . . . 674 mg.

GINGER-SCENTED BAKED MACKEREL

Mackerel is king of the sea when it comes to cholesterol-lowering omega-3 fatty acids. If you're concerned that the fish might be too strong for your taste, you needn't worry. Fresh mackerel is milder than canned, and the ginger and soy sauce in this recipe accent its flavor perfectly.

GINGER-SCENTED BAKED MACKEREL

4 scallions, thinly sliced

3 tablespoons minced fresh coriander

2 tablespoons reduced-sodium soy sauce

1–2 teaspoons grated fresh ginger

¼ teaspoon ground black pepper

12 ounces mackerel fillet, divided into 4 equal pieces

12 thin lime slices

8 ounces broad noodles

1. Cut 4 large squares of foil or brown paper. Coat the top side of each piece with no-stick spray.

2. In a medium bowl, toss the scallions, coriander, soy sauce, ginger and pepper together. Set aside.

3. Place a mackerel fillet on half of each piece of foil or paper. Divide the scallion mixture and the limes over the fillets.

4. Fold the empty half of the foil or paper over the fillet and crimp the edges to seal tightly. Place on a large cookie sheet.

5. Bake at 450° for about 8 minutes.

6. While the fish is baking, cook the noodles in a large pot of boiling water for 8 minutes, or until just tender. Drain and serve with the fish.

SERVES 4.

Preparation Time: 15 min.
Cooking Time: 10 min.

CHEF'S NOTES

■ ■ ■ ■ ■ ■ ■ ■ ■

VARIATIONS:
You may use other fish fillets, including halibut, salmon and orange roughy. You may bake the fish in a shallow casserole. Coat the dish with no-stick spray, add the fish and vegetables, and cover tightly with foil. Bake at 400° until the fish flakes easily, about 15 minutes.

NUTRITION AT A GLANCE ■■■

PER SERVING:

Calories 402
Fat . . . . 14 g. (31% of cal.)
Sat. fat . . . . . 2.8 g. (6% of cal.)
Cholesterol . . . . 60 mg.
Sodium . . . . 392 mg.

CANTONESE CATFISH

Catfish is a wonderful seafood that many people overlook. It's firm when cooked, so it doesn't fall apart. Yet it's tender, with a delicate flavor that complements a wide variety of foods. This Chinese dish pairs the fish with fiber-filled snow peas, carrots and pasta.

CANTONESE CATFISH

8 ounces spaghetti or other pasta
3 tablespoons unbleached flour
1 teaspoon dry mustard
1 pound catfish fillets
1 tablespoon sesame oil
1 cup julienned snow peas
1 cup julienned carrot
½ cup julienned scallions
1 clove garlic, minced
1 tablespoon reduced-sodium soy sauce
1 tablespoon toasted sesame seeds

1. Cook the pasta in a large pot of boiling water until just tender. Drain and keep warm in an oven on the lowest setting.

2. While the pasta is cooking, combine the flour and mustard in a shallow bowl. Dredge the catfish in the flour; shake off the excess.

3. In a large no-stick frying pan over medium-high heat, warm the oil. Add the catfish, cover and cook for 6 to 8 minutes, turning once. Transfer to a plate and keep warm. Add the peas, carrots, scallions and garlic to the frying pan. Sauté for 2 minutes. Add the soy sauce and mix well.

4. Add the pasta, toss well, cover and cook for 2 minutes. Transfer to a serving platter. Top with the catfish. Sprinkle with the sesame seeds.

SERVES 4.

Preparation Time: 15 min.
Cooking Time: 15 min.

CHEF'S NOTES

DO FIRST:
Julienne the vegetables: Cut the snow peas, carrots and scallions into matchstick-size pieces (about 2'' long and ⅛'' to ¼'' thick).

INGREDIENTS NOTE:
For the most flavor, use oriental sesame oil. It's dark in color and has a robust, toasted flavor. Look for the oil in supermarkets and oriental markets. Substituting pale, clear sesame oil will give an entirely different flavor.

VARIATION:
You may substitute other fish fillets for the catfish, such as perch, flounder or orange roughy.

NUTRITION AT A GLANCE

PER SERVING:
Calories 450
Fat . . . . . .11.3 g. (23% of cal.)
Sat. fat . . . . .1.9 g. (4% of cal.)
Cholesterol . . . . .66 mg.
Sodium . . . . .230 mg.

TUNA BURGERS WITH DILL SAUCE

These tuna burgers are simple to prepare, so you can whip them up in minutes for lunch or a light dinner. They're as satisfying as regular hamburgers but much lower in fat and cholesterol. And they have a bonus that beef lacks: heart-healthy omega-3's.

TUNA BURGERS WITH DILL SAUCE

DILL SAUCE

- ⅓ **cup nonfat mayonnaise or yogurt cheese**
- 2 **tablespoons minced gherkin pickles**
- 1 **tablespoon minced fresh dill or 1 teaspoon dried**
- 1 **tablespoon minced fresh parsley**
- 2 **teaspoons snipped chives**
- 1 **teaspoon lemon juice**
- ½ **teaspoon Dijon mustard**

TUNA BURGERS

- 1 **can (12½ ounces) low-sodium water-packed albacore tuna, drained and flaked**
- ½ **cup wheat germ**
- 2 **scallions, minced**

- 1 **tablespoon minced fresh parsley**
- ½ **teaspoon dried oregano**
- ½ **teaspoon ground black pepper**
- ⅛ **teaspoon ground red pepper**
- ¼ **cup nonfat mayonnaise**
- ¼ **cup fat-free egg substitute or 1 egg**
- 1 **tablespoon ketchup**
- 2 **teaspoons oil**
- 4 **Kaiser rolls or crusty hamburger rolls**
- 4 **thick tomato slices**
  Boston or romaine lettuce

1. *To make the dill sauce:* In a small bowl, combine the mayonnaise or yogurt cheese, pickles, dill, parsley, chives, lemon juice and mustard. Refrigerate until needed.

2. *To make the tuna burgers:* In a medium bowl, combine the tuna, wheat germ, scallions, parsley, oregano, black pepper and red pepper.

3. In a cup, combine the mayonnaise, egg and ketchup. Pour over the tuna and mix well.

4. Form the tuna into 4 patties.

5. In a large no-stick frying pan over medium heat, sauté the patties in the oil until browned and heated through, about 3 minutes per side.

6. Serve on the rolls, topped with the tomatoes, lettuce and dill sauce.

SERVES 4.

Preparation Time: 30 min.
Cooking Time: 10 min.

CHEF'S NOTES

■ ■ ■ ■ ■ ■ ■ ■

DO FIRST:
If using yogurt cheese, drain ⅔ cup yogurt in a cheesecloth-lined sieve for at least 30 minutes.

■

INGREDIENTS NOTE:
You may use fresh tuna. Poach, broil or sauté a 1-pound fillet. Cool, then flake with a fork.

■

ACCOMPANIMENTS:
Serve with cole slaw and oven-fried potatoes.

■

NUTRI-NOTE:
Most of the sodium in these burgers comes from the mayonnaise and the rolls. If you must cut back, seek out low-sodium brands.

NUTRITION AT A GLANCE ▬▬▬

PER SERVING:

Calories	406
Fat	8 g. (18% of cal.)
Sat. fat	1.4 g. (3% of cal.)
Cholesterol	37 mg.
Sodium	931 mg.

SAUTÉED SHRIMP WITH PARSLEY SAUCE

Stop thinking of parsley as a garnish! It's actually an admirable source of vitamins, such as A and C, so make it a prominent part of your meal. And remember that although shrimp does contain a fair amount of cholesterol, it is extremely low in saturated fat and is a decent source of heart-bolstering omega-3's. Added all up, shrimp is a better dietary choice than even the leanest red meats.

SAUTÉED SHRIMP WITH PARSLEY SAUCE

PARSLEY SAUCE
- **1** cup tightly packed chopped fresh parsley leaves
- **2** tablespoons defatted chicken stock
- **1** tablespoon olive oil
- **2** teaspoons Dijon mustard
- **½** teaspoon minced garlic
- **½** teaspoon lemon juice

SHRIMP
- **1** teaspoon olive oil
- **1** small zucchini, thinly sliced
- **1** small yellow squash, thinly sliced
- **1** carrot, thinly sliced
- **1** pound large shrimp, peeled and deveined
- **2** tablespoons defatted chicken stock
- **2** teaspoons minced fresh parsley
- **1** teaspoon lemon juice
- **½** teaspoon minced garlic
- **½** teaspoon grated lemon rind

1. *To make the parsley sauce:* Drop the parsley into boiling water for 5 seconds. Pour into a strainer and run under cold water for 10 seconds to stop cooking. Drain well, then shake off the remaining water.

2. Transfer to a blender. Add the stock, oil, mustard, garlic and lemon juice. Blend until smooth. Set aside.

3. *To make the shrimp:* Heat the oil in a large no-stick frying pan over medium heat. Add the zucchini, squash and carrots. Stir, cover and cook for 2 to 3 minutes, stirring occasionally. Transfer the vegetables to a platter and set aside.

4. Increase heat to medium high. Add the shrimp and cook for about 1 minute per side. Add the stock, parsley, lemon juice, garlic, lemon rind and cooked vegetables.

5. Cook for another minute, or until the vegetables are reheated and the shrimp is cooked through.

6. Divide among 4 dinner plates. Top each portion with parsley sauce.

SERVES 4.

Preparation Time: 20 min.
Cooking Time: 10 min.

CHEF'S NOTES

DO FIRST:
Prepare the shrimp: First take off shells, then remove the black vein that runs along the top of each shrimp. Simply run a knife tip down the length of the vein to expose it, then lift it out with the knife or your fingers.

PRESENTATION:
Serve with fettuccine, angel hair or other pasta. If desired, toss cooked pasta with parsley sauce. Then serve shrimp on top.

KITCHEN TRICK:
It's easier to grate the rind from the lemon if you do it before extracting the juice.

NUTRITION AT A GLANCE

PER SERVING:
Calories 190
Fat . . . . 6.8 g. (32% of cal.)
Sat. fat . . . . . . 1 g. (5% of cal.)
Cholesterol . . . . 172 mg.
Sodium . . . . 220 mg.

SHRIMP AND RICE ENCHILADAS

These seafood enchiladas are super-easy to prepare—the homemade salsa is ready in no time, and the shrimp filling cooks in a flash. Best of all, these Mexican delights are high in fiber and overflowing with vitamin A, calcium, iron and other essential nutrients.

SHRIMP AND RICE ENCHILADAS

SALSA

- **2 tablespoons minced onion**
- **1 teaspoon oil**
- **1 clove garlic, minced**
- **1 teaspoon ground cumin**
- **1 can (28 ounces) plum tomatoes**
- **2 tablespoons minced fresh coriander or basil**
- **¼ teaspoon ground black pepper**

ENCHILADAS

- **½ cup chopped green pepper**
- **½ teaspoon cumin seed**
- **1 teaspoon oil**
- **½ cup diced zucchini**
- **½ cup peeled and diced tomato**
- **8 ounces shrimp, peeled, deveined and coarsely chopped**
- **1 cup cooked rice**
- **¼ cup chopped red onion**
- **2 teaspoons minced jalapeño pepper**
- **½ cup shredded low-fat cheese**
- **8 corn tortillas**
- **8 thin slices avocado (optional)**
- **2 tablespoons minced fresh coriander**

1. *To make the salsa:* In a 2-quart saucepan over medium heat, sauté the onions in the oil until tender, about 5 minutes. Add the garlic and cumin.

2. Stir in the tomatoes (with juice). Use the side of a spoon to break up the tomatoes. Bring to a boil. Cook, stirring often, until the sauce thickens, about 15 minutes. Add the coriander or basil and pepper. Set aside.

3. *To make the enchiladas:* In a large no-stick frying pan, sauté the green peppers and cumin seeds in the oil for 2 minutes. Add the zucchini and tomatoes; sauté for 1 minute. Raise the heat to high. Add the shrimp, a few at a time, and stir-fry until they turn opaque. Stir in the rice, onions, jalapeño peppers and ¼ cup of the cheese. Mix well. Set aside.

4. Wrap the tortillas in foil. Bake them at 300° for 5 to 7 minutes, or until they're soft enough that they won't crack when rolled.

5. Divide the rice filling among the tortillas, placing it down the center of each. Top with a slice of avocado. Roll up the tortillas to enclose the filling.

6. Coat a 9" × 13" baking dish with no-stick spray. Add the tortillas, seam side down. Top with about half of the salsa. Sprinkle with the remaining ¼ cup cheese. Bake at 350° for 20 minutes, or until heated through. Sprinkle with the coriander. Serve with the remaining salsa.

SERVES 4.

Preparation Time: 25 min.
Cooking Time: 45 min.

CHEF'S NOTES

■ ■ ■ ■ ■ ■ ■ ■ ■

DO FIRST:

Peel, devein and chop the shrimp. Cook the rice.

■

VARIATIONS:

Substitute diced chicken, turkey or white fish fillets for the shrimp. Replace the rice with cooked bulgur, couscous or barley.

■

MICROWAVE OPTION:

To soften the tortillas in the microwave, wrap 4 at a time in a dampened paper towel. Microwave on high for 30 seconds, or until warm and pliable.

NUTRITION AT A GLANCE

PER SERVING:

Calories	378
Fat	9 g. (21% of cal.)
Sat. fat	2.1 g. (5% of cal.)
Cholesterol	94 mg.
Sodium	280 mg.

SEAFOOD SUPREME

Rich and creamy seafood casseroles are within a dieter's reach! This luscious shellfish dish features a basic white sauce but keeps fat, cholesterol and calorie levels down with skim milk and just a touch of margarine.

SEAFOOD SUPREME

WHITE SAUCE

- **1** tablespoon margarine
- **3** tablespoons unbleached flour
- **2** cups skim milk, heated
- **½** bay leaf
- **½** small onion
- **1** whole clove
- **⅛** teaspoon grated nutmeg
- **⅛** teaspoon ground white pepper

SEAFOOD

- **12** ounces mushrooms, sliced
- **1** sweet red pepper, thinly sliced (optional)
- **½** cup fish stock or defatted chicken stock
- **½** cup nonalcoholic white wine or defatted chicken stock
- **8** ounces shrimp, peeled and deveined
- **6** ounces sea scallops, whole or halved
- **6** ounces halibut, cut into ½″ cubes

1. *To make the white sauce:* In a 2-quart saucepan over low heat, melt the margarine. Stir in the flour and cook for 2 to 3 minutes without browning.

2. Gradually whisk in the milk. Bring the sauce to a boil, whisking constantly. Reduce the heat to a simmer.

3. Affix the bay leaf to the onion with the clove. Add the onion to the sauce. Simmer, stirring often, until the sauce is thickened, at least 20 minutes. Stir in the nutmeg and pepper. Discard the onion. Strain to remove any lumps.

4. *To make the seafood:* Place the mushrooms, peppers, stock and nonalcoholic wine or stock in a large frying pan. Bring to a boil over medium-high heat. Cook, stirring occasionally, until the vegetables are tender and the liquid has evaporated, about 10 minutes.

5. Add the shrimp, scallops and halibut. Cover, reduce the heat to medium and simmer until the seafood is opaque, about 5 minutes.

6. Stir in the white sauce. Heat briefly.

SERVES 6.

Preparation Time: 20 min.
Cooking Time: 25 min.

CHEF'S NOTES

■ ■ ■ ■ ■ ■ ■ ■ ■

DO FIRST:

Heat the milk in a 1-quart saucepan until hot but not boiling. Peel and devein the shrimp.

■

ACCOMPANIMENT:

Serve over rice, toast points or noodles.

■

VARIATIONS:

Vary the seafood; try other white fish or salmon. Or add cooked, shelled mussels or crab in step 5.

NUTRITION AT A GLANCE ▬▬

PER SERVING:

Calories 169
Fat . . . . 3 g. (16% of cal.)
Sat. fat . . . . . 0.4 g. (2% of cal.)
Cholesterol . . . . 63 mg.
Sodium . . . . 162 mg.

MARYLAND CRAB CAKES

These Chesapeake-style crab patties contain a surprise ingredient: tofu. It takes the place of the mayonnaise found in most crab cakes. Besides keeping the patties extra-moist, the tofu adds calcium for strong bones.

Fish and Shellfish

MARYLAND CRAB CAKES

⅓ **cup soft tofu**

2 **teaspoons Worcestershire sauce**

2 **teaspoons oil**

1 **teaspoon lemon juice**

⅛ **teaspoon ground black pepper**

⅛ **teaspoon powdered ginger**

⅛ **teaspoon paprika**

⅛ **teaspoon hot-pepper sauce**

1½ **cups backfin crab meat, flaked**

½ **cup soft whole wheat bread crumbs**

1 **egg white, lightly beaten**

2 **tablespoons minced onion**

2 **tablespoons minced celery**

1. In a food processor, blend the tofu, Worcestershire, 1 teaspoon of the oil, lemon juice, pepper, ginger, paprika and hot-pepper sauce until satiny smooth. Transfer to a large bowl.

2. Add the crab, bread crumbs, egg white, onions and celery. Mix well. Chill for 30 minutes to make handling easier.

3. Form into 4 large or 8 small patties.

4. In a large no-stick frying pan over medium heat, warm the remaining 1 teaspoon oil. Add the patties and brown on both sides.

SERVES 4.

Preparation Time: 10 min. + standing time
Cooking Time: 7 min.

CHEF'S NOTES

DO FIRST:
Pick over the crab meat to remove little pieces of cartilage and shell.

INGREDIENTS NOTE:
You may use fresh or canned crab or crab substitute.

ACCOMPANIMENTS:
Serve with low-fat tartar sauce (pickle relish mixed with nonfat mayonnaise or yogurt), a green salad and cooked vegetables, such as red beets or lightly sautéed cabbage.

VARIATIONS:
You may replace the crab with flaked cooked fish such as cod, haddock or salmon. Or you may use canned chunk white tuna.

NUTRITION AT A GLANCE

PER SERVING:
Calories 107
Fat . . . . . . .3.9 g. (33% of cal.)
Sat. fat . . . . .0.3 g. (3% of cal.)
Cholesterol . . . . .45 mg.
Sodium . . . . .256 mg.

CLAMS WITH FRESH TOMATO SAUCE

Clams are brimming with two blood-building nutrients most often associated with meat: iron and vitamin B_{12}. In fact, just one serving of this Italian-style clam dish supplies close to a full day's supply of iron and *12 times* the RDA of B_{12}! All that with barely a trace of fat.

CLAMS WITH FRESH TOMATO SAUCE

- 1 tablespoon olive oil
- 2 pounds tomatoes, chopped
- 1 onion, chopped
- 3 cloves garlic, thinly sliced
- 2 tablespoons tomato paste
- 1½ cups defatted chicken stock
- ½ cup chopped fresh coriander
- 2 teaspoons dried oregano
- ½ teaspoon hot-pepper sauce
- 3 dozen littleneck clams
- 8 ounces rigatoni or other pasta, cooked

1. Heat the oil in a large no-stick frying pan. Add the tomatoes, onions, garlic and tomato paste. Simmer over medium heat until saucy, 20 to 30 minutes, stirring occasionally.

2. Stir in the stock, coriander, oregano and hot-pepper sauce. Set the clams atop the sauce. Cover the pan, turn the heat up to high and cook until the clams open, about 6 minutes.

3. Serve the clams and sauce over the pasta. If desired, remove the clams from their shells first.

SERVES 4.

Preparation Time: 10 min.
Cooking Time: 40 min.

CHEF'S NOTES

DO FIRST:
Scrub the clams with a bristle brush under cold water. Discard any clams with gaping shells that won't close if you press the halves together. Fresh, live clams close at the slightest touch.

ACCOMPANIMENTS:
Serve with a mixed green salad and crusty bread.

VARIATIONS:
Replace the clams with mussels in the shell. Or use scallops or peeled shrimp.

KITCHEN TRICK:
If using homemade stock, chill it until any fat present floats to the surface and hardens. Skim it off with a spoon.

NUTRITION AT A GLANCE

PER SERVING:
Calories 262
Fat . . . . .6 g. (21% of cal.)
Sat. fat . . . . .0.7 g. (2% of cal.)
Cholesterol . . . . .28 mg.
Sodium . . . . .103 mg.

ONE-DISH MEALS

CHICKEN POTPIE

Is chicken potpie one of your favorites? Many classic recipes pack a whopping 40 grams of fat into a single serving (that's equivalent to 15 chocolate-chip cookies). Worse, much of that fat is often saturated, coming from butter or lard. We've trimmed this homey dish considerably by using light margarine (in moderation) and by having only a top crust.

CHICKEN POTPIE

CHICKEN FILLING

- **3 cups defatted chicken stock**
- **1 cup thinly sliced celery**
- **⅔ cup thinly sliced carrot**
- **⅔ cup sliced green beans**
- **⅔ cup diced sweet red pepper**
- **¼–½ cup low-fat milk**
- **½ cup chopped onion**
- **1 tablespoon light margarine**
- **3 tablespoons defatted chicken stock**
- **⅓ cup whole wheat flour**
- **2 tablespoons minced fresh parsley**
- **1 teaspoon reduced-sodium soy sauce**
- **½ teaspoon dried sage**
- **½ teaspoon dried thyme**
- **2 cups cubed cooked chicken breast**

BISCUITS

- **1 cup unbleached flour**
- **¾ cup whole wheat flour**
- **2 teaspoons baking powder**
- **½ teaspoon baking soda**
- **3 tablespoons light margarine**
- **¾–1 cup buttermilk**
- **1 teaspoon honey**
- **½ teaspoon reduced-sodium soy sauce**

1. *To make the chicken filling:* In a 3-quart saucepan combine 3 cups of stock, celery, carrots, beans and peppers. Boil for 5 minutes. Strain the stock into a 4-cup glass measuring cup and add enough milk to make 3 cups. Reserve the vegetables.

2. Sauté the onions in the margarine for 2 to 3 minutes. Mix in 3 tablespoons of stock. Stir in the flour and cook for 1 minute. Gradually whisk in the reserved stock. Add the parsley, soy sauce, sage and thyme. Cook over low heat, stirring constantly until thickened. Add the reserved vegetables and the chicken.

3. Coat 4 small casserole dishes (2 to 2½ cups) with no-stick spray. Divide the chicken mixture among them.

4. *To make the biscuits:* Sift the unbleached flour, whole wheat flour, baking powder and baking soda into a large bowl. Using 2 knives, cut the margarine into the flour until the mixture resembles coarse meal.

5. In a small bowl whisk together ¾ cup buttermilk, honey and soy sauce. Pour over the flour mixture and stir gently with a fork to moisten the flour. If the dough is too dry, mix in a little more buttermilk. Turn the dough out onto a lightly floured surface and divide it into 4 pieces. Pat each piece into a circle. Place over the chicken. Bake at 400° for 20 minutes.

SERVES 4.

Preparation Time: 30 min.
Cooking Time: 35 min.

CHEF'S NOTES

■ ■ ■ ■ ■ ■ ■ ■ ■

DO FIRST:
Cook the chicken: Start with 1 pound of boneless, skinless chicken breasts. Poach in water or stock until tender, 15 to 20 minutes.

■

PRESENTATION:
For an interesting presentation, bake the filling in small whole winter squash or individual pumpkins. Precook the containers until just tender.

■

NUTRI-NOTE:
One way to cut fat and calories even further is to replace the top crust with mashed white or sweet potatoes. Pipe them decoratively on top of the filling.

NUTRITION AT A GLANCE

PER SERVING:

Calories 589
Fat . . . . . . .14 g. (21% of cal.)
Sat. fat . . . . .2.1 g. (3% of cal.)
Cholesterol . . . . .62 mg.
Sodium . . . . .779 mg.

CHICKEN CASSOULET

Cassoulet is a marvelous bean dish from France. Although traditional recipes call for sausage, goose and even pork rind, those fatty ingredients are not at all necessary. Well-trimmed, skinless chicken thighs give this hearty main course robust flavor.

Chicken Cassoulet

- **1 pound boneless, skinless chicken thighs**
- **¾ teaspoon dried thyme**
- **¼ teaspoon ground allspice**
- **¾ teaspoon ground black pepper**
- **1 cup chopped onion**
- **3 cloves garlic, minced**
- **1½ cups chopped tomato**
- **1 large carrot, diced**
- **½ cup nonalcoholic white wine or defatted chicken stock**
- **Pinch of ground cloves**
- **2 tablespoons minced fresh parsley**
- **2 cups packed chopped spinach**
- **3½ cups cooked Great Northern beans**
- **1½ cups defatted chicken stock**
- **½ cup dry bread crumbs**

1. Trim all visible fat from the chicken and cut it into ¾'' cubes.

2. Coat a large no-stick frying pan with no-stick spray. Place over medium-high heat until hot. Add the chicken. Sprinkle with the thyme, allspice and ½ teaspoon of the pepper. Cook until brown. Transfer to a large bowl. Set aside.

3. Add the onions and garlic to the pan. Cook until tender, about 5 minutes. Add the tomatoes, carrots, wine or stock and cloves. Stir in 1 tablespoon of the parsley and the remaining ¼ teaspoon of the pepper. Cook until the carrots are almost tender, about 10 minutes. Add the spinach and cook until it wilts. Add to the chicken. Stir in the beans. Combine well.

4. Coat a 2½-quart casserole with no-stick spray. Add the chicken mixture. Pour the stock over the mixture just to cover.

5. Mix the bread crumbs with the remaining 1 tablespoon parsley. Sprinkle over the chicken and bake at 350° until the crumbs are golden brown, about 1½ hours.

SERVES 6.

Preparation Time: 25 min.
Cooking Time: 2 hr.

TURKEY SAUSAGE CASSEROLE

Turkey sausage is a lean alternative to pork links. This casserole combines sausage with oat-bran bread (for extra fiber) and fat-free egg substitute (to keep cholesterol down). Three kinds of peppers contribute vitamin C to help increase resistance to disease.

TURKEY SAUSAGE CASSEROLE

8 ounces mild or spicy turkey sausage

½ cup minced onion

½ cup thinly sliced green pepper

½ cup thinly sliced yellow pepper

⅓ cup chopped drained pimento

¼ cup shredded low-fat Cheddar cheese

1 tablespoon minced fresh parsley

½ teaspoon dried thyme

1½ tablespoons coarse mustard

2 teaspoons light margarine, softened

9 slices oat-bran bread, crusts removed

1 cup fat-free egg substitute

2 egg whites

2½ cups low-fat milk

¼ teaspoon ground white pepper

1. Remove any casing from the sausage. Crumble the meat into a large no-stick frying pan. Brown over medium heat, breaking up the pieces with a wooden spoon. Transfer to a large platter lined with several thicknesses of paper towels. Blot with more paper towels to soak up all surface fat. Set aside.

2. Wipe out the frying pan. Return it to the heat and add the onions, green peppers and yellow peppers. Sauté until tender, about 5 minutes. Remove from the heat and add the pimentos, Cheddar, parsley and thyme.

3. Coat a 9″ × 9″ baking dish with no-stick spray. In a small cup, mix the mustard and margarine. Cut the slices of bread in half and spread each half with a thin layer of the mustard mixture. Set aside 4 halves. Place the remaining bread, coated side down, in the dish to cover the bottom and come up the sides.

4. Cover with the pepper mixture. Sprinkle with half the sausage. Top with the remaining bread, mustard side up.

5. In a large bowl, whisk together the egg and egg whites. Whisk in the milk and white pepper. Pour over the bread. Top with the remaining sausage. Cover and refrigerate at least 2 hours or overnight to allow the bread to soak up the milk mixture.

6. Uncover and bake at 325° for 60 to 75 minutes, or until a knife inserted in the middle comes out clean. Let stand 10 to 20 minutes before serving.

SERVES 6.

Preparation Time: 25 min. + standing time
Cooking Time: 1½ hr.

CHEF'S NOTES

PRESENTATION:
Serve as a wonderful brunch dish with freshly squeezed orange juice, a light tossed salad and berries.

VARIATION:
Add 1 cup of steamed broccoli or 4 ounces of sliced mushrooms to the vegetable mixture.

NUTRI-NOTE:
Turkey sausage can vary widely in fat content, so read labels carefully. Drain the sausage as directed to remove as much fat as possible.

NUTRITION AT A GLANCE

PER SERVING:

Calories 347
Fat . . . . . . .12 g. (31% of cal.)
Sat. fat . . . . . .3 g. (8% of cal.)
Cholesterol . . . . .7 mg.
Sodium . . . . .500 mg.

BEEF AND NOODLE CASSEROLE

This is hot and hearty comfort food for chilly weather. And the B vitamins will give you lots of energy. To serve this casserole for weeknight dinners, assemble it ahead and pop it into the oven when you get home from work.

BEEF AND NOODLE CASSEROLE

1 cup finely chopped onion

1 cup diced sweet red, yellow or green pepper

1½ cups diced mushrooms

2 tablespoons water

8 ounces extra-lean ground beef

3 tablespoons unbleached flour

3 cups skim milk

2 tablespoons minced fresh dill or 1 teaspoon dried

1 tablespoon reduced-sodium soy sauce

1 teaspoon Worcestershire sauce

¼ teaspoon ground black pepper

6 ounces fine noodles

10 ounces frozen peas, thawed

3 ounces reduced-fat sharp Cheddar cheese, shredded

¼ cup unsalted shelled sunflower seeds

1. In a large frying pan over medium-high heat, cook the onions, peppers, mushrooms and water until the vegetables have softened and all the liquid has evaporated, about 8 minutes. Transfer to a large bowl and set aside.

2. Crumble the beef into the frying pan. Brown over medium-high heat, breaking up the pieces. Transfer to a large colander lined with paper towels and allow to drain for 5 minutes. Add to the vegetables and mix well. Set aside.

3. Place the flour in a 2-quart saucepan. Gradually whisk in the milk until smooth. Cook, stirring constantly, over medium heat until the milk comes to a boil and thickens. Stir in the dill, soy sauce, Worcestershire sauce and black pepper. Stir about half of the sauce into the beef mixture. Reserve the remaining sauce.

4. Cook the noodles in a large pot of boiling water until just tender, about 8 minutes. Drain well and return to the pot. Add the peas and the remaining white sauce.

5. Coat a 7″ × 11″ baking dish with no-stick spray. Add the noodle mixture. Top with the beef mixture. Sprinkle with the Cheddar.

6. Bake at 350° for 15 minutes. Sprinkle with the sunflower seeds. Bake for 10 minutes more.

SERVES 6.

Preparation Time: 30 min.
Cooking Time: 40 min.

CHEF'S NOTES

VARIATIONS:
Replace the beef with ground turkey or low-fat turkey sausage. Replace the sunflower seeds with pumpkin seeds or chopped nuts. Use other herbs, such as parsley, basil or sage.

CHEF'S SECRET:
To remove as much fat as possible from the beef after browning it, drain as directed then pat it dry with more paper towels.

NUTRITION AT A GLANCE

PER SERVING:
Calories 355
Fat . . . . 10 g. (25% of cal.)
Sat. fat . . . . 4.2 g. (11% of cal.)
Cholesterol . . . . 37 mg.
Sodium . . . . 322 mg.

VEGETABLE CHILI

Dried beans are an excellent source of blood-building iron. In fact, beans are the most iron-rich plant products around. But because the type of iron found in them is not as readily absorbed as that from meat, you should combine them with meat or foods high in vitamin C, such as red peppers.

VEGETABLE CHILI

2 tablespoons olive oil
1½ cups chopped onion
2 tablespoons minced garlic
2 cups diced sweet red pepper
2 teaspoons minced jalapeño pepper
2½ teaspoons chili powder
1 teaspoon ground cumin
⅛ teaspoon dried basil
1 can (28 ounces) whole tomatoes
1 cup defatted stock
½ cup mild or medium salsa
1 can (19 ounces) red kidney beans, drained and rinsed
1½ cups corn

1. Heat the oil in a large, heavy saucepan over medium-high heat. Add the onions and garlic. Sauté 3 to 4 minutes, stirring occasionally, until softened.

2. Stir in the red peppers and jalapeño peppers. Sauté 3 to 4 minutes, stirring occasionally, until softened.

3. Add the chili powder, cumin and basil. Sauté 1 minute, stirring occasionally.

4. Drain the tomatoes, reserving ½ cup of the juice. Add the juice to the pan. Crush the tomatoes or cut with scissors and add to the pan along with the stock and salsa. Bring to a boil.

5. Reduce heat to medium low and simmer for 10 minutes, stirring occasionally, until mixture has thickened slightly.

6. Add the beans and corn. Raise heat to medium and simmer for 6 to 8 minutes, until the beans and corn are heated.

SERVES 4.

Preparation Time: 15 min.
Cooking Time: 30 min.

CHEF'S NOTES

ACCOMPANIMENTS:

Serve with mix-and-match toppings: sliced scallions, sliced pickled jalapeños, diced avocados and nonfat yogurt.

VARIATIONS:

Use other beans, such as pintos. If using dried beans, soak and cook them ahead. You'll need 2 cups of cooked beans. Add ground turkey, chicken or lean sirloin to the chili. Brown the meat and add it along with the beans and corn.

NUTRI-NOTE:

When choosing a brand of salsa, look for one without fat or sugar. If you're on a sodium-restricted diet, check for the presence of salt in the tomatoes, stock and salsa. Rinsing the canned beans well will help remove most of their sodium.

NUTRITION AT A GLANCE

PER SERVING:
Calories 320
Fat . . . . .9 g. (25% of cal.)
Sat. fat . . . . .1.1 g. (3% of cal.)
Cholesterol . . . . .0 mg.
Sodium . . . . .442 mg.

FALAFEL POCKETS

Falafels are a Middle Eastern
specialty made of seasoned ground
chick-peas. Served in pita pockets,
they're great for a vegetarian lunch
or a light dinner. And this recipe
outshines commercial falafels because
the patties aren't deep-fried.

One-Dish Meals

FALAFEL POCKETS

SAUCE

- 1½ cups nonfat yogurt
- ¼ cup tahini (sesame seed paste)
- 1 teaspoon ground cumin
- ⅛–¼ teaspoon ground red pepper

FALAFELS

- ½ cup defatted chicken stock
- 2 tablespoons dried celery flakes, crumbled
- 1 tablespoon dried parsley, crumbled
- 1 clove garlic, minced
- ½ cup bulgur
- 1 can (19 ounces) chick-peas, rinsed and drained
- ¼ cup oat bran
- ¼ cup fat-free egg substitute or 1 egg
- ¼ cup minced fresh coriander
- 2 tablespoons tahini
- 1 tablespoon lemon juice
- 1 teaspoon ground cumin
- 1 teaspoon chili powder
- ¼ teaspoon ground black pepper
- ¼ teaspoon hot-pepper sauce
- 1–2 teaspoons olive oil

PITA POCKETS

- 6 pitas, halved and warmed
- 1 cup diced or sliced tomato
- 1 cup finely shredded carrot
- ½ cup torn lettuce
- ¼ cup minced fresh coriander

1. *To make the sauce:* Line a sieve with a double thickness of cheesecloth. Spoon in the yogurt and let drain for 20 minutes to thicken slightly. Transfer to a bowl. Stir in the tahini, cumin and pepper. Set aside.

2. *To make the falafels:* In a 1-quart saucepan, combine the stock, celery, parsley and garlic. Bring to a boil. Add the bulgur. Cover, remove from the heat and let stand 20 minutes, or until all the liquid has been absorbed. Fluff with a fork.

3. In a food processor, combine the chick-peas, oat bran, egg, coriander, tahini, lemon juice, cumin, chili powder, pepper and hot-pepper sauce. Puree. Transfer to a large bowl. Stir in the bulgur. Refrigerate for 20 minutes. Form into small balls, patties or logs about ½'' thick.

4. Heat a large no-stick frying pan over medium heat until warm. Add a little oil and a layer of falafels; do not crowd. Sauté until lightly browned on all sides. Repeat to use all falafels and just as much oil as needed.

5. *To make the pita pockets:* Place the falafels in the pita halves. Top with the tomatoes, carrots, lettuce, coriander and yogurt sauce.

SERVES 6.

Preparation Time: 40 min.
Cooking Time: 15 min.

CHEF'S NOTES

■ ■ ■ ■ ■ ■ ■ ■ ■

DO FIRST:
If using dried chick-peas, start with 2 cups. Soak, then cook them until very tender, at least 3 hours.

■

VARIATIONS:
For a slightly different taste, replace the tahini with peanut butter or another nut butter. You may replace the fresh coriander with parsley. For really quick falafels, use a store-bought mix. Serve it with the yogurt sauce, pita and other accompaniments listed.

■

MICROWAVE OPTION:
Reheat leftover falafels by micro-waving them on high until just warm.

NUTRITION AT A GLANCE

PER SERVING:
Calories	300
Fat	8.4 g. (25% of cal.)
Sat. fat	1 g. (3% of cal.)
Cholesterol	1 mg.
Sodium	85 mg.

ASPARAGUS QUESADILLAS

Asparagus contains three separate nutrients that doctors say may help fight cancer: carotene, vitamin C and the mineral selenium. That's good reason to enjoy these spears often. This particular recipe showcases them in crispy, low-calorie tortilla "sandwiches."

ASPARAGUS QUESADILLAS

FILLING
- **1 teaspoon olive oil**
- **1 large red onion, diced**
- **2 cloves garlic, minced**
- **½ teaspoon chili powder**
- **½ teaspoon ground cumin**
- **⅛ teaspoon ground cinnamon**
- **⅛ teaspoon ground red pepper**
- **1 pound asparagus spears, trimmed, cut into 2″ pieces and lightly steamed**
- **6 cherry tomatoes, quartered**
- **¼ cup minced fresh coriander**

QUESADILLA ASSEMBLY
- **6 flour tortillas**
- **2 ounces low-fat Monterey Jack cheese, shredded**
- **1 cup green or red salsa, warmed**
- **6 cherry tomatoes, halved or quartered**
- **¼ cup minced fresh coriander**

1. *To make the filling:* In a large no-stick frying pan over medium heat, warm the oil. Add the onions. Sauté for 3 to 4 minutes to soften. Add the garlic, chili powder, cumin, cinnamon and pepper. Stir for 1 minute.

2. Add the asparagus, tomatoes and coriander. Stir well and sauté for 3 to 4 minutes. Transfer to a large bowl.

3. *To assemble quesadillas:* Divide the filling among the tortillas, positioning it on half of each. Sprinkle with the Monterey Jack. Fold in half.

4. Clean the frying pan. Coat with no-stick spray and warm over medium-high heat. Add 2 tortillas and fry 2 minutes per side, until golden; press with a spatula to flatten slightly. Repeat to use all the tortillas.

5. To serve, cut each quesadilla in half and top with salsa, tomatoes and coriander.

SERVES 6.

Preparation Time: 25 min.
Cooking Time: 20 min.

CHEF'S NOTES
■ ■ ■ ■ ■ ■ ■ ■ ■

DO FIRST:
Trim the tough woody ends from the asparagus. Cut the spears into pieces and steam for about 5 minutes, or until just tender but not overcooked.

■

ACCOMPANIMENTS:
For a really hearty meal, serve with side dishes of beans and rice. Or use the quesadillas as an accompaniment to grilled fish, such as halibut or flounder.

■

VARIATION:
Replace the asparagus with other vegetables, such as broccoli or green beans.

NUTRITION AT A GLANCE

PER SERVING:
Calories 168
Fat . . . . . . .5.6 g. (30% of cal.)
Sat. fat . . . . .1.5 g. (7% of cal.)
Cholesterol . . . . .5 mg.
Sodium . . . . .181 mg.

SPICY FRIED RICE AND VEGETABLES

A vegetable medley like this is just brimming with dietary fiber—and that pays you double health benefits. The insoluble portion of the fiber is essential for digestive health. And the accompanying soluble fiber helps control cholesterol levels. The use of good-for-you olive oil and cholesterol-free egg substitute keeps this stir-fry ultra healthy.

SPICY FRIED RICE AND VEGETABLES

- 1 **broccoli stalk**
- 1½ **tablespoons olive oil**
- 4 **teaspoons minced garlic**
- 1 **teaspoon minced fresh ginger**
- 1 **sweet red pepper, cut into strips**
- 1 **onion, thinly sliced**
- ½ **cup vegetable or defatted chicken stock**
- 3 **cups cut Napa cabbage (1″ pieces)**
- 2 **cups sliced mushrooms**
- 1 **cup snow peas**
- 2 **tablespoons reduced-sodium soy sauce**
- 3 **cups cooked rice**
- 1½ **teaspoons hot-chili oil Pinch of red-pepper flakes**
- ½ **cup fat-free egg substitute**
- 2–3 **tablespoons chopped fresh coriander or Italian parsley**

1. Cut off the top portion of the broccoli and separate it into small florets. Halve the stalk portion lengthwise and slice thinly.

2. Heat the olive oil in a wok or large, heavy pot over high heat. Add the garlic and ginger and stir-fry for 30 seconds, just until fragrant.

3. Add the broccoli, peppers and onions; stir-fry for 1 minute, until well coated with oil. Pour in the stock, cover and simmer for 3 minutes, until the vegetables are nearly tender.

4. Add the cabbage, mushrooms, peas and 1 tablespoon soy sauce; stir-fry 1 minute, until the cabbage cooks down. Cover and simmer for 2 minutes, until the vegetables are tender.

5. Using a slotted spoon, transfer the vegetables to a bowl.

6. To liquid remaining in wok, add the rice, chili oil, red-pepper flakes and remaining 1 tablespoon soy sauce. Stir-fry for 1 to 2 minutes, until the rice is heated through.

7. Reduce heat to medium low. Pour in the egg and cook for 3 to 4 minutes, turning mixture occasionally with a spatula, until mixture is set. (Don't stir egg vigorously.)

8. Spoon the rice onto a large serving platter; top with vegetables and sprinkle with coriander or parsley.

SERVES 4.

Preparation Time: 20 min.
Cooking Time: 15 min.

CHEF'S NOTES

DO FIRST:

Cook the rice. But never rinse rice before cooking — you'll wash away nutrients.

VARIATION:

Mix and match vegetables according to availability.

NUTRI-NOTE:

For maximum nutrition, always choose broccoli that is deep green in color with tightly closed green or purplish green buds. Yellow patches and open buds indicate broccoli was picked past its prime.

KITCHEN TRICKS:

To peel ginger easily, use a vegetable peeler. Buy ginger in small quantities, store it in the refrigerator and use within 2 weeks.

NUTRITION AT A GLANCE

PER SERVING:

Calories	300
Fat	7 g. (21% of cal.)
Sat. fat	1 g. (3% of cal.)
Cholesterol	0 mg.
Sodium	393 mg.

MEDITERRANEAN EGGPLANT CASSEROLE

Eggplant Parmesan is traditionally made by breading eggplant and frying it in a great deal of oil. By microwaving the eggplant before assembling the casserole, we've slimmed down fat and calories considerably. Yet this dish is every bit as tasty as classic recipes!

MEDITERRANEAN EGGPLANT CASSEROLE

- **2 eggplants, peeled**
- **½ cup water**
- **4 ounces mushrooms, sliced**
- **1 onion, thinly sliced**
- **1 clove garlic, minced**
- **3 tablespoons minced fresh basil or 1 teaspoon dried**
- **½ teaspoon ground black pepper**
- **2½ cups tomato sauce**
- **6 ounces nonfat or part-skim mozzarella cheese, shredded**
- **½ cup grated Parmesan cheese**

1. Cut the eggplants crosswise into slices ⅜″ thick. Layer in a 7″ × 11″ glass baking dish. Sprinkle with ¼ cup of the water. Cover loosely with wax paper and microwave on high for 7 minutes. Redistribute the pieces, moving the soft ones to the center of the dish. Cover with wax paper and microwave on high for 8 minutes, or until all the slices are tender. (If you do not have a microwave, see Chef's Notes.)

2. Drain the eggplant. Transfer to a platter lined with several layers of paper towels. Cover with more towels and press out the excess liquid. Set aside.

3. Place the mushrooms, onions and garlic in a 2-quart casserole. Add the remaining ¼ cup water. Cover with a lid. Microwave on high for 4 minutes. Stir well, cover and microwave on high for 4 more minutes, or until tender. Drain well and stir in the basil and pepper. (If you do not have a microwave, see Chef's Notes.)

4. Coat a 7″ × 11″ baking dish with no-stick spray. Place 1 cup of the tomato sauce in the bottom. Top with half of the eggplant slices and all of the onion mixture. Add 1 cup of the remaining tomato sauce, 3 ounces of the mozzarella and ¼ cup of the Parmesan cheese. Top with the rest of the eggplant, the remaining ½ cup tomato sauce, the remaining 3 ounces of mozzarella and the remaining ¼ cup Parmesan.

5. Bake at 350° for 20 minutes, or until bubbly. Allow to stand for 10 minutes before serving.

SERVES 6.

Preparation Time: 15 min.
Cooking Time: 45 min.

CHEF'S NOTES

VARIATIONS:

Serve over cooked pasta. Or add a layer of lasagna noodles or other cooked pasta to the casserole itself. For a spicy dish, add minced hot peppers or pepper flakes.

TECHNIQUE:

If you do not have a microwave, bake the eggplant: Place in a single layer in jelly-roll pans coated with no-stick spray. Sprinkle with ¼ cup water, cover tightly with foil and bake at 350° for 30 minutes, or until tender. Drain well. Steam the mushrooms, onions and garlic until tender, about 10 minutes.

NUTRITION AT A GLANCE

PER SERVING:

Calories 170
Fat . . . . .3 g. (16% of cal.)
Sat. fat . . . . .1.6 g. (8% of cal.)
Cholesterol . . . . .7 mg.
Sodium . . . . .189 mg.

LEAN STUFFED CABBAGE

These low-fat cabbage rolls are just brimming with healing nutrients. B$_6$, niacin, iron and vitamin C are high on the list. Part of what makes these rolls so lean is the ground turkey used in the filling.

LEAN STUFFED CABBAGE

- **8 medium or 16 small cabbage leaves**
- **1 cup water**
- **¼ cup raisins**
- **½ cup minced onion**
- **1 teaspoon minced garlic**
- **1 pound lean ground turkey**
- **2 teaspoons ground cumin**
- **Grated rind of 2 lemons**
- **½ teaspoon ground black pepper**
- **½ teaspoon dried thyme**
- **2 large tomatoes, diced or cut into thin wedges**
- **2 tablespoons minced fresh parsley or basil**

1. Blanch the cabbage leaves in boiling water for 1 minute. Remove with a slotted spoon. Lay the leaves flat on a tray and set them aside.

2. In a 1-quart saucepan over medium heat, bring the water and raisins to a boil. Set aside.

3. In a large no-stick frying pan over medium heat, combine the onions, garlic and 2 teaspoons of the water from the raisins. Sauté until the onions turn translucent, about 5 minutes.

4. Add the turkey. Sauté, stirring constantly, until the meat has lost its color and is well broken up.

5. Drain the raisins, discarding the water. Add to the turkey. Add the cumin and lemon rind. Sauté for 5 minutes. Stir in the pepper and thyme.

6. Remove from the heat and allow to cool before handling.

7. Divide the filling among the cabbage leaves. Enclose the filling by tucking in the side edges and rolling up the leaves.

8. Coat a 9″ × 13″ baking dish with no-stick spray. Add the rolls, seam side down. Bake at 350° for 15 minutes.

9. Sprinkle the tomatoes with the parsley or basil. Serve with the cabbage rolls.

SERVES 4.

Preparation Time: 25 min.
Cooking Time: 35 min.

CHEF'S NOTES

VARIATIONS:

Add ½ to 1 cup of tomato sauce to the filling; top the rolls with additional tomato sauce or a low-fat white sauce before baking. You may also replace the meat with about 1½ cups of cooked rice.

CHEF'S SECRET:

To peel whole leaves from a head of cabbage without tearing them, first remove the core with a sharp knife. Then blanch the whole head in a large pot of boiling water for several minutes, until the leaves soften slightly and can be removed easily.

NUTRITION AT A GLANCE

PER SERVING:

Calories 219
Fat . . . . 2.6 g. (11% of cal.)
Sat. fat . . . . . 0.7 g. (3% of cal.)
Cholesterol . . . . 68 mg.
Sodium . . . . 104 mg.

EL PASO PILAF

Kidney beans, rice, corn and lentils combine to produce a protein-rich vegetarian entrée. And this Tex-Mex dish has over 8 grams of fiber, making a significant contribution toward the 20 to 35 grams a day that doctors recommend for optimum health.

El Paso Pilaf

½ cup chopped onion
2 teaspoons olive oil
1 can (15 ounces) red kidney beans, drained and rinsed
1¾ cups defatted chicken stock
1 cup long-grain white rice
1 cup corn

1 cup chunky salsa
¼ cup lentils
¼ cup chopped sweet red pepper
½ teaspoon chili powder
Pinch of garlic powder
4 large tomatoes, hollowed out (see Chef's Notes)

1. In a 3-quart saucepan over medium heat, cook the onions in the oil for 5 minutes, or until tender but not brown. Add the beans, stock, rice, corn, salsa, lentils, peppers, chili powder and garlic powder.

2. Bring to a boil, then reduce the heat so the mixture simmers. Cover and cook for 20 to 25 minutes, or until the rice and lentils are tender and most of the liquid has been absorbed.

3. Stuff the pilaf into the tomatoes. Serve any extra pilaf on the side.

SERVES 4.

Preparation Time: 15 min.
Cooking Time: 30 min.

CHEF'S NOTES

DO FIRST:

Rinse the beans well with cold water to remove excess sodium. If desired, you may also cook up dried beans. Start with about 1 cup of kidney beans. Soak overnight, then cook until tender, about 1½ hours.

VARIATIONS:

You may serve the pilaf over tomato slices. Or you may use it as a filling for tortillas.

KITCHEN TRICK:

The easiest way to hollow out tomatoes is to slice off the tops, then use a spoon to scoop out the interiors. Turn the tomatoes over and let drain for a few minutes.

NUTRITION AT A GLANCE

PER SERVING:

Calories 428
Fat . . . . 5.3 g. (11% of cal.)
Sat. fat . . . . . 0.7 g. (1% of cal.)
Cholesterol . . . . 0 mg.
Sodium . . . . 385 mg.

RICE-STUFFED PEPPERS

Incredible as it may seem, one green or yellow pepper has *more* vitamin C than the juice from two oranges. And red peppers contain almost twice that much! So eating vitamin C–rich dishes like this may help you tap into the vitamin's infection-fighting abilities. In one study, people getting more than 300 milligrams of C a day (that's five times the RDA) had fewer respiratory problems than those who consumed much less.

RICE-STUFFED PEPPERS

- 1⅔ cups defatted chicken stock
- ¾ cup long-grain white rice
- ¼ cup wild rice
- 4 sweet red, yellow or green peppers
- 2 tablespoons water
- 1 tablespoon olive oil
- ½ cup diced onion
- 1 clove garlic, minced
- ½ cup peas
- ½ cup corn
- ½ cup minced carrot
- ½ cup shredded part-skim mozzarella cheese
- ¼ teaspoon dried oregano
- 4 thin slices part-skim mozzarella cheese
- 2 cups warm tomato sauce

1. Combine the stock, white rice and wild rice in a 1-quart saucepan. Bring to a boil over medium heat. Cover, reduce the heat to medium low and simmer for about 20 minutes, or until the rice is tender and all the stock has been absorbed. Set aside.

2. Cut the tops off the peppers near the stem ends. Discard the stems, seeds and inner membranes.

3. Coat a deep 3-quart casserole dish with no-stick spray. Place the peppers upside down in the dish. Add the water. Cover with the lid or foil and bake at 350° for 20 minutes.

4. Heat the oil in a large no-stick frying pan over medium heat. Add the onions and garlic. Sauté, stirring, for 5 minutes or until tender. Add the peas, corn and carrots. Cover and cook over low heat for 5 minutes. Stir in the rice, shredded mozzarella and oregano.

5. Remove the peppers from the oven. Turn them right side up. Carefully fill them with the rice mixture, mounding the tops slightly. Top each with a slice of mozzarella.

6. Cover again with the lid and bake for 15 minutes. Remove the lid and bake 5 minutes longer. Serve with the tomato sauce.

SERVES 4.

Preparation Time: 20 min.
Cooking Time: 1¼ hr.

CHEF'S NOTES

■ ■ ■ ■ ■ ■ ■ ■ ■

ACCOMPANIMENT:
Serve with Italian Flat Bread with Fresh Herbs (page 279).

■

VARIATION:
Add sautéed ground meat, such as turkey breast or Italian-style turkey sausage (removed from the casings), to the rice mixture.

■

KITCHEN TRICKS:
Choose peppers with flat bottoms that will stand upright. Or prop them up with crumpled foil.

■

MAKE-AHEAD TIPS:
Bake the peppers ahead: Reheat in the oven at 350° for 10 minutes, in a frying pan with a little water or in the microwave (about 1 minute per half).

NUTRITION AT A GLANCE

PER SERVING:
Calories 375
Fat . . . . 8.3 g. (20% of cal.)
Sat. fat . . . . . 2.8 g. (7% of cal.)
Cholesterol . . . . 12 mg.
Sodium . . . . 196 mg.

BROCCOLI AND CHEESE FRITTATA

You don't have to give up eggs on a low-cholesterol diet. Egg substitutes—the foundation of this Italian-style omelet—are cholesterol free and low in fat. Made of egg whites, they come frozen in little cartons, just the size for quick meals. We've fortified this low-cal omelet with vitamin A-rich broccoli and high-fiber spuds.

BROCCOLI AND CHEESE FRITTATA

½ teaspoon oil
1½ cups fat-free egg substitute
1 tablespoon minced fresh basil or ½ teaspoon dried
½ teaspoon reduced-sodium soy sauce
½ cup diced cooked red-skinned potato

1 cup cooked broccoli florets
¼ cup sliced pimento
1 tablespoon minced scallions
⅓ cup grated low-fat Cheddar cheese
Pinch of ground black pepper

1. Heat the oil in a large no-stick frying pan over medium-high heat.

2. In a large bowl whisk together the eggs, basil and soy sauce. Add to the heated pan. As the eggs cook, gently push the outer edges toward the center with a spatula until eggs are about half set. Do not stir.

3. Sprinkle with potatoes, broccoli, pimentos and scallions.

4. Protect the handle of the pan by covering it with foil. Place the pan under the broiler, 5'' or 6'' from the heat. Broil for 3 minutes.

5. Sprinkle with the cheese and broil another 2 minutes, or until the cheese is melted.

6. Sprinkle with pepper. Slice into wedges. Serve immediately.

SERVES 4.

Preparation Time: 15 min.
Cooking Time: 15 min.

CHEF'S NOTES

■ ■ ■ ■ ■ ■ ■ ■

DO FIRST:
Cook the potatoes and broccoli: Steam the broccoli florets and small, whole red-skinned potatoes together until just tender when pierced with a sharp knife or skewer, about 5 minutes. If the broccoli is ready first, remove it with tongs and cook the potatoes a few minutes longer.

■

ACCOMPANIMENTS:
Serve for breakfast with whole-grain toast and fruit. Or make into a light lunch with rolls and a simple vegetable salad.

■

VARIATION:
Use other vegetables, such as zucchini, mushrooms, red peppers or carrots.

■

MAKE-AHEAD TIP:
Prepare the frittata ahead. Serve it cold, at room temperature or reheated in a toaster oven.

NUTRITION AT A GLANCE ▬▬

PER SERVING:
Calories 95
Fat . . . . .2 g. (19% of cal.)
Sat. fat . . . . .0.8 g. (8% of cal.)
Cholesterol . . . . .5 mg.
Sodium 209

SPINACH AND MUSHROOM PIE

One great way to cut calories and fat from pie recipes is to eliminate the crust. And with a thick, quichelike filling that holds together when baked, you can do just that. This pie contains plenty of rice, so it's nice and solid when served. Spinach, mushrooms and part-skim cheese add a nice complement of bone-building nutrients.

SPINACH AND MUSHROOM PIE

- **10 ounces frozen chopped spinach**
- **2 cups cooked rice**
- **½ cup shredded part-skim mozzarella cheese**
- **¼ cup minced scallions**
- **¼ cup minced sweet red pepper**
- **2 tablespoons minced fresh dill or 1½ teaspoons dried**
- **1 egg**
- **3 egg whites**
- **1½ cups low-fat milk**
- **2 teaspoons Dijon mustard**
- **¼ teaspoon ground white pepper**
- **¼ teaspoon hot-pepper sauce**
- **½ cup thinly sliced mushrooms**
- **1 tablespoon grated Parmesan cheese**
- **6 thin rings sweet red pepper**

1. Cook the spinach according to package directions. Transfer to a strainer to cool. Press with the back of a spoon and squeeze with your hands to remove as much liquid as possible.

2. In a large bowl combine the spinach with the rice, mozzarella, scallions, minced red peppers and dill. Stir to blend thoroughly.

3. In a small bowl whisk together the egg, egg whites, milk, mustard, white pepper and hot-pepper sauce.

4. Coat a 10'' pie plate with no-stick spray. Add the rice mixture in an even layer. At even intervals tuck mushrooms into the rice in a decorative pattern. Pour the egg mixture over rice; sprinkle with Parmesan.

5. Bake at 350° for 45 to 50 minutes, or until the custard is set and the top is golden. Cool for 10 minutes before cutting into wedges. Top with pepper rings.

SERVES 6.

Preparation Time: 25 min.
Cooking Time: 50 min.

CHEF'S NOTES

DO FIRST:

Cook the rice: Use either brown or white, but remember that you'll get more fiber from the brown. Let it cool a bit before adding it to other ingredients.

ACCOMPANIMENT:

Serve with a chunky vegetable salad of celery, cherry tomatoes, red onions and lima beans tossed with a zesty mustard vinaigrette.

MICROWAVE OPTION:

Thaw the spinach: Place in a glass pie plate and microwave on medium power for about 4 minutes, or until defrosted but not heated through.

NUTRITION AT A GLANCE

PER SERVING:

Calories	168
Fat	3.6 g. (19% of cal.)
Sat. fat	1.9 g. (10% of cal.)
Cholesterol	54 mg.
Sodium	191 mg.

VEGETABLE AND GRAIN SIDE DISHES

■ ■ ■ ■ ■ ■ ■ ■ ■ ■ ■ ■ ■ ■ ■ ■

MAPLE-GLAZED ACORN SQUASH

Here's a rich and luscious way to prepare acorn squash. Although the caramelized slices taste sinful and buttery, they're virtually fat free and nicely low in calories. And the addition of baked orange slices imparts extra vitamin C.

MAPLE-GLAZED ACORN SQUASH

1 large or 2 small acorn squash
⅓ cup orange juice
1 navel orange
3 tablespoons maple syrup
Pinch of grated nutmeg

1. Cut the squash into thick (½″ to ¾″) rings. Discard the seeds and stringy matter attached to them.

2. Coat a jelly-roll pan with no-stick spray. Add the squash in a single layer. Pour in the orange juice.

3. Cover the pan with foil. Bake at 400° for 10 minutes, or until the squash is almost tender when pierced with a fork.

4. If desired, remove the peel and underlying white membrane of the orange with a sharp knife. (You may also leave the skin on the orange.) Cut the orange crosswise into ¼″ rounds.

5. Remove the pan from the oven and add the orange slices, preferably in a single layer. Drizzle the oranges and squash with the syrup. Sprinkle with nutmeg.

6. Cover the pan and return it to the oven. Bake for 10 minutes. Remove the foil and bake for another 15 minutes, or until the squash is lightly caramelized and tender. (Flip the oranges and squash at least twice as they bake, and baste them with pan juices each time.)

SERVES 4.

Preparation Time: 15 min.
Cooking Time: 35 min.

CHEF'S NOTES

■ ■ ■ ■ ■ ■ ■ ■ ■

ACCOMPANIMENT:
Serve with Lean Veal Piccata (page 137) or Chicken Bow Ties (page 119).

■

VARIATION:
Use another spice, such as cinnamon or cardamom.

■

MICROWAVE OPTION:
Microwave the squash and orange juice (in batches, if necessary) for 3 or 4 minutes, until the squash is almost tender. Transfer to the oven and proceed with the recipe.

■

KITCHEN TRICK:
Hard-skinned winter squash can be difficult to cut. To make slicing easier, wrap the squash in waxed paper and microwave it on full power for about 2 minutes.

NUTRITION AT A GLANCE ■■■

PER SERVING:
Calories 91
Fat . . . . .0.2 g. (2% of cal.)
Sat. fat . . . . .0 g.
Cholesterol . . . . .0 mg.
Sodium . . . . .5 mg.

BROCCOLI WITH GARLIC AND RED PEPPERS

Broccoli, red peppers and garlic are an unbeatable health trio. Broccoli is a member of the cancer-fighting crucifer family and is rich in carotene, calcium and vitamin C. Red peppers are a stronghold of vitamins A and C. And garlic is said to have special heart-healthy benefits.

BROCCOLI WITH GARLIC AND RED PEPPERS

- **1 large bunch of broccoli (about 1½ pounds)**
- **1 teaspoon olive oil**
- **1 tablespoon minced garlic**
- **1 large sweet red pepper, cut into ⅛″ strips**
- **1 cup thinly sliced onion**
- **1 tablespoon balsamic vinegar or 2 teaspoons red-wine vinegar**
- **¼ teaspoon ground black pepper**
- **⅛ teaspoon red-pepper flakes (or to taste)**

1. Trim tough ends from the broccoli and pull off any leaves. Cut the stalks in half crosswise, then slice the tops and stalks into ½″-wide spears. (You should have about 8 cups.)

2. Pour enough water into a large, heavy pot or saucepan to reach 1″ up the sides. Cover and bring to a boil over high heat. Arrange the broccoli spears in a large steamer basket and suspend over boiling water. Cover and steam for 4 to 6 minutes, until broccoli is crisp-tender.

3. Remove the basket from the pot and set aside. Discard water and wipe the pot dry.

4. Add the oil to the pot and place over medium heat. Add the garlic and sauté for 30 seconds, until just fragrant.

5. Add the peppers and onions. Sauté 3 to 4 minutes, stirring frequently, until limp. Add the vinegar and let bubble about 1 minute, until nearly evaporated.

6. Add the broccoli to the pot. Season with black pepper and red-pepper flakes. Toss until heated through. Serve hot immediately or chill as a cold side dish.

SERVES 4.

Preparation Time: 10 min.
Cooking Time: 15 min.

CHEF'S NOTES

ACCOMPANIMENTS:
Serve with grilled chicken cutlets seasoned with lemon and basil. Add crusty whole-grain bread and ripe pears to round out the meal.

VARIATION:
You could make this recipe using broccoli rabe (also known as broccoli raab) or escarole instead of broccoli. Adjust steaming time accordingly.

MICROWAVE OPTION:
Microwave the broccoli: Cut stalks into uniform spears with about 3″ of stalk. Peel bottom 2″. Arrange in a glass pie plate with florets toward the center. Add a sprinkle of water, cover and microwave for about 8 minutes.

NUTRITION AT A GLANCE

PER SERVING:

Calories 78
Fat . . . . 1.9 g. (22% of cal.)
Sat. fat . . . . . 0.3 g. (3% of cal.)
Cholesterol . . . . 0 mg.
Sodium . . . . 49 mg.

CURRIED BRUSSELS SPROUTS

These delightful mini-cabbages share the cancer-fighting abilities of other cruciferous vegetables. And for that reason alone, they deserve an honored place on your table. But everyone—dieters especially—will relish this dish. Each serving has just 49 calories!

CURRIED BRUSSELS SPROUTS

- **2 cups trimmed brussels sprouts**
- **1 cup small or sliced mushrooms**
- **½ cup diced sweet red, yellow or green pepper**
- **¼ cup skim milk**
- **1 tablespoon light or nonfat mayonnaise**
- **2 teaspoons cornstarch**
- **1 tablespoon minced fresh parsley**
- **1 teaspoon curry powder**
- **¼ teaspoon ground black pepper**

1. In a steamer basket over simmering water, cook the brussels sprouts, partially covered, for 5 to 8 minutes, or until just tender.

2. Add the mushrooms and peppers and steam 2 minutes more. Remove the vegetables from the steamer. Retain ¼ cup of the steaming liquid in the pan.

3. In a cup, stir together the milk, mayonnaise and cornstarch until the cornstarch is dissolved. Add to the liquid in the pan. Cook over medium heat, whisking constantly, until the mixture thickens and bubbles.

4. Stir in the parsley, curry powder and black pepper. Add the cooked vegetables and heat through.

SERVES 4.

Preparation Time: 15 min.
Cooking Time: 15 min.

CHEF'S NOTES

MICROWAVE OPTIONS:

The vegetables can be cooked in the microwave. Place the brussels sprouts in a 1-quart casserole with 2 tablespoons of water. Cover and microwave about 3 to 4 minutes, stirring once. Let stand about 3 minutes.

Place the mushrooms and peppers in another bowl. Cover and microwave 1 minute.

KITCHEN TRICK:

Cutting a small X in the bottom of each sprout helps the thick core cook more evenly.

NUTRITION AT A GLANCE

PER SERVING:

Calories	49
Fat	1.4 g. (26% of cal.)
Sat. fat	0 g.
Cholesterol	2 mg.
Sodium	21 mg.

CARROTS WITH GARLIC AND BASIL

Carrots are super champs when it comes to beta-carotene—the plant form of vitamin A that has such cancer-fighting potential. That's why they should rate a recurring role on your table. This herb-flavored side dish is just one way to feature them.

Carrots with Garlic and Basil

- **1 pound carrots**
- **1 teaspoon olive oil**
- **1–2 cloves garlic, minced**
- **¼ cup minced fresh basil or 1 teaspoon dried**
- **1 teaspoon lemon juice**
- **Ground black pepper (to taste)**

1. Peel the carrots and cut as you wish: into sticks, coins or diagonal slices.

2. Pour enough water into a large, heavy pot or saucepan to reach 1'' up the sides. Cover and bring to a boil over high heat. Place the carrots in a large steamer basket and place over boiling water. Cover and steam until tender, 4 to 5 minutes. Remove the carrots from the basket. Pat them dry.

3. Heat the oil in a large no-stick frying pan over medium-high heat. Add the carrots, garlic, basil and lemon juice. Sauté until cooked through and fragrant, about 3 minutes. Sprinkle with pepper.

4. Serve at room temperature or very slightly chilled.

SERVES 4.

Preparation Time: 5 min.
Cooking Time: 10 min.

Chef's Notes

ACCOMPANIMENT:
Great with grilled chicken or fish.

VARIATION:
Substitute thyme for the basil.

MICROWAVE OPTION:
Instead of steaming, microwave sliced carrots. Place them in a 9'' glass pie plate with 2 tablespoons of water. Cover with vented plastic wrap and microwave on full power for about 3 minutes.

KITCHEN TRICKS:
For easy mincing of basil, use a small electric spice grinder. To peel garlic easily, first smash it with the broad side of a chef's knife. The peel will slip right off.

Nutrition at a Glance

PER SERVING:

Calories	56
Fat	1.3 g. (21% of cal.)
Sat. fat	0.2 g. (3% of cal.)
Cholesterol	0 mg.
Sodium	36 mg.

CORN AND SPINACH FRITTERS

These corn fritters are such a snap to prepare that you can serve them often. They get their appealing color from a combination of corn, spinach and carrots, giving them a nutritional edge over standard fried fritters. And they're nicely low in fat and calories—so dieters can indulge at will.

CORN AND SPINACH FRITTERS

1 cup packed spinach leaves, chopped into ½″ pieces

1 cup corn

¼ cup finely shredded carrot

¼ cup shredded part-skim mozzarella cheese

2 egg whites

1 tablespoon cornstarch

¼ teaspoon minced garlic (optional)

1 teaspoon olive oil

1. Place the spinach in a strainer and plunge into a pot of boiling water. Blanch until soft, about 1½ minutes. Drain well and pat dry.

2. Transfer the spinach to a medium bowl. Add the corn, carrots, mozzarella, egg whites, cornstarch and garlic. Stir well to combine.

3. Heat a large, well-seasoned, cast-iron or no-stick frying pan on medium high. Add the oil. Use a tablespoon to measure out well-rounded scoops of the batter and form them into patties. They'll be a bit loose. As they're formed, place the patties in the frying pan and flatten them gently with a spatula.

4. Sizzle the fritters until lightly browned, about 3 minutes on each side. Serve warm.

SERVES 4.

Preparation Time: 15 min.
Cooking Time: 20 min.

CHEF'S NOTES

■ ■ ■ ■ ■ ■ ■ ■ ■

INGREDIENTS NOTE:

You may use fresh, frozen or canned corn. If using fresh, cut the kernels from the cob with a serrated knife. You may use a frozen, 10-ounce box of chopped spinach. Thaw and squeeze dry. Use half and reserve the rest for another use.

■

ACCOMPANIMENT:

Serve with grilled lamb, roast chicken or lightly sautéed fish.

■

VARIATION:

Use other greens, such as kale, lettuce or even dandelion leaves.

■

KITCHEN TRICK:

To easily chop fresh spinach, stack the leaves, roll them up and slice.

NUTRITION AT A GLANCE ■■■

PER SERVING:

Calories 83
Fat . . . . 2.8 g. (30% of cal.)
Sat. fat . . . . 1.1 g. (11% of cal.)
Cholesterol . . . . 4 mg.
Sodium . . . . 80 mg.

PARSNIPS AND TOMATOES AU GRATIN

For a nice change of pace, try parsnips. They have a sweet, nutty flavor that complements most meat, seafood and poultry dishes. This recipe pairs them with garden-ripe tomatoes, herbs and a bit of reduced-fat cheese for a delicious side dish.

PARSNIPS AND TOMATOES AU GRATIN

- **1 pound parsnips, julienned**
- **1 large onion, thinly sliced**
- **½–¾ cup defatted chicken stock**
- **¼ teaspoon dried thyme or tarragon**
- **1 large tomato**
- **2 tablespoons minced fresh parsley**
- **⅓ cup shredded low-fat Swiss cheese**

1. In a large frying pan, combine the parsnips, onions, ½ cup stock and thyme or tarragon. Cover and cook over medium heat until the parsnips are tender, about 10 minutes. If the liquid boils away before the parsnips are tender, add a bit more.

2. Uncover the pan and let the liquid evaporate.

3. Coat a 9″ pie plate with no-stick spray. Add the parsnips.

4. Core the tomato and slice it half crosswise. Gently squeeze each half to remove the seeds and juice. Cut the flesh into thin slices.

5. Arrange the tomatoes over the parsnips. Sprinkle with the parsley and top with the cheese.

6. Broil about 4″ from the heat until the cheese is melted and bubbly, about 4 minutes.

SERVES 4.

Preparation Time: 15 min.
Cooking Time: 20 min.

CHEF'S NOTES

ACCOMPANIMENT:

Serve as a side dish with broiled fish, poached chicken or grilled burgers.

VARIATIONS:

Replace the parsnips with icicle radishes or carrots. Use another type of cheese in place of the Swiss. Use other herbs, such as basil or oregano.

MICROWAVE OPTION:

You may cook the parsnips in the microwave. Place in a large casserole with the onions and 2 tablespoons stock. Cover with a lid and cook on full power, stirring several times, for about 8 minutes, or until tender. Drain off excess liquid. Add the herbs.

NUTRITION AT A GLANCE

PER SERVING:

Calories	122
Fat	2.4 g. (18% of cal.)
Sat. fat	0.1 g. (<1% of cal.)
Cholesterol	5 mg.
Sodium	32 mg.

HOT-TOPPED POTATOES

Potatoes—both regular white and sweet—may offer protection from stroke. Both are high in potassium, a nutrient that doctors have linked directly with a lowered incidence of stroke. In one study just 400 extra milligrams of potassium a day translated to a 40 percent reduction in stroke risk.

HOT-TOPPED POTATOES

REDS WITH MEXICAN CONFETTI

- **1 pound small potatoes**
- **½ avocado, diced**
- **½ cup cooked corn**
- **¼ cup diced tomato**
- **3 tablespoons nonfat yogurt**
- **2 tablespoons minced fresh coriander**
- **1 tablespoon lime juice**
- **1 scallion, thinly sliced**
- **1 clove garlic, minced**
- **½ teaspoon reduced-sodium soy sauce**
- **Pinch of ground red pepper**

1. Steam the potatoes until tender, about 20 minutes. In a medium bowl combine the avocados, corn, tomatoes, yogurt, coriander, lime juice, scallions, garlic, soy sauce and pepper. Serve on the potatoes.

Preparation Time: 10 min.
Cooking Time: 20 min.

YAMS WITH HONEY AND CINNAMON

- **2 large sweet potatoes**
- **½ cup low-fat cottage cheese**
- **¼ cup diced firm tofu**
- **1 tablespoon honey**
- **1 teaspoon minced shallot**
- **¼ teaspoon ground cinnamon**
- **¼ teaspoon reduced-sodium soy sauce**
- **⅛ teaspoon grated nutmeg**
- **Pinch of ground red pepper**
- **2 teaspoons snipped chives**

1. Bake the potatoes at 375° for 1 hour and 15 minutes, or until easily pierced. In a food processor combine the cottage cheese, tofu, honey, shallots, cinnamon, soy sauce, nutmeg and pepper. Process until smooth. Stir in the chives. Halve the potatoes. Serve with the topping.

Preparation Time: 5 min.
Cooking Time: 1¼ hr.

BAKERS WITH EMERALD TOPPING

- **2 large baking potatoes**
- **½ cup cooked peas**
- **¼ cup low-fat cottage cheese**
- **2 tablespoons nonfat yogurt**
- **½ teaspoon dried dill**
- **¼ teaspoon reduced-sodium soy sauce**
- **½ cup grated carrot**

1. Bake the potatoes at 375° for 1 hour, or until easily pierced. In a food processor combine the peas, cottage cheese, yogurt, dill and soy sauce. Process until smooth. Halve the potatoes. Serve with the topping; sprinkle with the carrots.

Preparation Time: 5 min.
Cooking Time: 1 hr.

EACH RECIPE SERVES 4.

CHEF'S NOTES

VARIATIONS:

Make the potatoes into light main dishes serving two: Add chicken or ground beef to the Mexican Confetti topping. Double the topping for the yams. Add cooked shrimp to the Emerald Topping.

NUTRITION AT A GLANCE

PER SERVING:

REDS WITH MEXICAN CONFETTI

Calories	183
Fat	2.7 g. (13% of cal.)
Sat. fat	0.5 g. (3% of cal.)
Cholesterol	0 mg.
Sodium	48 mg.

YAMS WITH HONEY AND CINNAMON

Calories	181
Fat	2 g. (10% of cal.)
Sat. fat	0.4 g. (2% of cal.)
Cholesterol	1 mg.
Sodium	145 mg.

BAKERS WITH EMERALD TOPPING

Calories	161
Fat	0.4 g. (2% of cal.)
Sat. fat	0.1 g. (<1% of cal.)
Cholesterol	0 mg.
Sodium	107 mg.

MAPLE-GLAZED RADISHES AND CARROTS

If you've never eaten cooked radishes, you're in for a treat. Slow simmering tames their fiery flavor and brings out a sweet mellowness that complements cooked carrots. And weight-watchers will appreciate this side dish—it has just 87 calories per serving.

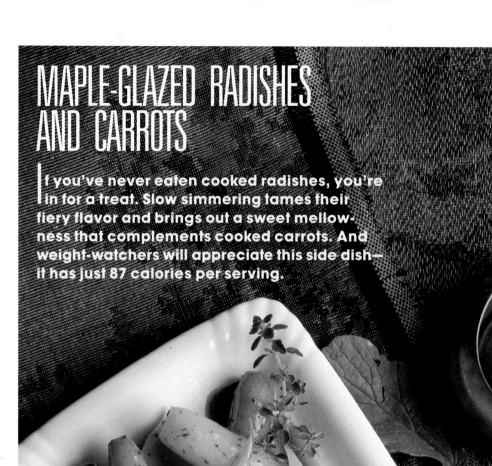

Vegetable and Grain Side Dishes

Maple-glazed radishes and carrots

10 ounces mini carrots, trimmed

10 ounces icicle radishes, trimmed

⅔ cup apple cider

2 tablespoons maple syrup

2 tablespoons apple-cider vinegar

2 teaspoons Dijon mustard

½ teaspoon dried thyme

1. Peel the carrots and radishes. Halve the radishes lengthwise. If the carrots are larger than ½'' in diameter, cut to the same size as the radishes.

2. In a large frying pan, combine the cider, syrup, vinegar, mustard and thyme. Bring to a boil.

3. Add the carrots. Cover and cook over medium heat for 5 minutes. Add the radishes. Cover and cook until the vegetables are just tender, 20 to 25 minutes.

4. Remove the lid and raise the heat to medium high. Cook, stirring often, until the liquid is reduced to a glaze, about 5 minutes.

SERVES 4.

Preparation Time: 15 min.
Cooking Time: 35 min.

CHEF'S NOTES

ACCOMPANIMENT:

Serve with meat or poultry, such as Lean Veal Piccata (page 137) or Roast Chicken Legs with Basil and Garlic (page 167).

VARIATIONS:

Use daikon radishes cut to the same size as the carrots. Or replace the radishes with parsnips. If you don't have mini carrots, simply cut regular ones into thin finger shapes.

KITCHEN TRICK:

To ensure even cooking, make sure the carrots and radishes are about the same size.

MAKE-AHEAD TIP:

Cook the vegetables through step 3. Cover and refrigerate. Finish step 4 just before serving.

NUTRITION AT A GLANCE

PER SERVING:

Calories	87
Fat	0.3 g. (3% of cal.)
Sat. fat	0 g.
Cholesterol	0 mg.
Sodium	73 mg.

RUTABAGAS AU GRATIN

Have you ever wondered what to do with rutabagas? These oversize yellow turnips are members of the cancer-preventing cabbage family. And their slightly sweet flavor when cooked complements other vegetables. This low-fat casserole pairs them with potatoes, which have a similar texture.

RUTABAGAS AU GRATIN

1 pound rutabagas, thinly sliced

1 pound red potatoes, thinly sliced

1 bay leaf

1 clove garlic

½ cup defatted chicken stock

½ cup evaporated skim milk

2 tablespoons unbleached flour

½ cup minced fresh parsley

½ cup fresh bread crumbs

3 shallots, minced

1. In a 3-quart saucepan, combine the rutabagas, potatoes, bay leaf, garlic and enough cold water to cover. Bring to a boil. Reduce the heat and simmer, stirring often, for about 10 minutes, or until the vegetables are just firm to the bite. Drain in a colander. Remove and discard the bay leaf and garlic.

2. Coat a 9″ × 9″ baking dish with no-stick spray. Add the rutabagas and potatoes.

3. Place the stock, milk and flour in a blender. Process until smooth. Pour into a 1-quart saucepan. Bring to a boil over medium heat and whisk until thickened, about 5 minutes. Add ¼ cup of the parsley. Pour over the vegetables.

4. In a small bowl, combine the bread crumbs and shallots. Sprinkle over the casserole.

5. Bake at 400° for 20 minutes. Sprinkle with the remaining ¼ cup parsley.

SERVES 4.

Preparation Time: 15 min.
Cooking Time: 35 min.

CHEF'S NOTES

DO FIRST:

Remove the thick wax coating from the rutabagas with a sturdy vegetable peeler or a very sharp paring knife. If desired, you may peel the potatoes, but they're prettier if the red skins are left on.

INGREDIENTS NOTE:

Buy rutabagas that are smooth, free of punctures and heavy for their size.

PRESENTATION:

You may also bake this casserole in individual gratin dishes.

ACCOMPANIMENTS:

Serve with roast turkey, oyster filling and carrots for a holiday meal. This recipe is easily doubled.

NUTRITION AT A GLANCE

PER SERVING:

Calories 182
Fat . . . . .0.8 g. (4% of cal.)
Sat. fat . . .0.1 g. (<1% of cal.)
Cholesterol . . . . .1 mg.
Sodium . . . . .107 mg.

SPAGHETTI SQUASH PARMESAN

This unusual vegetable is amazingly low in fat and calories, as befits a vegetable, and it's a wonderful source of dietary fiber like its pasta namesake. Just don't overcook it or you'll lose its distinctive texture.

SPAGHETTI SQUASH PARMESAN

- **1 spaghetti squash (about 2 pounds), quartered**
- **1 cup water**
- **1½ cups shredded zucchini**
- **½ cup thinly sliced or diced tomato**
- **⅓ cup sliced scallion**
- **2–4 tablespoons grated Parmesan cheese**
- **1 tablespoon lemon juice**
- **1 teaspoon dried basil**
- **¼ teaspoon dried dill**
- **¼ teaspoon ground black pepper**

1. Place the squash, cut side up, in a Dutch oven or deep electric frying pan. Add the water. Cover and bring to a boil. Then reduce the heat and simmer for 13 to 17 minutes, or until the squash fibers pull apart easily with a fork. Remove the squash from the pan and drain well. Scoop out and discard the seeds. Using 2 forks, fluff the flesh into strands.

2. In a steamer basket over simmering water, steam the zucchini, covered, for 3 minutes; remove from the heat.

3. Discard the cooking liquid from the Dutch oven or frying pan and dry the pan well.

4. Add the squash, zucchini, tomatoes and scallions to the pan. Stir in the Parmesan, lemon juice, basil, dill and pepper. Toss well to coat with sauce. Cook 1 minute over medium-high heat to heat through.

SERVES 6.

Preparation Time: 15 min.
Cooking Time: 20 min.

CHEF'S NOTES

INGREDIENTS NOTE:

Choose squash that is hard and smooth with an even pale yellow color. Avoid those with a greenish tinge, which indicates immaturity, and those with soft or damaged spots. Squash can be stored at room temperature for up to three weeks.

ACCOMPANIMENT:

Serve with poultry, such as Spicy Turkey Breast with Cranberries (page 171), or serve with fish, such as Herbed Monkfish with Fresh Tomato Salsa (page 191).

MICROWAVE OPTION:

If the squash is too hard to cut easily, wrap it in wax paper and microwave on full power for 2 to 3 minutes.

NUTRITION AT A GLANCE

PER SERVING:

Calories 54
Fat . . . . . . 1.3 g. (22% of cal.)
Sat. fat . . . . 0.5 g. (9% of cal.)
Cholesterol . . . . 2 mg.
Sodium . . . . 71 mg.

SAVORY BAKED BEANS

Baby lima beans have a meaty texture that gives this low-fat side dish real substance. And these beans have a good portion of vitamin C—thanks to carrots and apples—for enhanced immunity and possible protection against certain types of cancer.

Vegetable and Grain Side Dishes

SAVORY BAKED BEANS

12 ounces dried baby lima beans, soaked overnight
2 cups diced carrot
1½ cups diced onion
1 tart apple, diced
2 cups defatted chicken stock
½ cup maple syrup
½ cup reduced-sodium ketchup
1 tablespoon dry mustard
¼ teaspoon dried thyme
¼ teaspoon ground cloves
¼ teaspoon ground black pepper

1. Drain the lima beans and place them in a 3-quart saucepan. Add cold water to cover. Bring to a boil and skim off any foam. Cook over medium to medium-low heat, skimming occasionally, until tender, about 1 hour. (Add more hot water to the pan as needed to keep the beans covered.)

2. Drain the beans and transfer them to a 3-quart casserole. Stir in the carrots, onions and apples.

3. Rinse out the saucepan. In it, combine the stock, syrup, ketchup, mustard, thyme, cloves and pepper. Bring to a simmer over medium-high heat. Pour over the beans and stir well.

4. Cover the casserole and bake at 325°, stirring occasionally, for 2½ hours. Remove the cover. Bake, stirring occasionally, for 1 hour, or until the beans are tender and the sauce is very thick.

SERVES 10.

Preparation Time: 20 min. + standing time
Cooking Time: 3½ hr.

CHEF'S NOTES

DO FIRST:

Soak the beans. For quick micro-wave directions, see White Bean and Corn Soup (page 57).

VARIATIONS:

Use other beans, such as navy, Great Northern, pinto or pea beans. Replace the cloves with ground allspice. Add 1 cup diced sweet red or green peppers.

MICROWAVE OPTION:

To reheat leftovers, place a single serving on a plate and cover with wax paper to prevent spattering. Heat on high for 35 seconds or until warmed through.

NUTRITION AT A GLANCE

PER SERVING:

Calories 166
Fat . . . . .0.8 g. (5% of cal.)
Sat. fat . . .0.1 g. (<1% of cal.)
Cholesterol . . . . .0 mg.
Sodium . . . . .111 mg.

BARLEY WITH TOASTED PECANS

This satisfying side dish is loaded with fiber. Each serving has 9 grams—that's about one-third of the amount that experts recommend you consume each day. Besides satisfying your hunger, fiber may also dilute and help remove cancer-causing toxins from the intestinal tract. In fact, numerous studies have suggested that a diet high in fiber can help prevent colon cancer.

BARLEY WITH TOASTED PECANS

2½ cups defatted stock
1 thick onion slice
1 clove garlic, crushed
1 bay leaf
1 cup pearl barley
2 tablespoons broken pecans
1 tablespoon olive oil

½ cup diced carrot
1 clove garlic, minced
½ cup small broccoli florets
¼ cup sliced scallions
1 tablespoon rice-wine vinegar

1. In a 3-quart saucepan combine the stock, onion slice, crushed garlic and bay leaf. Bring to a boil. Stir in the barley. Cover and cook over low heat until the liquid is absorbed and the barley is tender, about 40 minutes. Set aside.

2. In a large no-stick frying pan stir the pecans over medium-low heat until fragrant and lightly toasted, about 3 minutes. Transfer to a small dish.

3. Heat the oil in the frying pan over medium heat. Add the carrots and minced garlic; stir-fry until the carrot is crisp-tender but not brown, about 3 minutes. Stir in the broccoli and scallions; stir-fry until the vegetables are crisp-tender, about 2 minutes. Do not overcook the vegetables.

4. Fluff the barley with a fork and remove the onion slice, crushed garlic and bay leaf. Add the stir-fried vegetables. Sprinkle with the vinegar and toss to blend. Top with the toasted pecans.

SERVES 6.

Preparation Time: 10 min.
Cooking Time: 45 min.

CHEF'S NOTES

ACCOMPANIMENTS:

Serve as a side dish with veal, chicken or turkey. Or add low-fat cheese and chopped chicken and serve as a light lunch.

KITCHEN TRICK:

If you're in a hurry, try the quick-cooking type of barley. The grains are rolled flat like oats and need only about 12 minutes on the stove. Use the amount of liquid called for in the recipe and, if necessary, drain off any excess for another use.

MAKE-AHEAD TIP:

Prepare the barley ahead. Reheat in a frying pan or place in the microwave for 2 minutes.

NUTRITION AT A GLANCE

PER SERVING:

Calories 157
Fat . . . . 4.8 g. (28% of cal.)
Sat. fat . . . . . 0.9 g. (4% of cal.)
Cholesterol . . . . 0 mg.
Sodium . . . . 38 mg.

MILLET WITH BROCCOLI AND GARLIC

Expand your side-dish repertoire with millet, an oft-neglected grain. Millet contains B vitamins, fiber, iron, potassium and protein—all of which contribute to overall good health. This pilaf recipe perks up millet's mild flavor with broccoli, onions and garlic, all cancer-fighting vegetables.

MILLET WITH BROCCOLI AND GARLIC

2 cups defatted chicken or beef stock

1 cup millet

2–3 cups broccoli florets

1 onion, halved and cut into thin wedges

1–2 cloves garlic, thinly sliced

⅛–½ teaspoon red-pepper flakes

1 tablespoon olive oil

2 tablespoons red-wine vinegar

¼ teaspoon ground black pepper

2 tablespoons grated Parmesan cheese (optional)

1. In a 2-quart saucepan over high heat, bring the stock to a boil. Stir in the millet. Reduce the heat to medium low, cover the pan and cook for 25 minutes, or until the millet is tender and all the liquid has been absorbed. Remove from the heat, uncover and let stand for 10 minutes. Fluff with a fork.

2. If desired, cut the broccoli into bite-size pieces. Steam broccoli until just tender, about 5 minutes. Set aside.

3. In a large no-stick frying pan over medium-low heat, cook the onions, garlic and pepper flakes in the oil for 10 to 20 minutes, until the onions are the color of pale straw; do not let them brown.

4. Stir in the vinegar, black pepper, broccoli and millet. Toss well to combine. Transfer to a serving dish and sprinkle with the Parmesan.

SERVES 8.

Preparation Time: 15 min.
Cooking Time: 45 min.

CHEF'S NOTES

DO FIRST:

Prepare the broccoli: Cut off the stems about 1'' below the florets and reserve for another use.

INGREDIENTS NOTE:

For the most flavorful millet, start with rich-tasting stock. If necessary, boil it down to concentrate the flavor.

ACCOMPANIMENT:

Serve with grilled chicken, roast turkey breast or kabobs.

VARIATION:

Replace the broccoli with julienned zucchini, diced carrots, sliced red peppers, peas or corn.

NUTRITION AT A GLANCE

PER SERVING:

Calories 128
Fat . . . . . . .3.1 g. (22% of cal.)
Sat. fat . . . . .0.3 g. (2% of cal.)
Cholesterol . . . . .0 mg.
Sodium . . . . .23 mg.

RICE AND LENTIL PILAF

Over half the world's population virtually lives on rice. And there's good reason: It's inexpensive yet high in hunger-satisfying complex carbohydrates. In addition, rice is low in calories, fat and sodium—with no cholesterol. All of which is great for controlling weight, blood pressure and cholesterol levels! So make rice a regular part of your meals with easy casseroles like this pilaf.

RICE AND LENTIL PILAF

2 teaspoons olive oil
1 cup diced carrot
1 cup diced sweet red pepper
¼ cup finely chopped onion
¾ cup rice
¼ cup lentils

2 cups defatted chicken stock
1 bay leaf
½ teaspoon ground cumin
1 cup peas

1. In a 2-quart saucepan heat the oil over medium-high heat. Add the carrots, peppers and onions. Sauté for 1 to 2 minutes.

2. Add the rice and lentils. Continue to sauté until the grains are coated, about 2 minutes.

3. Add the stock, bay leaf and cumin. Bring to a boil. Stir once, cover with a tight lid and turn the heat down to a simmer. Cook for approximately 12 minutes.

4. Add the peas. Cover and cook for another 5 to 7 minutes, or until the rice is tender and the liquid has been absorbed. Discard the bay leaf before serving.

SERVES 4.

Preparation Time: 10 min.
Cooking Time: 25 min.

CHEF'S NOTES

DO FIRST:
Pick over the lentils to remove any small stones or other foreign objects. If using fresh peas, you'll need about 1 pound to get 1 cup of shelled peas.

ACCOMPANIMENT:
Serve with marinated and grilled chicken or fish.

VARIATIONS:
For a Mexican flavor, add oregano. Then replace the lentils with kidney beans and use corn instead of the peas.

KITCHEN TRICK:
Chill any leftover pilaf and serve it as a salad with a light vinaigrette.

NUTRITION AT A GLANCE

PER SERVING:
Calories 254
Fat . . . . . . .3.6 g. (13% of cal.)
Sat. fat . . . .0.4 g. (10% of cal.)
Cholesterol . . . . .0 mg.
Sodium . . . . .54 mg.

BREADS AND BATTERS

GOLDEN GRAIN AND HERB LOAVES

Rolled oats, skim milk, olive oil and onions give these savory loaves cholesterol-lowering ability that most ordinary breads lack. And the blend of herbs makes them extra tasty, so you won't need butter to enhance their flavor.

Golden grain and herb loaves

2 cups rolled oats
1½ cups boiling water
2 tablespoons active dry yeast
½ cup warm water (about 115°)
1 cup skim milk
¼ cup honey
¼ cup olive oil
1 teaspoon salt (optional)
½ cup minced onion
⅓ cup minced celery leaves
¼ cup minced fresh parsley

1 tablespoon minced fresh sage or 1 teaspoon dried
1 tablespoon minced fresh marjoram or 1 teaspoon dried
1 tablespoon minced fresh thyme or 1 teaspoon dried
2 cups whole wheat flour
4–4½ cups unbleached flour
1 egg white
1 tablespoon water
2 tablespoons lightly ground rolled oats

1. In a medium bowl, combine 2 cups rolled oats and the boiling water. Let cool until lukewarm.

2. In a large bowl, dissolve the yeast in the warm water. Let stand in a warm place until foamy, about 5 minutes.

3. In a 1-quart saucepan, combine the milk, honey, oil and salt. Heat until lukewarm. Stir in the onions, celery, parsley, sage, marjoram and thyme. Add to the yeast mixture.

4. Stir in the whole wheat flour and the oats. Stir in about 4 cups of the unbleached flour to make a kneadable dough. Let stand for 15 minutes.

5. Turn the dough out onto a lightly floured surface. Knead, adding more flour as necessary, for about 10 minutes, or until smooth and elastic.

6. Coat a large bowl with no-stick spray. Add the dough and turn to coat all sides. Cover and set in a warm place until doubled, about 1¼ hours.

7. Divide the dough in half and let rest for 10 minutes. Roll each half into a 14″ × 7″ rectangle. Starting at a short end, roll the dough into a log.

8. Coat 2 loaf pans (9″ × 5″) with no-stick spray. Add the dough, seam side down. Cover and set in a warm place until doubled, 30 to 45 minutes.

9. In a cup, lightly beat together the egg white and 1 tablespoon water. Brush over the loaves. Sprinkle with the ground oats. Bake at 375° for 45 to 50 minutes, or until the breads are lightly browned.

MAKES 2 LOAVES; 16 SLICES EACH.

Preparation Time: 25 min. + standing time
Cooking Time: 50 min.

CHEF'S NOTES

INGREDIENTS NOTE:
You may use either old-fashioned rolled oats or the quick-cooking variety. Do not, however, use instant oatmeal. To lightly grind oats, place them in a food processor or blender and chop until about one-quarter their original size.

VARIATION:
You may remove all the savory ingredients (onions, celery, herbs) and replace them with 1 teaspoon of pumpkin pie spices and ½ cup raisins or currants.

NUTRI-NOTE:
Using the optional salt, which helps the bread to rise, raises sodium to 75 milligrams per slice.

NUTRITION AT A GLANCE

PER SLICE:
Calories 134
Fat . . . . . . .2.3 g. (15% of cal.)
Sat. fat . . . . .0.4 g. (3% of cal.)
Cholesterol . . . . .0 mg.
Sodium . . . . .9 mg.

BRAIDED FRENCH BREAD WITH HERB SPREAD

Whole-grain bread is a staple in the health-lover's kitchen. It's a satisfying source of fiber and complex carbohydrates. When you make this braided French loaf, serve it with a creamy herb spread that's much lower in fat than ordinary herb butter.

BRAIDED FRENCH BREAD WITH HERB SPREAD

BRAIDED FRENCH BREAD

½ **cup skim milk**	3¾ **cups sifted whole wheat flour**
1 **cup boiling water**	1 **egg white**
1 **package active dry yeast**	1 **teaspoon water**
¼ **cup warm water (115°)**	1 **tablespoon poppy seeds or sesame seeds**
1½ **tablespoons olive oil**	
1 **tablespoon honey**	
½ **teaspoon salt**	

1. In a 1-quart saucepan, scald the milk. Add the boiling water. Set aside until lukewarm. In a large bowl, dissolve the yeast in the warm water. Stir in the oil, honey and salt. Let stand until foamy.

2. Add the milk mixture to the yeast bowl and whisk thoroughly. Add the flour 1 cup at a time, stirring until a soft dough forms. Form it into a ball. Leave the dough in the bowl and cover with a damp cloth. Set in a warm, draft-free place until doubled in bulk (about 2 hours).

3. Punch down the dough. Place on a lightly floured board and roll into a 10″ × 14″ rectangle. Cut lengthwise into 6 strips. Using 3 strips at a time, braid the dough into 2 loaves.

4. Coat a cookie sheet with no-stick spray. Place the dough on the sheet and set in a warm place until doubled (about 45 minutes).

5. In a cup, whisk together the egg white and 1 teaspoon water. Brush over the top of each loaf. Sprinkle with the poppy seeds or sesame seeds.

6. Bake at 400° for 10 minutes. Then lower the temperature to 350° and bake for 10 minutes, or until golden brown. Let cool at least 20 minutes.

MAKES 2 LOAVES; 16 SLICES EACH.

Preparation Time: 25 min. + standing time
Cooking Time: 20 min.

HERB SPREAD

¼ **cup nonfat yogurt cheese (see Chef's Notes)**	1 **tablespoon minced fresh basil**
¼ **cup light margarine, softened**	1 **tablespoon minced fresh dill**
¼ **cup nonfat mayonnaise**	¼ **teaspoon minced garlic**

1. In a small bowl, whisk together the yogurt cheese, margarine and mayonnaise. Stir in the basil, dill and garlic.

MAKES ABOUT ¾ CUP.

Preparation Time: 5 min.

CHEF'S NOTES

INGREDIENTS NOTE:
To make yogurt cheese, spoon nonfat yogurt into a cheesecloth-lined strainer and let drain for at least 2 hours.

VARIATION:
For a lighter loaf, use 2 cups whole wheat flour and 1¾ cups unbleached flour or bread flour.

NUTRITION AT A GLANCE

BRAIDED FRENCH BREAD
PER SLICE:

Calories	58
Fat	1 g. (16% of cal.)
Sat. fat	0.3 g. (5% of cal.)
Cholesterol	0 mg.
Sodium	70 mg.

HERB SPREAD
PER 2 TEASPOONS:

Calories	22
Fat	1.6 g. (65% of cal.)
Sat. fat	0 g.
Cholesterol	0 mg.
Sodium	17 mg.

WILD RICE ROLLS

Wild rice gives these whole-grain dinner rolls a marvelous chewy texture and an irresistible aroma. And although they may seem exotic, these rolls are as easy to prepare as any other homemade bread.

WILD RICE ROLLS

1½ **cups water**	⅓ **cup warm water (115°)**
½ **cup wild rice, rinsed**	1½ **cups whole wheat flour**
2 **cups skim milk**	½ **cup rye flour (optional)**
½ **cup honey**	½ **cup bran**
½ **cup rolled oats**	4–5 **cups unbleached flour**
2 **tablespoons oil**	2 **tablespoons fat-free egg substitute**
1 **teaspoon salt (optional)**	
1 **package quick-rise active dry yeast**	¼ **cup shelled sunflower seeds (optional)**

1. In a 1-quart saucepan, bring the water to a boil. Add the rice. Cover the pan, reduce the heat to medium low and cook for 50 minutes, or until the rice is tender. Drain well and set aside.

2. In a 2-quart saucepan over medium heat, scald the milk (do not let it boil). Remove from the heat and stir in the honey, oats, oil and salt. Add the cooked rice. Set aside and cool to lukewarm.

3. In a cup, combine the yeast and warm water. Set aside for 5 minutes.

4. In a very large bowl, combine the whole wheat flour, rye flour and bran. Add 3½ cups of the unbleached flour. Stir in the milk mixture and the yeast. Mix well with a wooden spoon. Stir in enough of the remaining unbleached flour to form a kneadable dough. Knead the dough on a floured surface until smooth and elastic, about 10 minutes.

5. Place the dough in an oiled bowl and turn to coat on all sides. Cover the bowl with plastic wrap and set in a warm, draft-free place until the dough has doubled in bulk, about 45 minutes.

6. Punch down the dough. Divide it into 4 pieces. Form each piece into a log about 12″ long. Cut each log into 6 equal pieces. Form each piece into a ball. You'll have 24 balls in all.

7. Coat 2 cake pans (9″) with no-stick spray. Place 4 rolls in the center of each pan in a square formation. Surround each square with 8 rolls. It is not necessary that all the rolls touch. Set in a warm, draft-free place until doubled in bulk, 25 to 30 minutes. Brush lightly with the egg. Sprinkle with the sunflower seeds. Bake at 375° for 20 minutes, or until browned.

8. Unmold the rolls onto a cookie sheet. Bake for 5 minutes to crisp the bottoms. Carefully flip the rolls onto wire racks. Cool for 5 minutes.

MAKES 24.

Preparation Time: 35 min. + standing time
Cooking Time: 1¼ hr.

CHEF'S NOTES

VARIATIONS:

For very delicious plain rolls, omit the wild rice. Sprinkle the rolls with sesame or caraway seeds. You may also form the dough into loaves. After the first rise, form into 2 loaves and place in oiled 9″ × 5″ pans. Let rise until doubled. Bake for 30 minutes. Brush with egg, sprinkle with seeds and bake for 15 minutes.

NUTRI-NOTE:

Adding the optional salt increases sodium to 106 milligrams per roll.

CHEF'S SECRET:

An easy way to cut the dough is with heavy thread or dental floss. Position it under the dough, pull up and cross the ends to cut through.

NUTRITION AT A GLANCE

PER ROLL:

Calories	167
Fat	1.7 g. (9% of cal.)
Sat. fat	0.2 g. (1% of cal.)
Cholesterol	0 mg.
Sodium	18 mg.

ITALIAN FLAT BREAD WITH FRESH HERBS

This Italian flat bread was just made to go with herb-flavored olive oil. That makes it doubly good for your heart: There's no cholesterol in the bread itself, and the oil is a wonderful source of monounsaturated fat, which has shown such good results lowering elevated cholesterol.

ITALIAN FLAT BREAD WITH FRESH HERBS

- **1 cup warm water (about 115°)**
- **1 tablespoon active dry yeast**
- **2 teaspoons honey**
- **1 tablespoon olive oil**
- **1⅓ cups whole wheat bread flour**
- **1⅓ cups unbleached flour**
- **½ teaspoon salt (optional)**
- **¼ cup minced fresh herbs**
- **2 cloves garlic, slivered**

1. Combine ½ cup of the water and yeast in a large bowl. Stir in the honey and 2 teaspoons of oil.

2. Stir in the bread flour, unbleached flour, salt and herbs. Add enough additional water to make a soft, kneadable dough.

3. Knead the dough on a floured surface until smooth, about 8 minutes.

4. Place the dough in an oiled bowl and turn to coat on all sides. Cover the bowl with plastic wrap and set in a warm, draft-free place until the dough has doubled in bulk, about 40 minutes.

5. Punch down the dough, cover again and let rise a second time until doubled in bulk, about 40 minutes. Punch down.

6. Place a sheet of parchment paper on a large cookie sheet. Transfer the dough to the paper and use your hands to form it into a 14″ round, about ½″ thick. Poke garlic pieces into the dough at intervals. Rub the surface with the remaining oil.

7. Bake at 400° until cooked through and lightly browned on top, about 15 to 20 minutes. Transfer to a wire rack to cool.

8. To serve, cut into wedges with kitchen shears. If desired, toast under the broiler.

MAKES 1 LOAF; SERVES 8.

Preparation Time: 20 min. + standing time
Cooking Time: 20 min.

CHEF'S NOTES

ACCOMPANIMENT:
Serve with fruity olive oil liberally laced with minced fresh basil. Dip bread lightly into the oil or simply drizzle the oil on.

VARIATIONS:
Substitute shallots for the garlic. Take your pick of fresh herbs for the bread itself: rosemary, sage, basil and thyme are all excellent, alone or in combination.

NUTRI-NOTE:
Although this recipe does call for an optional amount of salt to help the dough rise, you can omit it if you're on a low-sodium diet. The sodium level given below is without the salt. With salt, the figure is 269 milligrams.

NUTRITION AT A GLANCE

PER SERVING:
Calories 167
Fat . . . . . . .2.2 g. (12% of cal.)
Sat. fat . . . . .0.4 g. (2% of cal.)
Cholesterol . . . . .0 mg.
Sodium . . . . .3 mg.

BLUEBERRY BREAD AND FRENCH TOAST

Yes, you *can* enjoy French toast on a low-cholesterol, low-fat diet. Forget those old recipes that demand heavy cream, butter and whole eggs. Instead, whip up a hearty fruit, oat-bran and egg-white bread as the basis for your toast. Then keep it healthy by soaking it in a mixture of egg whites and white grape juice.

BLUEBERRY BREAD AND FRENCH TOAST

BLUEBERRY BREAD

1 cup unbleached flour	**1 cup blueberries**
½ cup oat bran	**¾ cup evaporated skim milk**
½ cup cornmeal	**2 egg whites**
2 teaspoons baking soda	**¼ cup honey**
¾ teaspoon ground cinnamon	**2 tablespoons oil**

1. In a large bowl mix the flour, oat bran, cornmeal, baking soda and cinnamon. Stir in the blueberries.

2. In a medium bowl combine the milk, egg whites, honey and oil. Pour into the flour bowl. Mix just until the flour is moistened.

3. Coat a 4½'' × 8½'' loaf pan with no-stick spray. Spoon in the batter. Bake at 325° for 20 minutes. Lightly cover with foil. Bake another 30 to 40 minutes, or until a cake tester inserted in the center comes out clean. Cool on a wire rack before slicing.

MAKES 1 LOAF; 16 SLICES.

Preparation Time: 15 min.
Cooking Time: 1 hr.

FRENCH TOAST

2 egg whites	**2 teaspoons oil**
¼ cup white grape juice	**4 peaches, sliced**
8 slices Blueberry Bread (above)	

1. Lightly beat the egg whites and juice in a shallow baking dish. Add the bread. Flip the slices after 2 minutes and let them soak until all the liquid is absorbed.

2. Heat 1 teaspoon of the oil in a well-seasoned cast-iron frying pan. Add half of the slices and let them sizzle on medium high until toasty brown, 2 to 3 minutes on each side. Repeat with remaining oil and bread. Serve warm with the peaches.

SERVES 4.

Preparation Time: 5 min.
Cooking Time: 15 min.

CHEF'S NOTES

ACCOMPANIMENTS:

Serve both the bread and the French toast with all-fruit preserves. Serve the French toast with warm maple syrup and additional fruit, such as raspberries or sliced strawberries.

KITCHEN TRICKS:

If using frozen blueberries, don't defrost them before adding them to the bread batter. Wild Maine blueberries, which are much smaller than cultivated berries, are particularly nice for this recipe. They're available frozen and canned. If they're canned in heavy syrup, drain them and use paper towels to pat off some of the excess liquid so the bread doesn't become soggy.

NUTRITION AT A GLANCE

BLUEBERRY BREAD

PER SLICE:

Calories 99
Fat . . . . . . .2.2 g. (20% of cal.)
Sat. fat . . . . .0.2 g. (2% of cal.)
Cholesterol . . . . .0 mg.
Sodium . . . . .125 mg.

FRENCH TOAST

PER SERVING:

Calories 269
Fat . . . . . . .6.6 g. (22% of cal.)
Sat. fat . . . . .0.5 g. (2% of cal.)
Cholesterol . . . . .0 mg.
Sodium . . . . .275 mg.

CHILI CORN BREAD

This south-of-the-border bread is virtually cholesterol free. Traditional recipes call for whole eggs and butter or bacon drippings—all of which add up to too much cholesterol, too much saturated fat and way too many calories! We've kept this corn bread heart-healthy by using only egg whites and just a small amount of vegetable oil.

CHILI CORN BREAD

⅔ cup yellow cornmeal
⅔ cup unbleached flour
1 tablespoon baking powder
1 teaspoon chili powder
1 cup corn
2 mild or hot green chili peppers, seeded and minced

2 scallions, minced
3 egg whites
½ cup skim milk
2 tablespoons honey
1 tablespoon vegetable oil

1. In a large bowl combine the cornmeal, flour, baking powder and chili powder. Stir in the corn, peppers and scallions.

2. In a medium bowl whisk together the egg whites, milk, honey and oil. Pour into the dry ingredients and stir to combine; don't overmix.

3. Coat a 9″ glass pie plate with no-stick spray. Spoon in the batter and level the top.

4. Bake at 350° until a toothpick inserted in the center comes out clean, about 25 minutes. Serve warm.

SERVES 8.

Preparation Time: 15 min.
Cooking Time: 25 min.

CHEF'S NOTES

ACCOMPANIMENTS:

Serve with Mexican dishes, such as enchiladas or chicken with rice, or tomato-based soups. Or serve warm topped with Vegetable Chili (page 221).

VARIATION:

Use cooked pinto beans instead of the corn.

MAKE-AHEAD TIPS:

The bread will keep at room temperature, covered loosely with waxed paper, for several days. To reheat, wrap in foil and bake at 350° for 5 minutes, or until warm. Or heat individual pieces in a toaster oven. If desired, serve drizzled with honey.

NUTRITION AT A GLANCE

PER SERVING:

Calories 138
Fat . . . . 2.3 g. (15% of cal.)
Sat. fat . . . . . 0.4 g. (3% of cal.)
Cholesterol . . . . 0 mg.
Sodium . . . . 161 mg.

COFFEE CAKE WITH APRICOT SWIRLS

This not-too-sweet coffee cake is perfect for breakfast. Its dried apricots contribute valuable cancer-fighting fiber and beta-carotene to your diet. And as a bonus, the apricots and molasses add a welcome share of iron.

COFFEE CAKE WITH APRICOT SWIRLS

- **1 pound dried apricots, chopped**
- **2 teaspoons ground cinnamon**
- **1 cup whole wheat pastry flour**
- **2½ cups unbleached flour**
- **1 tablespoon baking powder**
- **½ teaspoon baking soda**
- **1 cup nonfat yogurt**
- **1 cup all-fruit apple butter**
- **6 egg whites**
- **⅓ cup canola oil**
- **3 tablespoons blackstrap or other molasses**
- **2 teaspoons vanilla**
- **¼ cup all-fruit apricot preserves**

1. In a medium bowl, mix the apricots and cinnamon.

2. In a large bowl, stir together the pastry flour, unbleached flour, baking powder and baking soda.

3. In another medium bowl using an electric mixer on medium speed, beat the yogurt, apple butter, egg whites, oil, molasses and vanilla for 2 minutes, until smooth. Pour over the flour and combine well with a rubber spatula.

4. Coat a 12-cup decorative tube pan with no-stick spray. Spread one-third of the batter in the pan. Sprinkle with one-third of the fruit. Add half the remaining batter and spread it evenly with a spatula (it will be sticky). Add half the remaining fruit. Repeat with the rest of the batter and fruit, ending with the fruit.

5. Bake at 350° for 45 minutes, or until a skewer or toothpick inserted in the center comes out clean. If the top browns too fast, cover with foil.

6. Transfer to a wire rack and let the cake cool, uncovered, for 15 minutes before unmolding onto a plate.

7. In a 1-quart saucepan, heat the preserves until melted. Drizzle over the top of the cake. Let cool before slicing.

SERVES 16.

Preparation Time: 15 min.
Cooking Time: 45 min.

CHEF'S NOTES

ACCOMPANIMENT:
Serve with sliced fresh apricots or additional all-fruit preserves.

VARIATION:
Use other dried fruit, such as dates, raisins, peaches or apples.

MICROWAVE OPTION:
To make the glaze, place the preserves in a small bowl and microwave uncovered on full power until melted, about 30 seconds. Stir before drizzling over the cake.

KITCHEN TRICK:
Chop the fruit in a food processor. If it begins to stick to the blades, toss in a bit of flour.

NUTRITION AT A GLANCE

PER SERVING:

Calories 266
Fat . . . . 5.2 g. (18% of cal.)
Sat. fat . . . . . 0.3 g. (1% of cal.)
Cholesterol . . . . 0 mg.
Sodium . . . . 132 mg.

CORN CUSTARD SPOON BREAD

Spoon bread is a southern favorite. This version has a dense corn bread base with a layer of creamy custard on the top. But thanks to low-fat buttermilk, skim milk and egg substitute, it's much lower in fat and cholesterol than you'd ever imagine.

CORN CUSTARD SPOON BREAD

- **1 cup white or yellow cornmeal**
- **½ cup unbleached flour**
- **1 teaspoon baking soda**
- **1 cup buttermilk**
- **½ cup fat-free egg substitute**
- **2 tablespoons honey**
- **2 tablespoons snipped chives**
- **1½ cups skim milk**
- **1 cup corn**

1. In a large bowl, combine the cornmeal, flour and baking soda.

2. In a medium bowl, whisk together the buttermilk, egg, honey and chives. Add 1 cup of the milk and the corn; stir well.

3. Pour the liquid ingredients over the dry ones. Stir well to mix, but don't overbeat.

4. Coat a 10″ cast-iron frying pan or a 9″ × 9″ baking dish with no-stick spray. Pour in the batter.

5. Place the pan on a rack in the middle of the oven. Carefully and slowly pour the remaining ½ cup of milk over the top of the batter.

6. Bake at 400° for 30 to 35 minutes, or until the top is golden brown and a toothpick inserted in the center comes out clean.

7. Remove from the oven and let stand about 10 minutes before cutting or spooning from the pan.

SERVES 8.

Preparation Time: 10 min.
Cooking Time: 35 min.

CHEF'S NOTES

INGREDIENTS NOTE:
You may use fresh, frozen or canned corn. (Tender white kernels are especially good.) Thaw frozen corn; drain canned corn.

ACCOMPANIMENT:
Although this bread is perfectly delicious plain, you may also serve it with honey or maple syrup.

VARIATION:
Replace the chives with other herbs, such as sage, basil, parsley or thyme.

MICROWAVE OPTION:
Reheat leftovers in a toaster oven or microwave for 30 seconds on high.

NUTRITION AT A GLANCE

PER SERVING:

Calories 149
Fat . . . . .1.2 g. (7% of cal.)
Sat. fat . . . . .0.3 g. (2% of cal.)
Cholesterol . . . . .2 mg.
Sodium . . . . .187 mg.

PRUNE-BANANA MUFFINS WITH CRANBERRY SPREAD

These muffins and their accompanying cranberry spread are a superb way to increase your intake of potassium, a mineral that's valued for its effect on blood pressure. Consuming an adequate amount helps the body counteract the pressure-raising tendencies of sodium. The bananas, prunes, raisins, molasses and flour contribute the most potassium to these breakfast favorites, but even the yogurt, bran and apple juice kick in a nice amount.

PRUNE-BANANA MUFFINS WITH CRANBERRY SPREAD

PRUNE-BANANA MUFFINS

1 **cup mashed banana**	½ **cup coarsely chopped pitted prunes**
½ **cup nonfat yogurt**	½ **cup molasses**
½ **cup bran**	¼ **cup oil**
1½ **cups whole wheat flour**	¼ **cup fat-free egg substitute**
1 **teaspoon baking powder**	
½ **teaspoon baking soda**	
½ **teaspoon ground cinnamon**	

1. In a small bowl mix the bananas, yogurt and bran.

2. In a large bowl sift together the flour, baking powder, baking soda and cinnamon. Add the prunes and toss to coat.

3. In a small bowl combine the molasses, oil and eggs. Pour into the flour mixture along with the banana mixture. Carefully fold together with a rubber spatula until just blended; do not overmix.

4. Coat 12 muffin cups with no-stick spray. Spoon the batter into the cups, filling them about two-thirds. Bake at 400° for 20 to 25 minutes, or until the edges pull away from the sides of the cups.

MAKES 12.

Preparation Time: 15 min.
Cooking Time: 25 min.

CRANBERRY SPREAD

12 **ounces whole cranberries**	½ **cup maple syrup**
1 **cup apple juice**	½ **cup raisins**

1. In a 2-quart saucepan combine the cranberries, apple juice, syrup and raisins. Bring to a boil over high heat. Reduce the heat to medium and cook until the mixture is thickened and reduced, about 15 minutes. Stir the mixture occasionally as it cooks and press on the cranberries to break them.

2. Spoon the spread into small jars. Cool, cover and refrigerate.

MAKES 2 CUPS.

Preparation Time: 5 min.
Cooking Time: 20 min.

CHEF'S NOTES

DO FIRST:

Pick over the cranberries to remove very soft and unripe ones. You may also want to remove any stems mixed in with the berries.

VARIATION:

Replace the prunes in the muffins with other dried fruit, such as apricots, peaches or currants.

NUTRI-NOTE:

Baking powder and baking soda both contain a lot of sodium and account for most of the sodium in the muffins. There are low-sodium baking powders available for those who would like to reduce sodium in baked products.

NUTRITION AT A GLANCE

PRUNE-BANANA MUFFINS

PER MUFFIN:

Calories 175
Fat . . . . .5 g. (26% of cal.)
Sat. fat . . . . 0.7 g. (4% of cal.)
Cholesterol . . . . 0 mg.
Sodium . . . . 82 mg.

CRANBERRY SPREAD

PER TABLESPOON:

Calories 28
Fat . . . . .0 g.
Sat. fat . . . . 0 g.
Cholesterol . . . . .0 mg.
Sodium . . . . .1 mg.

CARROT MUFFINS WITH BERRY SPREAD

Carrots make a smart addition to muffins for many reasons: They can help lower cholesterol, they're full of dietary fiber, and they're naturally sweet, so you can reduce other sweeteners in your recipe. Paired with a luscious strawberry-yogurt spread, these muffins are a great breakfast treat.

CARROT MUFFINS WITH BERRY SPREAD

LEMON-CARROT MUFFINS

- **1 cup whole wheat pastry flour**
- **1 cup unbleached flour**
- **2½ teaspoons baking powder**
- **½ teaspoon baking soda**
- **¼ teaspoon powdered ginger**
- **1 cup nonfat or low-fat sour cream**
- **⅓ cup maple syrup**
- **¼ cup fat-free egg substitute or 1 egg**
- **3 tablespoons canola oil**
- **1 teaspoon vanilla**
- **1 cup loosely packed finely shredded carrot**
- **⅓ cup golden raisins, chopped**
- **2 teaspoons grated lemon rind**
- **Poppy seeds or chopped nuts**

1. In a large bowl, combine the pastry flour, unbleached flour, baking powder, baking soda and ginger. Make a well in the center.

2. In a medium bowl, whisk together the sour cream, syrup, egg, oil and vanilla. Stir in the carrots, raisins and lemon rind.

3. Pour the liquid ingredients into the well in the dry ingredients. Using a rubber spatula, mix just enough to moisten the dry ingredients. Do not overmix.

4. Coat 12 muffin cups with no-stick spray. Spoon the batter into the cups. Sprinkle lightly with the poppy seeds or nuts. Bake at 400° for 18 to 20 minutes, or until golden. Let cool a few minutes in the pan, then transfer to a wire rack.

MAKES 12.

Preparation Time: 20 min.
Cooking Time: 20 min.

STRAWBERRY SPREAD

- **1 cup sliced strawberries**
- **1 cup nonfat yogurt cheese (see Chef's Notes)**
- **2 teaspoons honey**
- **¼ teaspoon almond extract**

1. Puree the strawberries in a food processor or blender. Transfer to a medium bowl. Add the yogurt, honey and almond extract. Fold together until thoroughly blended.

MAKES ABOUT 2 CUPS.

Preparation Time: 5 min.

CHEF'S NOTES

■ ■ ■ ■ ■ ■ ■ ■ ■

DO FIRST:
Shred the carrots for the muffins.

Make the yogurt cheese: Place 2 cups of nonfat yogurt in a strainer lined with cheesecloth or a paper coffee filter. Drain until thick.

■

INGREDIENTS NOTE:
Nonfat and reduced-fat sour cream are good low-cal, low-fat substitutes for regular sour cream. If you don't have any, use nonfat yogurt that you've drained for 20 minutes.

NUTRITION AT A GLANCE ▬▬▬

LEMON-CARROT MUFFINS
PER MUFFIN:

Calories	157
Fat	4 g. (23% of cal.)
Sat. fat	0.3 g. (2% of cal.)
Cholesterol	0 mg.
Sodium	129 mg.

STRAWBERRY SPREAD
PER 2 TABLESPOONS:

Calories	21
Fat	0.4 g. (17% of cal.)
Sat. fat	0 g.
Cholesterol	0 mg.
Sodium	0 mg.

FILLED PINEAPPLE MUFFINS

Pineapple could be called Hawaii's gift to health: It's low in fat, calories and cholesterol but brimming with fiber and potassium. Start the day with a taste of the tropics by treating yourself to these breakfast muffins.

Breads and Batters

FILLED PINEAPPLE MUFFINS

FILLING
- ⅔ cup part-skim or nonfat ricotta cheese
- 1 tablespoon fat-free egg substitute or lightly beaten egg white

MUFFINS
- 1½ cups quick-cooking rolled oats
- 1 cup unbleached flour
- ⅓ cup oat bran
- 1 tablespoon baking powder
- 1 tablespoon poppy seeds
- ¼ cup currants
- ⅔ cup skim milk
- ¼ cup nonfat dry milk
- ⅓ cup honey
- ¼ cup fat-free egg substitute or 1 egg
- 1 tablespoon oil
- 1 can (8 ounces) crushed pineapple

1. *To make the filling:* In a small bowl, combine the ricotta and 1 tablespoon egg substitute or egg white. Set aside.

2. *To make the muffins:* In a large bowl, combine the oats, flour, bran, baking powder and poppy seeds until well-mixed. Stir in the currants.

3. In a medium bowl, whisk together the skim milk and dry milk. Add the honey, egg and oil. Mix well. Stir in the pineapple (with juice).

4. Pour the pineapple mixture into the flour mixture. Stir to moisten the dry ingredients. Do not overmix.

5. Coat 12 muffin cups with no-stick spray. Divide the batter among the cups. Use the back of a spoon to form a hollow in the middle of each muffin large enough to hold about 1 tablespoon of filling.

6. Place a scant tablespoon of the ricotta mixture in the hollow of each muffin.

7. Bake at 375° for 22 to 25 minutes, or until the muffins are golden on top; they are best served warm.

MAKES 12.

Preparation Time: 20 min.
Cooking Time: 25 min.

CHEF'S NOTES

ACCOMPANIMENT:
Serve with fruit preserves or a homemade spread, such as mashed bananas sweetened with orange-juice concentrate.

VARIATIONS:
Omit the filling entirely or replace it with all-fruit preserves (use a rounded teaspoon per muffin).

MICROWAVE OPTION:
To reheat the muffins, wrap each in a damp paper towel and microwave on full power for about 30 seconds.

CHEF'S SECRET:
For the lightest, most tender muffins, don't overbeat the batter. Simply stir until the dry ingredients are moistened.

NUTRITION AT A GLANCE

PER MUFFIN:
Calories 174
Fat . . . . 3.5 g. (18% of cal.)
Sat. fat . . . . . 0.9 g. (5% of cal.)
Cholesterol . . . . 4 mg.
Sodium . . . . 120 mg.

DOUBLE-OAT PANCAKES WITH WARM PEAR SAUCE

Say good morning to good nutrition! These pancakes are more than simply delicious—they're loaded with cholesterol-lowering oats and oat bran. Then for extra measure they're topped with a fiber- and pectin-rich fruit sauce, all the better to zap cholesterol.

DOUBLE-OAT PANCAKES WITH WARM PEAR SAUCE

PEAR SAUCE
- **2 ripe pears, chopped**
- **6 dried apricots**
- **¼ cup orange juice**

PANCAKES
- **¾ cup unbleached flour or whole wheat pastry flour**
- **⅓ cup rolled oats**
- **¼ cup oat bran**
- **1 teaspoon baking powder**
- **½ teaspoon ground cinnamon**
- **3 tablespoons maple syrup**
- **2 egg whites, lightly beaten**
- **½ cup skim milk**
- **2 teaspoons oil**

TOPPING
- **1½ cups blueberries**

1. *To make the pear sauce:* Combine the pears, apricots and orange juice in a small saucepan and bring to a boil. Reduce the heat to medium and simmer until the fruit is soft, about 3 to 4 minutes. Let cool for about 5 minutes, then pour into a food processor or blender and puree. Set aside.

2. *To make the pancakes:* In a medium bowl combine the flour, oats, oat bran, baking powder and cinnamon.

3. In a small bowl whisk together the syrup, egg whites and milk.

4. Pour the wet ingredients into the flour and combine until all the flour is moistened. Don't overmix.

5. Heat a well-seasoned cast-iron skillet on medium-high heat. Pour in 1 teaspoon of oil, spread it around and immediately reduce the heat to medium.

6. Drop in batter by slightly rounded tablespoons. You'll probably be able to get 6 pancakes in the skillet at a time. Let sizzle until lightly browned on bottom, about 4 minutes. Then flip and brown the other side.

7. For the second batch, pour in remaining oil and repeat the procedure.

8. Serve pancakes warm, topped with blueberries and warm sauce.

SERVES 4.

Preparation Time: 25 min.
Cooking Time: 15 min.

CHEF'S NOTES

VARIATIONS:

For sauce: Use apples instead of pears. If desired, add a few cranberries for a rosy color. Cook sauce until cranberries pop.

MICROWAVE OPTION:

Cook the fruit in the microwave. Place pears, apricots and orange juice in a 9'' glass pie plate. Cover with vented plastic wrap and microwave until tender, about 4 minutes.

MAKE-AHEAD TIPS:

Prepare sauce ahead, refrigerate and reheat just before serving. Make pancakes ahead and reheat in a toaster oven.

NUTRITION AT A GLANCE

PER SERVING:
Calories 320
Fat . . . . 3.9 g. (11% of cal.)
Sat. fat . . . . . 0.5 g. (1% of cal.)
Cholesterol . . . . 0 mg.
Sodium . . . . 141 mg.

PUMPKIN PANCAKES WITH FRUIT SAUCE

Don't wait for Halloween to try these fruit-topped pumpkin pancakes. They're very low in fat but high in fiber—a combination that's ideal for combating many health problems, including high cholesterol, overweight and digestive disorders.

Pumpkin Pancakes with Fruit Sauce

PUMPKIN PANCAKES

- **2 cups warm water (about 115°)**
- **1 package active dry yeast**
- **2 cups whole wheat flour**
- **1 tablespoon nonfat yogurt**
- **1 cup unbleached or whole wheat flour**
- **1 cup canned pumpkin**
- **1 cup skim milk**
- **½ cup water**
- **¼ cup honey**
- **½ teaspoon baking soda**
- **½ teaspoon grated orange rind**
- **½ teaspoon ground cinnamon**
- **¼ teaspoon grated nutmeg**
- **Nonfat vanilla yogurt**
- **Maple syrup**

1. To make the sourdough starter, combine the warm water and the yeast in a large bowl. Stir well to dissolve the yeast. Add 2 cups whole wheat flour and 1 tablespoon yogurt. Stir until smooth. Cover and set in a warm place for several hours or overnight.

2. Stir the starter well. With a whisk or wooden spoon, beat in 1 cup unbleached or whole wheat flour. Add the pumpkin, milk, ½ cup water, honey, baking soda, orange rind, cinnamon and nutmeg. Stir until well-blended, then let the batter stand for 15 or 20 minutes.

3. Coat a large no-stick frying pan with no-stick spray. Place over medium heat until hot. Ladle scant tablespoonfuls of batter into the pan. Cook until the bubbles that form on the tops break and the tops begin to look dry. Flip and cook until lightly browned. Serve the pancakes with fruit sauce, vanilla yogurt and syrup.

MAKES ABOUT 72; SERVES 12.

Preparation Time: 20 min. + standing time
Cooking Time: 15 min.

FRUIT SAUCE

- **2 cups orange juice**
- **2 tablespoons cornstarch**
- **¼ cup water**
- **2 teaspoons grated orange rind**
- **2 cups orange sections**
- **2 cups sliced plums, blueberries or raisins**
- **2 tablespoons honey or other sweetener**

1. Place the juice in a 2-quart saucepan. In a cup, dissolve the cornstarch in the water and add to the pan. Add the orange rind. Cook over medium heat, stirring constantly, until the sauce thickens, about 5 minutes. Remove from the heat and stir in the oranges and plums, blueberries or raisins. Add the honey or other sweetener. Serve warm or chilled.

MAKES ABOUT 4 CUPS; SERVES 12.

Preparation Time: 10 min.
Cooking Time: 5 min.

CHEF'S NOTES

VARIATION:
Serve the pancakes as a savory appetizer or entrée by topping them with steamed vegetables and a low-fat white sauce instead of a sweet sauce.

MICROWAVE OPTION:
To reheat chilled or frozen pancakes, place six on a plate and micro-wave on full power for about 30 seconds.

KITCHEN TRICKS:
To cut the time needed to make the starter, use quick-rise yeast. Place the starter in a warm place for about 2 hours, or until quite bubbly. To reduce total cooking time, use two griddles or frying pans.

NUTRITION AT A GLANCE

PER SERVING:

Calories	196
Fat	0.7 g. (3% of cal.)
Sat. fat	0.2 g. (<1% of cal.)
Cholesterol	0 mg.
Sodium	50 mg.

BUCKWHEAT WAFFLES

What a way to start the day! These golden waffles owe their goodness to buckwheat, which is a better source of muscle-building protein than most any other grain. And unlike traditional breakfast meats, it's cholesterol free and low in fat. As a bonus, the blackberries are especially rich in fiber, and the mango is a storehouse of vitamin A—both of which have anticancer properties.

Breads and Batters

BUCKWHEAT WAFFLES

MANGO SAUCE
- **1 mango**
- **¼ cup honey**
- **3 tablespoons cornstarch**
- **2 tablespoons lime juice**
- **1 cup evaporated skim milk**
- **1 tablespoon margarine**
- **¼ teaspoon ground cinnamon**

WAFFLES
- **¾ cup whole wheat pastry flour**
- **¾ cup unbleached flour**
- **1½ teaspoons baking powder**
- **1 cup cooked buckwheat groats**
- **1½ cups buttermilk**
- **3 tablespoons maple syrup**
- **3 egg whites, lightly beaten**
- **1 tablespoon oil**
- **1 teaspoon vanilla**
- **2 cups blackberries**

1. *To make the mango sauce:* Peel the mango. Using a serrated knife, slice the flesh from the pit. Chop it and place in a blender or food processor. Add the honey, cornstarch and lime juice. Process until smooth.

2. Transfer to a 1-quart saucepan. Whisk in the milk. Cook over medium heat, whisking constantly, until thickened, about 10 minutes. Stir in the margarine and cinnamon. Keep warm.

3. *To make the waffles:* Coat the grids of a waffle iron with no-stick spray. Preheat the iron according to the manufacturer's instructions.

4. In a medium bowl sift together the pastry flour, unbleached flour and baking powder. Stir in the buckwheat.

5. In another medium bowl whisk together the buttermilk, syrup, egg whites, oil and vanilla. Pour into the flour. Stir until just combined; don't overmix.

6. Spoon enough batter into the waffle iron to cover two-thirds of the bottom grid. Bake according to the manufacturer's instructions, about 4 minutes. Serve with the mango sauce and blackberries.

SERVES 8.

Preparation Time: 25 min.
Cooking Time: 20 min.

DESSERTS

ALL-AMERICAN SUNDAES

Red, white and blue—these summer-fresh sundaes are a treat any time of the year. The strawberries contain a substance called ellagic acid that doctors say can help fight cancer. And the creamy-smooth frozen yogurt supplies bone-building calcium.

ALL-AMERICAN SUNDAES

FROZEN YOGURT
- **1 cup sliced strawberries**
- **¾ cup sliced banana**
- **2 cups nonfat vanilla yogurt**
- **½ cup nonfat plain yogurt**

STRAWBERRY SAUCE
- **⅓ cup water**
- **1 tablespoon cornstarch**
- **3 tablespoons all-fruit strawberry preserves**
- **1 teaspoon lemon juice**
- **1½ cups sliced strawberries, lightly crushed**

SUNDAES
- **2 large ripe bananas**
- **2 cups blueberries**
- **2 tablespoons sliced almonds (optional)**

1. *To make the frozen yogurt:* Place the strawberries and bananas in a large bowl. Use a potato masher to crush thoroughly. Stir in the vanilla yogurt and plain yogurt to combine well.

2. Transfer to the container of an ice-cream maker and process according to the manufacturer's directions. (If you do not have an ice-cream maker, see Chef's Notes.)

3. Form the frozen yogurt into balls with an ice-cream scoop and place on a large plate lined with wax paper. Freeze until firm but not solid, about 20 minutes.

4. *To make the strawberry sauce:* While the yogurt is being processed, mix the water and cornstarch in a 1-quart saucepan until the cornstarch is dissolved. Whisk over medium heat for 5 minutes, until clear, thick and just boiling. Remove from the heat. Whisk in the preserves and lemon juice until smooth. Let cool 5 minutes. Add the berries to the sauce. Refrigerate until chilled, about 30 minutes.

5. *To make the sundaes:* Cut the bananas as desired and divide among serving bowls or banana-split dishes. Top with the frozen yogurt, strawberry sauce and blueberries. Sprinkle with the almonds.

SERVES 6.

Preparation Time: 40 min. + standing time
Cooking Time: 5 min.

CHEF'S NOTES

VARIATION:
Use other fruit. Try raspberries, peaches, blueberries or pineapple.

KITCHEN TRICKS:
If you do not have an ice-cream maker, place the yogurt mixture in a 9'' × 9'' metal pan. Freeze for 20 minutes. Beat well with a wooden spoon or electric mixer for 1 minute to break up the forming ice crystals. Return the pan to the freezer. Beat well every 15 to 20 minutes for 2½ to 3 hours, or until the mixture holds its shape when formed into balls. For the smoothest texture, transfer the mixture to a food processor for the final few beatings.

NUTRITION AT A GLANCE

PER SERVING:
Calories 170
Fat . . . . .0.7 g. (4% of cal.)
Sat. fat . . . . .0.3 g. (2% of cal.)
Cholesterol . . . . .0 mg.
Sodium . . . . .65 mg.

FRUIT ICES

What a light, refreshing way to end a meal! These colorful ices are made from fresh fruit—with just a little sweetener and a bit of citrus juice to enhance the fruit's natural flavors. That makes them dieters' delights: low cal with no cholesterol and barely a trace of sodium or fat. They're a perfect alternative to high-fat ice cream.

FRUIT ICES

PAPAYA ICE

1½ cups papaya puree
¾ cup water
2 tablespoons honey
(or to taste)

1 tablespoon lemon juice

1. Combine the papaya, water, honey and lemon juice in a blender. Process about 10 seconds. Transfer to a bowl or shallow pan. Place in the freezer.

2. Stir or beat the mixture every 15 to 20 minutes to break up the ice crystals and to prevent the mixture from freezing solid too fast. Finished ice will be ready in 2 to 3 hours (8 to 12 vigorous stirrings). Serve either slushy or frozen enough to scoop.

SERVES 4.

Preparation Time: 3 hr.

RASPBERRY ICE

2 cups raspberry puree
⅔ cup water

3 tablespoons maple syrup
½ teaspoon lemon juice

1. Combine the raspberries, water, syrup and lemon juice. Transfer to a bowl or shallow pan. Place in the freezer.

2. Stir or beat the mixture every 15 to 20 minutes to break up the ice crystals and to prevent the mixture from freezing solid too fast. Finished ice will be ready in 2 to 3 hours (8 to 12 vigorous stirrings). Serve either slushy or frozen enough to scoop.

SERVES 4.

Preparation Time: 3 hr.

HONEYDEW ICE

2 cups honeydew puree
¼ cup maple syrup
½ teaspoon lime juice

½ teaspoon ground
cinnamon

1. Combine the honeydew, syrup, lime juice and cinnamon. Transfer to a bowl or shallow pan. Place in the freezer.

2. Stir or beat the mixture every 15 to 20 minutes to break up the ice crystals and to prevent the mixture from freezing solid too fast. Finished ice will be ready in 2 to 3 hours (8 to 12 vigorous stirrings). Serve either slushy or frozen enough to scoop.

SERVES 4.

Preparation Time: 3 hr.

DEVILISH RASPBERRY CAKE

Yes, you can enjoy a chocolate dessert on a heart-healthy diet! Using cocoa powder instead of unsweetened chocolate cuts a lot of saturated fat from cake recipes. And canola oil (in place of butter) reduces saturates even more. Serve with a raspberry topping for lots of beneficial fiber.

DEVILISH RASPBERRY CAKE

COCOA CAKE

- **1 cup whole wheat flour or unbleached flour**
- **1 cup unbleached flour**
- **¾ cup packed light brown sugar**
- **½ cup cocoa powder**
- **1 teaspoon baking powder**
- **1 teaspoon baking soda**
- **1¼ cups nonfat plain or vanilla yogurt**
- **½ cup canola oil**
- **½ cup fat-free egg substitute**
- **1 teaspoon vanilla**

RASPBERRY SAUCE

- **3 cups raspberries**
- **⅓ cup all-fruit raspberry preserves**
- **1 teaspoon lemon juice**
- **Low-fat whipped topping (optional)**

1. *To make the cocoa cake:* In a large bowl, thoroughly mix the whole wheat flour, unbleached flour, brown sugar, cocoa, baking powder and baking soda.

2. Place the yogurt, oil, egg and vanilla in another large bowl. Using an electric mixer on low speed, beat for about 30 seconds to combine.

3. Add the dry ingredients and beat on low speed until just combined. Increase the speed to high and beat for about 3 minutes.

4. Coat a 9" × 9" baking dish or a 9" springform pan with no-stick spray. If you intend to unmold the cake, cut a piece of wax paper to fit the bottom and spray the paper. Pour the batter into the pan. Bake at 350° for 35 to 45 minutes, or until a toothpick inserted in the center comes out clean.

5. Let cool on a wire rack. (If unmolding, let cool on the rack for 10 minutes. Unmold onto a plate and peel off the paper; let cool completely.)

6. *To make the raspberry sauce:* Puree 1 cup of the raspberries. Set aside.

7. In a 2-quart saucepan over medium-low heat, melt the preserves. Stir in the lemon juice and pureed raspberries. Heat for 1 minute. Add the remaining 2 cups of raspberries and stir well to coat them with glaze. Set aside to cool.

8. To serve, cut the cake into pieces and transfer to dessert plates. Spoon sauce over the cake and add topping.

SERVES 12.

Preparation Time: 20 min.
Cooking Time: 45 min.

CHEF'S NOTES

PRESENTATION:

If desired, cut the cake in half horizontally to make two layers. Fill the middle with a layer of low-fat whipped topping.

NUTRI-NOTE:

Cocoa may help those with lactose intolerance digest milk. In one study, people who drank cocoa-spiked low-fat milk didn't suffer the bloating or cramping usually caused by milk.

KITCHEN TRICK:

To replace unsweetened chocolate in any recipe, use 3 tablespoons cocoa powder and 1 tablespoon oil for each 1-ounce square of the chocolate.

NUTRITION AT A GLANCE

PER SERVING:

Calories	261
Fat	10 g. (34% of cal.)
Sat. fat	1.1 g. (4% of cal.)
Cholesterol	1 mg.
Sodium	139 mg.

BOTTOMS-UP PEACH CAKE

This variation on classic pineapple upside-down cake is much lighter than standard recipes. We slashed both cholesterol and fat by using egg substitute rather than whole eggs and just a small amount of reduced-calorie margarine rather than a lot of highly saturated butter.

BOTTOMS-UP PEACH CAKE

1 tablespoon light margarine, melted

2–3 tablespoons maple syrup

¼ teaspoon almond extract

1½–2 cups thinly sliced peaches

½ cup raspberries or cranberries

½ cup whole wheat flour

½ cup unbleached flour

1½ teaspoons baking powder

⅓ cup evaporated skim milk

⅓ cup honey

¼ cup oil

¼ cup fat-free egg substitute or 1 egg

1 teaspoon vanilla extract

1. Coat a 9″ round baking pan with no-stick spray. Line the bottom with wax paper and coat with spray.

2. In a cup, combine the margarine, syrup and almond extract. Pour into the prepared pan and swirl to coat the bottom evenly. Arrange the peaches and raspberries or cranberries on top of the mixture in a decorative pattern.

3. In a large bowl, combine the whole wheat flour, unbleached flour and baking powder.

4. In a medium bowl, combine the milk, honey, oil, egg and vanilla. Pour over the flour. Stir to combine thoroughly.

5. Pour the batter over the fruit and smooth the top with a rubber spatula. Bake at 350° until puffed and lightly brown, 30 to 35 minutes.

6. Remove from the oven and let stand on a wire rack for 10 minutes. Invert the cake onto a serving platter. Serve warm.

SERVES 8.

Preparation Time: 20 min.
Cooking Time: 35 min.

CHEF'S NOTES

DO FIRST:

Prepare the peaches: Peel fresh peaches by immersing them in boiling water for 20 seconds. Use a sharp knife to remove the peel; slice the flesh into ¼″ to ⅜″ pieces. If using frozen peaches, allow to soften until pliable. Slice as needed. If using canned peaches, start with halves, drain well and pat dry. Cut as above.

ACCOMPANIMENT:

Serve with more fruit or frozen yogurt.

VARIATION:

Use other fruit, including drained pineapple, blueberries, sliced plums or sliced nectarines.

NUTRITION AT A GLANCE

PER SERVING:

Calories 207
Fat . . . . .8 g. (35% of cal.)
Sat. fat . . . . .0.4 g. (2% of cal.)
Cholesterol . . . . .0 mg.
Sodium . . . . .100 mg.

HEAVENLY ORANGE CAKE

The oranges and cherries served with this spongy cake contribute fiber and disease-fighting vitamin C—something many desserts lack. Just ten cherries contain 1 gram of fiber, much of it in the soluble form that lowers cholesterol. And oranges, of course, are champions of vitamin C.

HEAVENLY ORANGE CAKE

ORANGE CREAM
- **1 cup nonfat cottage cheese**
- **1 cup nonfat vanilla yogurt**
- **⅓ cup orange-juice concentrate**

CAKE
- **¾ cup sifted unbleached flour**
- **¼ cup sifted whole wheat pastry flour**

- **12 egg whites, at room temperature**
- **1 teaspoon cream of tartar**
- **1½ teaspoons orange extract**
- **½ cup honey**
- **2 cups orange sections**
- **1 cup sweet cherries, pitted**

1. *To make the orange cream:* In a food processor puree the cottage cheese until completely smooth (about 4 minutes; stop frequently to scrape down the sides of the container). Transfer to a small bowl. Lightly whisk in the yogurt and orange-juice concentrate. Chill.

2. *To make the cake:* Sift the unbleached flour and pastry flour together. Return the flour to the sifter.

3. In a 5- or 6-quart bowl beat the egg whites until bubbly. Add the cream of tartar and orange extract. Beat on medium speed until the whites form soft peaks. Gradually beat in the honey until the whites are stiff.

4. Sift about ¼ cup of the flour over the whites. Carefully fold it in with a large spatula. Repeat until all the flour has been incorporated.

5. Spoon the batter into an ungreased 9″ or 10″ tube pan with removable bottom. Level the top with a spatula.

6. Bake at 325° for 40 to 50 minutes, or until the top is golden and springs back when lightly touched. Invert the pan onto a wire rack and let the cake cool for 1 hour.

7. To remove the cake from the pan, run a thin knife around the outside edges. Remove the outer portion of the pan. Run a thin knife around the center tube and also around the bottom of the cake. Slice the cake and serve with the orange cream, oranges and cherries.

SERVES 10.

Preparation Time: 20 min.
Cooking Time: 50 min.

CHEF'S NOTES

DO FIRST:
Separate the eggs and let the whites come to room temperature. Make sure no traces of yolk are mixed in with the whites or they won't beat up properly. If any specks of yolk accidentally fall in, dab them up with a piece of eggshell or a piece of bread.

VARIATIONS:
Flavor the cake with another extract, such as almond, cherry, maple, peppermint or black walnut. Serve with other fruit, such as raspberries, blueberries, peaches or strawberries.

KITCHEN TRICK:
Pit the cherries just before serving to prevent discoloration.

NUTRITION AT A GLANCE

PER SERVING:
Calories 186
Fat . . . . .0.4 g. (2% of cal.)
Sat. fat . . . . .0 g.
Cholesterol . . . . .2 mg.
Sodium . . . . .100 mg.

FESTIVE CAKE ROLL

You needn't reserve this dessert just for holidays. It's made with egg whites and egg substitute, so levels of fat and cholesterol are kept low. Filled with skinny frozen yogurt and topped with fresh fruit, this is a "splurge" you can enjoy often.

FESTIVE CAKE ROLL

CAKE
- **5 egg whites**
- **½ teaspoon cream of tartar**
- **½ cup fat-free egg substitute**
- **½ cup honey, warmed slightly**
- **1 tablespoon vanilla**
- **¾ cup whole wheat flour or whole wheat pastry flour**

FILLING AND TOPPING
- **3 pints low-fat or nonfat frozen yogurt**
- **2 cups sliced peaches**
- **2 cups sliced strawberries**
- **2 tablespoons maple syrup**
- **1 teaspoon lemon juice**
- **1 teaspoon vanilla**

1. *To make the cake:* Oil a 10″ × 15″ jelly-roll pan. Line with wax paper. Oil the paper generously, then dust with flour.

2. In a medium bowl, beat the egg whites with an electric mixer until frothy. Add the cream of tartar. Beat until stiff peaks form. Set aside.

3. In a large bowl, beat the egg substitute, honey and vanilla with the mixer for 1 minute.

4. Gently fold a third of the whites into the honey mixture. Then sift in ¼ cup of the flour and gently fold together. Repeat twice more to incorporate all the whites and flour. Do not overmix.

5. Spread the batter in the prepared pan. Bake at 375° until the cake is puffed and golden, 12 to 15 minutes. Remove from the oven and immediately cover with a sheet of wax paper and a baking sheet. Invert the cake onto the baking sheet. Carefully peel the wax paper off the bottom of the cake. Starting at one short end—and using the paper under the cake to help you—roll up the warm cake. Set on a wire rack to cool.

6. *To make the filling and topping:* Soften the frozen yogurt in the refrigerator for about 30 minutes. Working quickly, unroll the cake and spread with the yogurt. Reroll the cake and place in the freezer to harden, at least 30 minutes.

7. In a medium bowl, combine the peaches, strawberries, syrup, lemon juice and vanilla.

8. To serve, cut the log into slices and top with the fruit.

SERVES 8.

Preparation Time: 45 min. + standing time
Cooking Time: 15 min.

CHEF'S NOTES

DO FIRST:
Ready the egg whites: Separate the whites from the yolks while the eggs are still cold; discard the yolks. Place the whites in a large bowl; let stand at room temperature for about 20 minutes so they'll achieve proper volume when beaten.

INGREDIENTS NOTE:
You may use any flavor frozen yogurt. You may also substitute ice milk. If desired, vary the fruit topping to complement it—for instance, use raspberries with raspberry frozen yogurt.

MAKE-AHEAD TIP:
Wrap the filled roll tightly in heavy-duty plastic or foil and store in the freezer for up to 1 week.

NUTRITION AT A GLANCE

PER SERVING:
Calories 259
Fat . . . . .1.2 g. (4% of cal.)
Sat. fat . . . . .0 g.
Cholesterol . . . . .10 mg.
Sodium . . . . .59 mg.

FRUIT AND NUT CAKE

This no-fuss fruitcake is packed with fiber, thanks to whole wheat flour, dates, raisins and other fruit. As the cake bakes, its fragrant spices will fill the house with a wonderful holiday aroma—any time of the year.

Fruit and nut cake

1 cup whole wheat flour	**½ cup golden raisins**
1 cup unbleached flour	**¼ cup chopped pecans**
1½ teaspoons baking powder	**½ cup apple juice concentrate**
½ teaspoon baking soda	**½ cup fat-free egg substitute or 2 eggs**
½ teaspoon ground cinnamon	**1 can (8 ounces) crushed pineapple**
½ teaspoon powdered ginger	**1 apple, coarsely shredded**
¼ teaspoon ground allspice	**1 teaspoon vanilla**
½ cup chopped dates	

1. In a large bowl, combine the whole wheat flour, unbleached flour, baking powder, baking soda, cinnamon, ginger and allspice. Stir in the dates, raisins and pecans.

2. In a medium bowl, combine the juice concentrate, eggs, pineapple (with juice), apples and vanilla.

3. Stir the liquid ingredients into the flour mixture until well-combined.

4. Coat a 6-cup Bundt pan or other decorative tube pan with no-stick spray. Spoon in the cake batter and smooth the top with a spatula. Bake at 325° for about 1 hour, or until a skewer inserted in the middle of the cake comes out clean.

5. Unmold onto a wire rack. Let cool 30 minutes before slicing.

SERVES 12.

Preparation Time: 25 min.
Cooking Time: 1 hr.

CHEF'S NOTES

ACCOMPANIMENT:

Serve with a low-fat version of classic hard sauce: Mix equal parts reduced-fat soft margarine and honey. Season with vanilla or brandy extract, grated orange rind and nutmeg. Use a small dollop for each slice.

VARIATIONS:

Use other dried fruit, such as chopped prunes, apricots, figs or peaches. Use other nuts or sunflower seeds. Replace the apple with a pear.

CHEF'S SECRET:

When chopping dates or other dried fruit, sprinkle the knife and fruit with flour to keep sticking to a minimum.

NUTRITION AT A GLANCE

PER SERVING:

Calories	162
Fat	2 g. (11% of cal.)
Sat. fat	0.2 g. (1% of cal.)
Cholesterol	0 mg.
Sodium	94 mg.

FRESH PLUM TART

Plum delicious! That pretty well describes this no-cholesterol, low-fat tart. Fresh plums, rolled oats and almonds pack it full of fiber, so you can indulge in this luscious dessert without guilt.

Desserts

Fresh Plum Tart

FILLING
- **3 tablespoons honey or other sweetener**
- **1 tablespoon lemon juice**
- **½ teaspoon cornstarch**
- **½ teaspoon grated orange rind**
- **⅛ teaspoon almond extract**
- **4 cups sliced large red or purple plums**

CRUST
- **1 cup unbleached flour**
- **1 cup rolled oats**
- **¼ cup toasted sliced almonds**
- **¼ cup orange juice**
- **3 tablespoons reduced-fat margarine**
- **2 tablespoons honey or other sweetener**

TOPPING
- **1 cup nonfat yogurt**
- **1 tablespoon honey or other sweetener**
- **⅛ teaspoon ground cinnamon**
- **⅛ teaspoon grated nutmeg**

1. *To make the filling:* In a large bowl, combine the honey or other sweetener, lemon juice, cornstarch, orange rind and almond extract. Add the plums and stir to coat. Set aside.

2. *To make the crust:* In a food processor, combine the flour, oats, almonds, orange juice, margarine and honey or other sweetener. Process with on/off turns, stopping to scrape down the sides of the container as needed, until the mixture is combined and will form a ball if pressed together.

3. Coat a 9″ French tart pan (with removable bottom) with no-stick spray. Press the dough evenly into the pan, coming about 1″ up the sides. Bake at 425° for 5 minutes. Let cool for about 10 minutes.

4. Arrange the plums in a decorative pattern in the crust. Pour any extra juices from the bowl over the plums.

5. Bake at 425° for 25 to 30 minutes, or until the plums are soft. Cool on a wire rack for 1 hour. Remove the sides of the pan.

6. *To make the topping:* In a small bowl, combine the yogurt, honey or other sweetener, cinnamon and nutmeg. Refrigerate until needed.

7. Cut the tart and serve each slice with a dollop of the topping.

SERVES 8.

Preparation Time: 40 min.
Cooking Time: 35 min.

CHEF'S NOTES

VARIATIONS:
Replace the plums with sliced peaches or apricots. Use a home-made whipped topping: Freeze ⅓ cup skim milk in a small bowl for 20 minutes. Add ⅓ cup nonfat dry milk and whip with an electric mixer until soft peaks form. Sweeten to taste. Use within 15 minutes.

CHEF'S SECRETS:
If you don't have a French tart pan, use a springform pan or deep-dish pie plate. To remove the sides from a French tart pan, place the pan on top of a can. Gently wiggle the outer rim to loosen it. Pull the rim down and out of the way.

NUTRITION AT A GLANCE

PER SERVING:
- **Calories** 255
- **Fat** . . . . . . .5.9 g. (21% of cal.)
- **Sat. fat** . . . . .0.4 g. (1% of cal.)
- **Cholesterol** . . . . .0 mg.
- **Sodium** . . . . .48 mg.

PIE IN A PUMPKIN

If you love creamy pumpkin pie but can do without a fattening crust, try this novel approach. Bake the filling in tiny pumpkin shells. You'll get lots less fat and calories—and you'll serve yourself an extra helping of cancer-fighting vitamins A and C.

Desserts

PIE IN A PUMPKIN

6 **Jack Be Little pumpkins, 3½″ in diameter (6–8 ounces each)**
½ **cup honey**
1 **cup fat-free egg substitute**
1 **cup low-fat milk**
¾ **cup canned pumpkin**
3 **tablespoons light molasses**
1 **teaspoon grated orange rind**
½ **teaspoon ground cinnamon**
⅛ **teaspoon grated nutmeg**
Pinch of ground allspice
Pinch of powdered ginger

1. Wash and dry the pumpkins. Cut off the tops about 1″ down. Scoop out the seeds and fiber, being careful not to pierce the bottoms. Put the tops back on and place the shells in a 9″ × 13″ baking dish. Bake at 350° for 25 to 35 minutes, or until the flesh is tender but the shells are not in danger of collapsing. (To test, remove a top and insert a fork into the flesh, but be careful not to pierce the outer skin.) Set aside to cool.

2. When the shells are cool enough to handle, brush the insides with a little of the honey.

3. In a large bowl, whisk together the remaining honey, egg, milk, pumpkin, molasses, orange rind, cinnamon, nutmeg, allspice and ginger.

4. Set aside the lids until later. Divide the custard mixture among the shells, filling them almost to the top, about ½ cup per shell. (If you have extra filling, see Chef's Notes.) Place the pumpkins in a baking dish large enough to hold them without crowding.

5. Bake at 350° for 30 to 45 minutes, or until the filling does not jiggle in the center when gently shaken (if you bake the filling until a knife inserted in the center comes out clean, it will be a little too dry). Serve warm or chilled with the lid in place. Spoon out the flesh along with the custard filling. Eat the skin too, if tender.

SERVES 6.

Preparation Time: 30 min.
Cooking Time: 1½ hr.

CHEF'S NOTES

INGREDIENTS NOTE:

If tiny pumpkins are not available, use little squash (such as Sweet Dumpling). Or use butternut squash (1 pound each). Cut off the necks to expose the seed cavities. Scoop out the seeds and fill the cavities with custard. Expect a little longer baking time.

PRESENTATION:

If desired, serve with a dollop of frozen yogurt or low-cal whipped topping.

VARIATION:

Replace the custard with a bread pudding mixture.

KITCHEN TRICK:

Bake extra filling in 4-ounce custard cups placed in a pan with 1″ of water; bake as in step 5.

NUTRITION AT A GLANCE

PER SERVING:
Calories 202
Fat . . . . 1.1 g. (5% of cal.)
Sat. fat . . . . 0.3 g. (1% of cal.)
Cholesterol . . . . 0 mg.
Sodium . . . . 60 mg.

RASPBERRY BREAD PUDDING

Raspberries are worth their weight in gold! They're very low in calories, fat and sodium but amazingly high in fiber. One cup of the little beauties contains as much dietary fiber as ¼ cup of bran, but the berries are much more fun to eat. And although nobody needs to be coaxed into consuming more raspberries, this bread pudding is a very nice way to enjoy them.

Desserts

RASPBERRY BREAD PUDDING

2 cups low-fat milk	**5 cups bread cubes**
½ cup fat-free egg substitute	**4 cups raspberries**
½ cup honey or maple syrup	**1 tablespoon light margarine**
¼ cup oat bran	**1 cup nonfat vanilla yogurt**
2 teaspoons vanilla	
¼ teaspoon ground cinnamon	

1. In a large bowl whisk together the milk, eggs, honey or syrup, bran, vanilla and cinnamon. Stir in the bread. Set aside for 10 minutes for the bread cubes to soak up the milk mixture.

2. Fold in 2 cups of raspberries.

3. Preheat the oven to 350°. Coat an 8″ × 8″ baking dish with no-stick spray. Transfer the bread mixture to the pan. Cut the margarine into tiny pieces and distribute it on top of the bread pudding.

4. Place the bread pudding in the oven and reduce the temperature to 300°. Bake for 45 minutes. Raise the temperature to 425° and bake another 10 minutes, or until the bread pudding is puffed and lightly browned on top.

5. Serve warm or cold with additional raspberries and yogurt.

SERVES 6.

Preparation Time: 25 min.
Cooking Time: 55 min.

CHEF'S NOTES

ACCOMPANIMENT:

If desired, serve with a sauce made of pureed raspberries and honey to taste.

VARIATION:

Replace the raspberries with blueberries or sliced peaches, apricots or plums.

KITCHEN TRICKS:

Bread puddings often have a more interesting texture when made with stale bread. If you don't have any, cut fresh bread into cubes and dry it out in the oven at a low temperature for about 20 or 30 minutes. Stir the cubes occasionally. If using frozen berries, you needn't thaw them first.

NUTRITION AT A GLANCE

PER SERVING:

Calories 294
Fat . . . . . . .3.8 g. (12% of cal.)
Sat. fat . . . . .0.7 g. (2% of cal.)
Cholesterol . . . . .4 mg.
Sodium . . . . .233 mg.

ROYAL RICE

This milk-based dessert has lots of calcium, which is celebrated for its bone-strengthening merits. But calcium might also protect against colon cancer. Studies have shown that people without the disease have higher intakes of calcium than those with the cancer. Because a high-fat diet also seems to increase risk, low-fat foods like this dessert make extra nutritional sense.

ROYAL RICE

1 can (8 ounces) crushed pineapple
⅔ cup arborio rice
¼ cup raisins
¼ teaspoon ground cinnamon
¼ teaspoon grated nutmeg
1 tablespoon cornstarch
2 cups low-fat milk
¼ cup honey
¼ cup maple syrup
½ cup fat-free egg substitute
1½ teaspoons vanilla
1½ cups sliced strawberries
3 tablespoons slivered toasted almonds

1. Place the pineapple in a strainer set over a measuring cup. Press as much liquid as possible from the pineapple. Set the pineapple aside.

2. You should have about ½ cup of pineapple juice. Add enough water to equal 1⅓ cups.

3. In a 1-quart saucepan combine the liquid with the rice. Bring to a boil, reduce the heat to medium low, partially cover the pan and cook the rice for 5 minutes.

4. Stir the rice with a fork. Cover the pan tightly and cook for another 5 to 15 minutes, or until all the liquid has been absorbed. Stir in the pineapple, raisins, cinnamon and nutmeg.

5. In a 2-quart saucepan whisk the cornstarch with 2 tablespoons of the milk until smooth. Whisk in the remaining milk plus the honey and syrup.

6. Cook the sauce over medium heat, whisking constantly, until it starts to thicken and the milk just comes to a boil, about 10 minutes. Remove from the heat.

7. Place the eggs in a cup. Slowly whisk about ¼ cup of the heated sauce into them. Whisk the mixture into the rest of the sauce.

8. Return the pan to the heat and whisk constantly until the sauce comes to a boil.

9. Remove from the heat and stir in the vanilla and cooked rice. Transfer to a large bowl, cover and chill. Just before serving, fold in the strawberries and almonds.

SERVES 6.

Preparation Time: 20 min.
Cooking Time: 35 min.

CHEF'S NOTES

ACCOMPANIMENTS:

If you really love fruit, mix in additional selections, such as blueberries, raspberries, sliced peaches, apricots or nectarines. Or serve a small portion as a sweet breakfast-cereal dish to accompany Broccoli and Cheese Frittata (page 237).

VARIATION:

Arborio is a short-grain Italian rice that is very creamy when cooked. Although the results will be somewhat different, you may substitute long-grain rice. The cooking time will be the same for long-grain white rice; it will increase to about 45 minutes for brown. (If the rice is not tender by the time all the liquid has been absorbed, add a little more juice or water and continue cooking.)

NUTRITION AT A GLANCE

PER SERVING:

Calories	276
Fat	3 g. (10% of cal.)
Sat. fat	1.3 g. (3% of cal.)
Cholesterol	3 mg.
Sodium	72 mg.

SUNSHINE FRUITS WITH APRICOT SAUCE

This refreshing dessert has an impressive amount of fiber, thanks to the different types of fruit used. Further, the full-day's supply of vitamin C a single serving provides will help enhance the absorption of iron from other foods eaten at the same meal.

SUNSHINE FRUITS WITH APRICOT SAUCE

APRICOT SAUCE

- **1 cup fresh apricot halves**
- **¼ cup nonfat apricot yogurt**
- **1–2 tablespoons honey or other sweetener**
- **¼ teaspoon almond extract**
- **2 teaspoons unflavored gelatin**
- **1 tablespoon orange-juice concentrate**
- **1 ice cube**

FRUIT

- **1 pint strawberries, halved, quartered or sliced**
- **2 kiwifruit, peeled, halved lengthwise and thinly sliced**
- **1 large navel orange, sectioned**
- **1 teaspoon grated orange rind**
- **1 banana**
- **2 tablespoons toasted slivered almonds**
- **Julienned orange rind**

1. *To make the apricot sauce:* In a blender, combine the apricots, yogurt, honey or other sweetener and almond extract. Process until smooth.

2. In a custard cup, sprinkle the gelatin over the orange-juice concentrate. Let stand to soften. Warm by microwaving for a few seconds or by standing the cup in warm water. Add to the blender, along with the ice cube.

3. Process on high speed until the ice cube is well-blended and the sauce has a smooth, fluffy consistency. Transfer to a bowl and refrigerate at least 30 minutes before serving.

4. *To make the fruit:* In a large bowl, combine the strawberries, kiwifruit, oranges and grated rind. Refrigerate until needed. Just before serving, slice and stir in the bananas.

5. To serve, divide the fruit among parfait glasses or decorative bowls. Top with the sauce. Sprinkle with the almonds and julienned rind.

SERVES 6.

Preparation Time: 20 min. + standing time

CHEF'S NOTES

■ ■ ■ ■ ■ ■ ■ ■ ■

DO FIRST:
Toast the almonds at 350° for 8 minutes, stirring often to prevent burning.

■

INGREDIENTS NOTE:
If fresh apricots are not available, use 1 can (16 ounces) packed in juice or water. Drain well.

■

VARIATIONS:
Make the sauce from peaches or cantaloupe. Serve with grapes, raspberries, fresh figs, chopped melons, sliced nectarines or other fruit.

■

NUTRI-NOTE:
Apricots are a storehouse of beta-carotene, the plant form of vitamin A. Three raw apricots provide half the RDA of 5,000 I.U.

NUTRITION AT A GLANCE ▬▬

PER SERVING:
Calories 110
Fat . . . . . . .1.8 g. (15% of cal.)
Sat. fat . . . . .0.2 g. (2% of cal.)
Cholesterol . . . . .0 mg.
Sodium . . . . .11 mg.

FRUIT-FILLED MERINGUE BASKETS

Here's a dessert that actually promotes weight loss. These elegant little baskets are very low in calories and virtually devoid of fat, cholesterol and sodium. What's more, the fruit filling has them brimming with vitamin C. So serve them in good conscience.

Desserts

FRUIT-FILLED MERINGUE BASKETS

- **2 egg whites, at room temperature**
- **½ teaspoon lemon juice**
- **2 tablespoons maple syrup**
- **⅛ teaspoon cream of tartar**
- **3 cups chopped or sliced peaches**
- **3 cups sliced raspberries**

1. Preheat the oven to 275°.

2. Line a cookie sheet with parchment or brown paper and draw 4 (3″) circles on it with a light pencil.

3. In a medium bowl beat the egg whites with an electric mixer until bubbly. Add the lemon juice, syrup and cream of tartar. Beat on high speed until stiff and glossy, about 3 to 5 minutes. Do not beat until dry.

4. Spoon meringue into a pastry bag fitted with a ¼″ plain or star tip.

5. To make baskets, pipe out meringue onto parchment following the outline of each circle. Do not fill in the middle of the circle, but build up the sides with at least 5 tiers of meringue.

6. Bake the baskets on the middle oven rack until just lightly browned, about 8 to 10 minutes. Turn off the oven and leave baskets in for about an hour with the door closed. Use at once or store in a very tightly covered container for up to a day.

7. If desired, puree 1 cup of the peaches or raspberries to make a sauce.

8. To serve, set each basket on a dessert plate, spoon in fruit and top with sauce.

SERVES 4.

Preparation Time: 15 min. + standing time
Cooking Time: 10 min.

CHEF'S NOTES

■ ■ ■ ■ ■ ■ ■ ■ ■

DO FIRST:
Remove the egg whites from the refrigerator ahead of time. Eggs are easier to separate when cold, but whites achieve more volume when they're beaten while at room temperature.

■

VARIATIONS:
Fill with other fruit, such as strawberries and blueberries, or use low-fat mousse or frozen yogurt. An alternate way to form meringues is to spoon 4 mounds onto the parchment. Use the back of a spoon to create hollowed-out baskets.

■

KITCHEN TRICK:
Don't make meringues when the weather is very humid; they will absorb moisture from the air and become soft in short order.

NUTRITION AT A GLANCE

PER SERVING:
Calories 112
Fat . . . . .0.5 g. (4% of cal.)
Sat. fat . . . . .0 g.
Cholesterol . . . . .0 mg.
Sodium . . . . .36 mg.

HEALTHY COOKING HINTS

PLAY IT SAFE!

■ ■ ■ ■ ■ ■ ■ ■ ■ ■ ■ ■   ■ ■ ■ ■ ■

You try to eat right. You make smart food choices and use cooking methods that will maximize nutrients. But are you really doing everything you can to safeguard your family's health?

Food poisoning is more common than you might think. (Some estimates say over four million people a year are affected.) The symptoms can range from mild to quite serious, but in many cases the problem could have been avoided entirely by using common sense when buying, preparing and storing foods.

Just remember that meat, poultry, eggs and other foods do not have to smell bad or look spoiled to make you ill. All food harbors bacteria that are potentially harmful. So mishandling food at any point can put you at risk. Here are some ways to minimize the risk.

SHOP RIGHT

■ When shopping, get meat, poultry, fish and other refrigerated or frozen items last so they stay cold. Buy foods labeled "keep refrigerated" only if they are stored in a refrigerated case and are cold to the touch.

■ Keep raw meat and poultry products separate from other foods, both in your grocery cart and in carry-home bags. That means bagging the meat and poultry in their own sack — preferably plastic — so any bacteria-laden juices can't leak onto other foods that may be eaten raw.

■ If you have a long drive, put all perishables in a cooler. And in hot weather, keep the cooler in the passenger compartment of the car; it's not as hot as the trunk. Go directly home — don't stop for other errands.

■ For home storage, make sure raw meat and poultry are wrapped securely so they can't contaminate other foods or surfaces. Use plastic bags over commercial packaging or place the items on plates to contain raw juices. Freeze raw meat or poultry that you know you won't be using within a day or two.

■ To keep foods cold, make sure your refrigerator registers 40° or lower and your freezer 0° or lower. Use a refrigerator thermometer to monitor the temperatures in both areas. Cold won't kill all harmful bacteria, but it will keep many of them from multiplying.

■ Refrigerate eggs in their original carton. Don't wash them; they contain a natural film that protects against spoilage. Discard any with cracked shells — they may be contaminated with salmonella bacteria. Use fresh eggs within five weeks of purchase. And never keep eggs out of the refrigerator for more than 2 hours.

■ Store highly perishable foods, such as milk, in the main part of the refrigerator. The door does not stay as cold as the rest of the refrigerator. Use the door for condiments such as ketchup, mustard and mayonnaise, which are much more stable.

■ Make sure the arrangement of items in your refrigerator and freezer allows the cold air to circulate freely.

■ Don't store food under the sink. If cleaning products are also stored there, they could leak and soak through cardboard boxes or bags. Also, leaking pipes could rust cans and damage boxes. And openings in the walls for pipes could give pests easy access to the area.

COUNTER MEASURES

■ Proper handling at the time of food preparation is crucial. Make sure everything that touches the food — from your hands to the kitchen counter — is scrupulously clean. Start by washing your hands with soap and warm water for at least 20 seconds before beginning food preparation. And always scrub your hands thoroughly after handling raw chicken or meat. If you don't, bacteria on your hands could be transferred to foods that won't be cooked.

■ If you have a cut or skin infection, wear rubber or plastic gloves.

■ To reduce the risk of salmonella, rinse chicken thoroughly with cold water before cooking. Pat it dry with paper towels.

■ Rinse all produce thoroughly. Use a vegetable brush to vigorously scrub potatoes, carrots, turnips, beets and other vegetables that grow underground. ▲

■ Have at least two cutting boards to reduce the chances of bacterial cross contamination. Use one for foods that will be eaten raw, such as bread, fruits, vegetables, salad materials and already cooked meat, poultry and seafood. Have another that you reserve for raw meat, chicken, other poultry items and fish. ▼

■ To clean cutting boards used for raw meat, fish and poultry, wash them in very hot, soapy water. Every few days, douse them with a solution of 1 part bleach to 8 parts water. And occasionally scrub the entire surface with a wire brush.

■ Use paper towels to clean anything that comes into contact with raw poultry, meat or fish. Sponges and cloth towels are difficult to sterilize, and you may be tempted to reuse them on other surfaces before you launder them.

NOW YOU'RE COOKING

■ Most food-borne illness is caused by bacteria that multiply rapidly at temperatures between 60° and 125°. To control any bacteria that may be present, keep hot foods *hot*—at 140° or above. Likewise, keep cold foods, such as chicken salad, at 40° or below. These guidelines are particularly important for parties or picnics, where food might be on the table longer than usual.

■ Cook meat and poultry thoroughly. Use a meat thermometer to make sure meat reaches an internal temperature of 160° and poultry 180°. And always finish cooking food in a single step. In other words, don't partially cook dishes and set them aside to be finished later.

■ Don't roast meat or poultry at temperatures lower than 325°. Although slow cooking can produce a juicy turkey, the low temperature may not be sufficient to kill bacteria. And if the turkey contains stuffing, the center portions may not get hot enough to be safe.

■ Never stuff poultry ahead of time; bacteria can multiply readily in the stuffing. Refrigerate the bird and stuffing separately until just before cooking. Then be sure not to pack the stuffing too tightly into the cavity, so it can heat through properly. After dinner, separate leftover stuffing from the meat and store it in its own container.

■ To thaw meat and poultry safely, defrost it in the refrigerator, not on the kitchen counter. Bacteria multiply rapidly at room temperature. Place the food on a plate to catch any drippings as it thaws. If any raw meat juices do spill in the refrigerator, thoroughly wipe them up.

■ If you're in a hurry to thaw something, place it in a plastic bag immersed in a pan of *cold* water. Change the water every half hour. And cook the meat as soon as it's pliable.

DEALING WITH LEFTOVERS

■ Never leave perishable food out for more than 2 hours. Then refrigerate it properly. The faster foods are cooled, the less time there is for bacteria to grow. So store leftovers in small portions in shallow containers.

■ If you need to store a large amount of very hot food, like a big pot of soup or stew, partially submerge the pot in a sink full of ice water. Stir it for several minutes until it stops steaming. Then transfer to small containers and refrigerate them.

■ Thoroughly reheat leftovers. Cover them to retain moisture and to guarantee that heat will be distributed evenly throughout the food. Bring gravies and soups—which are particularly susceptible to bacterial growth—to a rolling boil before serving.

HEALTHY MICROWAVE COOKING

■ ■ ■ ■ ■ ■ ■ ■ ■ ■ ■ ■   ■

The microwave is more than a handy appliance for reheating pizza in a flash or boiling water right in your teacup. It's an essential part of the healthy cook's kitchen — giving new meaning to the concept of "fast food." With a microwave, you can take shortcuts galore and still dish out delicious, low-fat meals any day of the week.

Foods cook so quickly that their natural moisture doesn't evaporate. And because there's no dry heat involved, foods just don't stick to the pan. That means you can really slash — or totally eliminate — added fat in all sorts of recipes.

Valuable nutrients that might be destroyed by heat during boiling, baking or long simmering are retained. So are the savory flavors and textures of fresh foods, so you don't need to jazz them up with salty or fatty sauces. And nutrient-dense vegetables, such as winter squash and potatoes, cook so quickly that you can serve them often.

Just remember that microwaving is different from other cooking methods. Here's how to use this appliance to its best advantage.

THE NEW WAVE

■ Although microwaves do not directly heat cookware, heat building up in food can be transferred to the dish. So containers can become *very hot*. Always use pot holders when removing dishes from the microwave.

■ If you have a microwave with a built-in carousel (preferably one you can remove or turn off when necessary), you will be able to cut down on some — but not all — of the stirring, rotating and rearranging needed for even cooking.

■ Microwaving goes so fast that small variations in many factors can affect cooking time. Things to consider:
1. *Starting temperature.* The colder the food, the more time it will require.
2. *Amount.* A large quantity of food takes longer than a small amount.
3. *Density.* Porous foods, such as bread, heat more quickly than dense foods of the same size.
4. *Composition.* Fat and sugar attract microwaves. Fatty ground beef will cook faster than extra lean; foods high in sugar will heat quickly.
5. *Size.* Small, uniform pieces and round shapes cook more quickly and evenly than assorted or irregular ones.
6. *Placement.* Where food is placed affects how evenly it cooks. Stirring or rearranging is often necessary.

■ Standing time is crucial to success. Foods continue to cook after they're out of the microwave, so you'll need to remove them a little before they're "done." Whole potatoes, for example, should have a small uncooked area in the center; after standing 5 minutes, they'll be ready.

■ Remove meat from the microwave before it's quite reached the standard internal temperature. Cover it to hold in the heat, then let it stand until the temperature rises. Use a probe or meat thermometer. Check in several places, avoiding fat and bone.

■ With poultry, covering the meat and letting it stand are extra important. They allow heat to be distributed evenly so that harmful bacteria, such as salmonella, on the surface can be killed. Cool spots in the microwave might otherwise leave them untouched.

THE MICRO KITCHEN

■ Suitable dishes for microwaving include heat-resistant glass, oven-tempered glass, glass-ceramic cookware, clay pots and clay cookers. Pottery, porcelain, fine china and stoneware are usually good if they don't have a metallic glaze or trim. Oven cooking bags are fine; always use the plastic ties that come with them, not twist ties containing metal. Paper plates, towels and napkins are okay for short-term cooking and reheating. Wood and straw products without metal staples, joints or handles are usable for reheating.

■ If you are unsure whether a container is safe for the microwave, try the following test: Fill a glass measure with 1 cup of tap water. Place it and the dish you wish to test in the microwave (with space between them). Microwave on high for 1 minute. If the dish remains cool, it is safe for microwaving. If it is hot or even slightly warm, do not use it.

■ When purchasing cookware, make sure the dish will fit the cavity. If you have a built-in turntable, be sure the dish can rotate without hitting the walls. Rectangular dishes fit best when they have rounded corners.

■ Covering food promotes steam for even cooking and shortens the cooking time. Casseroles, vegetables, poultry, meat and seafood are often covered. Suitable are microwave-casserole lids, plates, plastic wrap (fold back a corner for steam to escape), wax paper, parchment and most paper towels. Use the paper products when doing food that might turn soggy, such as sandwiches.

SAFETY FIRST

■ Do not use newspapers, brown grocery bags or *recycled* paper towels. All may contain metal fragments that could spark a fire.

■ Never turn on an empty microwave. Running a microwave with nothing in it may damage the unit.

■ Don't use the microwave if anything is caught in the door, if the door doesn't close firmly or if the door is in any way damaged. If your door has a soft mesh gasket, check it periodically for deterioration.

■ Never use a microwave that has been damaged. And don't use one that has had a fire — get it checked by a qualified service center.

■ Don't do home canning in the microwave. Food must be conventionally heated or pressure canned to a specified temperature throughout to avoid botulism. And never deep-fry in the microwave; it's dangerous.

■ To clean your microwave, wipe the interior with a damp sponge. For baked-on particles, bring a cup of water to a boil; it'll create steam that will soften the spots. Don't use scouring powder, steel wool or other abrasives unless they're marked "microwave-safe."

■ If odors cling to your microwave, wipe it out with a solution of baking soda and water. Never use products containing ammonia — the odor might linger and get into food. Don't use oven cleaners not designed specifically for microwaves.

FOR KIDS' SAKE

■ Keep the microwave *out of reach* until children are old enough to use it without supervision — they should have sufficient motor skills to handle foods in the microwave and be able to read and follow directions.

■ On those occasions when you do let young children use the microwave under your supervision, limit them to small tasks, such as pushing a button or closing the door.

■ When children are old enough to use the microwave alone, place it within easy reach — on a low counter or a cart — to simplify the task of placing food in the appliance, to allow safe removal of hot food and to lessen the chances of accidentally pushing the wrong buttons.

■ Take the time to teach children how to cook their favorite meals and snacks. Show them how to pierce foods that have a membrane or skin, such as hot dogs and potatoes. Remind them never to cook an egg in its shell — it may explode. Tell them to stir or turn foods *slowly,* with the proper utensils, to avoid splashing themselves with hot liquids.

■ Have children use pot holders. Teach them that although the inside of the microwave remains cool, dishes and other cooking containers can be hot and the food inside even hotter. Also warn them that foods may heat unevenly. Foods that are cool on the surface may be very hot inside. That's a particular danger with jelly doughnuts, for example.

■ Show kids how to uncover dishes in a safe way — *away* from their faces — and show them how to open popcorn bags safely so steam can escape and they don't get burns.

FOLLOW A PATTERN

Exactly how you position food in the microwave affects how evenly it cooks. Food at the edges of containers cooks faster than food in the center, for instance. And food that is irregular in shape absorbs microwaves in an uneven pattern, increasing the odds that some portions will be overcooked while others remain raw or underdone. Here are ways to ensure that foods cook uniformly:

■ If doing one potato, muffin, mug of beverage or other individual item, position it in the very center of the microwave. Place two items side by side, with about 1″ between them. Do three in a triangle pattern; four in a square and five or more in a circle. If cooking more than eight such items, do them in batches.

■ If cooking cut pieces, take care to make them all the same size and shape. That applies to fruits and vegetables as well as meat, poultry and seafood. If preparing whole pieces, such as chicken legs, chops or baking potatoes, try to choose pieces that are about the same size and basic shape.

■ Arrange cut foods or small items in an even layer. And stir them often during microwaving to bring the pieces from the center or bottom to the sides and top. Cover the container to help build steam, which contributes to even cooking.

■ With whole vegetables that have both tender and dense areas, such as asparagus and broccoli spears, arrange the food in a spoke fashion with the tender tips at the center of the dish.

The stalks will receive the brunt of the microwaves, allowing them to cook through. The tips will receive a little less exposure so they won't be overdone.

■ Rotate the dish a half or quarter turn several times during cooking to help compensate for any unevenness in the way the microwaves are distributed. Rotation is essential for foods that cannot be stirred or otherwise rearranged, such as lasagna or cake.

■ Position fish steaks, such as salmon, with the thin ends facing inward. Place shelled shrimp around the edge of a large plate, with the tail ends facing inward. (If you don't want them to curl, skewer each straight with a toothpick.) With clams and oysters, position them in a circle at the edge of a plate with their opening edges facing the center.

■ When cooking fish fillets, boneless chicken breasts or other foods that taper at one end, turn the thin portion underneath so the whole piece is a consistent thickness. It will cook more evenly.

THE MEAT OF THE MATTER

■ Bone shields meat from microwaves, preventing meat from cooking properly. Always position the bony parts of chops, chicken legs and such toward the center of the dish. Keep the meatiest parts facing outward, where they'll get the most exposure to microwaves. Rotate and rearrange the pieces during cooking.

■ Large pieces of meat should be turned frequently. Covering them with

wax paper or preparing them in an oven cooking bag helps to hold in heat and moisture, facilitating more even cooking.

■ When cooking large cuts of meat or poultry, use a medium setting (50% power). The on/off cycling of power that occurs with a lower power setting gives heat time to penetrate the food without overcooking it.

■ When grilling, broiling or pan-frying burgers, make extras for later meals. Then cool and freeze. To serve, microwave until completely heated through.

■ Drain excess fat from ground meat by cooking it in a microwave-safe colander set over a bowl. Stir often as the meat cooks to break it up. Fat will drain into the bowl for easy removal. After cooking, spread the meat on several layers of paper towels to soak up any remaining fat.

■ For a quick chicken stock, combine 1 pound of chicken bones, cut into 2″ pieces, and 2 cups water in a 2-quart casserole. Add minced onions, celery or parsley. Cover and cook on high for 12 minutes. Strain, chill and remove congealed fat.

BE EXTRA CAREFUL

■ When microwaving whole foods that have a peel or membrane — such as potatoes, squash, eggplant, apples, pears, sausages or beets — prick them all over to allow steam to escape. Otherwise the foods might explode.

■ Do not, under any circumstances, microwave eggs in their shell — they will explode. If cooking whole egg yolks, such as for poached eggs or sunny-side-up eggs, pierce them with a pick.

■ If cooking a mixture of fruits or vegetables, try to choose those that are similar in texture. Do root vegetables together, for instance. Or cook a compote of apples, pears and quinces.

■ When making stir-fries or other dishes that call for vegetables or fruits of different textures, add them in stages. Start with the denser varieties, such as carrots and broccoli. As they start to soften, add the more tender ones, like snow peas and peppers. Finish with the most fragile items, such as shredded greens.

■ Use ring-shaped pans for meat loaves, cakes and casseroles that can't be stirred. If you don't have a commercial microwave-safe ring pan, make your own: Place an upside-down custard cup in the center of a round baking dish.

■ Foods tend to cook most evenly if they're at room temperature before microwaving. If you don't want to let fish, poultry or meat stand out of the refrigerator for any extended time, especially in summer, use the microwave to take the chill off them. Use low power (10%) for a minute or two. Then proceed with your recipe.

VEGETABLE BASICS

■ To retain the most flavor and nutrients, cook vegetables only until bright in color and crisp-tender. Cook dense vegetables such as potatoes, sweet potatoes and winter squash until they give slightly when pressed.

Allow to stand for a few minutes to finish cooking.

■ An easy way to blanch vegetables for crudité platters: Slightly undercook them in the microwave. Let stand, covered, for 1 minute, then plunge them into ice water to stop the cooking. Dry with paper towels.

■ Here's a quick, one-dish way to make mashed potatoes. Peel and cube the potatoes and place in a cook-and-serve casserole dish. Add a small amount of water. Cover tightly and microwave on high until soft. Mash right in the dish using a potato masher, add a little buttermilk or low-fat milk and season with pepper or herbs and butter-flavored sprinkles.

■ When you want to peel fresh tomatoes for soups and sauces, microwave them on full power for approximately 1 minute (adjust this time according to size and ripeness).

■ To quickly and effortlessly remove the skin from a fresh pepper, microwave it on full power for 3 minutes, turning the pepper three times. Then wrap it loosely and place it in the freezer until cool.

■ The tough outer skins of winter squash will be easier to cut if you microwave the whole vegetable for 1 to 2 minutes on high. Let stand another 1 to 2 minutes before slicing.

BAKING TIPS

■ Here's a time-saving way to check whether your yeast is alive before baking bread: Mix the yeast with the recipe's sweetener, the liquid and ¼ cup of the recipe's flour. Cover and

microwave on the lowest power (10%) for 1 minute. If the yeast becomes bubbly, it's okay to use.

■ To reduce the time needed to make yeast breads, let them rise in the microwave. Place 3 cups hot tap water in a 4-cup glass measure. Microwave on high until the water boils. Add the bowl containing your dough. Cover with a plate and microwave on the lowest setting (10% power) for 5 minutes. Let stand for 5 minutes. Repeat once or twice, until the dough has doubled in bulk. Punch down the dough, form it into a loaf, place in a glass pan and repeat the procedure until the dough has again doubled.

■ When making muffins, remember that they'll need a few minutes of standing time to finish cooking outside the microwave. To keep the bottoms from turning soggy, unmold the muffins and place on a wire rack during this time. To make unmolding easier, line the muffin pan with cupcake papers.

■ To recapture the just-baked moistness and soft texture of muffins or quick breads, reheat them in the microwave. Wrap a muffin or a slice of bread in a dampened microwave-safe paper towel, then microwave on high for 15 to 35 seconds. Do two pieces on high for 30 to 60 seconds.

■ Reheat rolls in a dry paper towel to absorb moisture that would make the rolls soggy. One roll takes about 10 seconds on high. Overheating will toughen the bread.

■ To soften honey that's too firm to pour, microwave it in its glass or plastic container until liquefied, about 30 seconds for a half-cup.

TIPS FOR THE BERRY RICH

■ ■ ■ ■ ■ ■ ■ ■ ■ ■ ■ ■　　■ ■ ■ ■

There are few foods more elegantly simple — and simply elegant — than fresh berries. They're the very condensation of summer's sweetness — any time of the year. But berries offer more than eye appeal and palate-pleasing goodness. They have an abundance of nutrients, including potassium for healthy blood pressure, vitamin A for cancer protection and vitamin C for immunity to many diseases.

Berries are also full of fiber, especially the soluble form, called pectin, that helps lower cholesterol. Those fruits with lots of seeds, such as raspberries and blackberries, are very high in insoluble fiber for excellent digestive health.

These fruits are low in sodium — and they don't need salt to enhance their flavors. And berries are so low in calories that you can eat them by the cupful as part of a weight-controlling diet.

MAKING GOOD BUYS

■ Trust your eyes and sense of smell to locate the most succulent berries. Look for firm, plump, brightly colored fruit that is uniform in size. If possible, smell the berries and choose only those with a heady fragrance. Many great-looking berries have little flavor; fragrance is a clue to taste.

■ Try to peek beyond the top layer to see if berries below show signs of mold, softness or bruises. Avoid any boxes with juice stains on the bottom; that indicates crushed fruit within.

■ Whenever possible, buy local berries in season. Although many berries are available year-round, their quality is often poor, and they're very expensive. A better approach is to buy extra in season and freeze the excess.

■ If you can't locate the berries you want in a supermarket, check your local newspaper for nearby berry farms. Gooseberries and fresh currants, for example, rarely see the inside of a supermarket but are available to those willing to go out of their way a little. Even large cities often have picking areas within a few hours' drive.

■ In general, 1 pound of fresh berries equals about 4 cups or 1 quart. And 1 pint equals about 2 cups.

KEEPING AND FREEZING

■ To keep berries in peak condition, remove the fruit from its carton as soon as you get it home. Look closely for any mold or bruising.

■ If your berries are organically grown, you needn't wash them unless they show signs of dirt. Otherwise, just before using, rinse the berries lightly. Use cold — even iced — water. Warm water may soften fruit. Gently pat the berries dry.

■ Line a large platter or baking sheet with a dish towel or paper towels. Add the berries in a single layer. If you aren't going to use them within a few hours, cover lightly with plastic wrap and refrigerate.

■ Never soak berries — they'll disintegrate or become waterlogged, and water-soluble vitamins, such as C, will be lost.

■ If you can't use very ripe or fragile berries within 2 days, puree them into a sauce.

■ Choose fruit for freezing that is at its peak. Freezing softens fruit, so berries that are already soft will turn to mush as they thaw.

■ To freeze fruit for easy retrieval, line a baking sheet with wax paper. Spread the berries in a single layer and freeze for several hours. Transfer to plastic containers or freezer bags. The pieces will remain separate.

■ An alternate freezing method is to lightly sweeten whole or sliced berries, then pack into pint containers. You'll need to thaw the whole container when ready to use.

■ Thaw solid-pack fruit in the refrigerator in its sealed container. Thaw loose-pack berries as needed. For best texture, eat while still icy.

■ You may also thaw fruit in the microwave. Use medium power and very short times. Check the berries often to keep from thawing them too far or cooking them.

BERRIES AT THEIR BEST

Here's a basketful of berries — all exceptional taste treats. Some are old favorites; others are a rare find but available to those lucky enough to live where they're plentiful. All are simply the best.

BERRY	DESCRIPTION
Blackberries	Purplish black; the largest of the wild berries. Look for berries without hulls (which would indicate immaturity and tartness). Available May through August. Very high in fiber.
Blueberries	Deep blue. Should be plump, well-rounded, firm and covered with a silvery frost that indicates freshness.
Boysenberries	Purplish black to purple-red with sweet-tart flavor; resemble large raspberries. A hybrid cross of raspberries, blackberries and loganberries.
Cranberries	Shiny scarlet; very tart and are best combined with other fruits. Available most of winter, packaged in plastic bags. Discard discolored or shriveled berries. Can be eaten raw, but best cooked.
Currants	Black, red or white; related to gooseberries. Red and white berries are good for out-of-hand eating; black ones generally used for preserves. Choose plump berries without hulls. Store up to four days. Don't confuse with the tiny dried raisins also known as (Zante) currants.
Elderberries	Purple-black; tart fruit most often used cooked, as in jams and pies.
Fraises des bois/ Alpine strawberries	Red; tiny wild strawberries from Europe that can be grown in home gardens. Use as you would regular strawberries.
Gooseberries	Green, white, yellow or red; tart berries the size of large currants. May be smooth or fuzzy. Choose ones that are fairly firm and evenly colored. Green berries must be cooked. Often available canned.
Huckleberries	Blue-black; resemble blueberries with thicker skins, less sweet flavor and larger seeds. Good raw or cooked.
Lingonberries	Red; tiny, tart, related to cranberries. Grow in the wild, notably in Maine. Also available as preserves.
Loganberries	Purple-red; a cross between red raspberries and blackberries. Juicy, sweetly tart. Best for jams and jellies.
Mulberries	Black or red; resemble blackberries. Sweet-sour flavor. Grow wild. Eat raw or in jams and jellies.
Raspberries	Black, red or golden. Choose brightly colored berries without hulls. Very fragile. Check carefully for signs of bruising or mold. Very high in fiber.
Strawberries	Red, juicy and cone-shaped. Come in large and small sizes, with the small often being sweeter. Choose brightly colored berries with their caps attached. Remove caps just before using. Avoid berries with white shoulders or tips.

A TASTE OF THE TROPICS

■ ■ ■ ■ ■ ■ ■ ■ ■ ■ ■ ■

When every calorie has to count, indulge yourself with tropical fruits. These ambrosial delights often have luscious, creamy textures that seem rich and fattening, but most are really quite low in fat and calories. Further, they tend to be high in cancer-preventing vitamins A and C, with potassium for stroke protection and fiber for healthy digestion.

Below are some of the tropics' finest offerings.

■ When you get tropical fruits home from the market, treat them kindly. Remember that they grew in a warm environment, not one the temperature of your refrigerator. A good rule of thumb is to keep them on the kitchen counter until they're perfectly ripe.

■ Because many tropicals must travel a great distance, they're often picked a little green. To speed the ripening process, place the fruit in a paper bag. Check daily. Most fruits should become soft (but not mushy) to the touch, with a characteristic aroma.

■ Eat these fruits out-of-hand. Or enjoy a tropical slush: Peel, slice and freeze individual fruits. Then let them thaw slightly and puree in a food processor or blender until smooth. Mamey, papaya, mango, kiwi, pineapple and banana work well.

■ Mix tropical fruits into chicken, turkey, tuna, shrimp, crab and pasta salads. Or lightly sauté or grill along with cutlets, stir-fries and kabobs.

■ **Avocados** owe their silken, buttery texture to heart-healthy monounsaturated fat. Let ripen until the skin yields to gentle pressure.

■ **Bananas** also have a luscious creamy texture but without any fat. They're high in potassium and magnesium for healthy blood pressure. And they have a nice helping of fiber. Seek out red, black and other types. Ripen at room temperature.

■ **Citrus fruits** encompass everything from oranges, lemons and limes to grapefruit, ugli fruit and kumquats. They're great sources of vitamin C, which helps boost immunity and heal wounds. And they contain cholesterol-lowering pectin. Those with colored flesh, such as pink grapefruit, also have some cancer-fighting beta-carotene.

■ **Guavas** are packed with vitamin C — almost three times the RDA in a single fruit. And they're high in fiber. Guavas range from round to pear shape and from pale yellow to purple-black. Ripe fruit will give slightly when squeezed, releasing a rose-like aroma. Serve plain, add to compotes or puree as a sauce for chicken.

■ **Kiwifruit** are wonderfully low in calories, fat and sodium. They're also high in fiber, vitamin C and potassium. Kiwis are ripe when they yield to gentle pressure. Peel off the fuzzy brown skin and slice the fruit.

■ **Mamey** (or mamey sapote) is a football-sized fruit with creamy flamingo-colored flesh. Though rock-hard when picked, the fruit softens to a silky smoothness and yields to gentle pressure. Eat straight from the shell or puree into thick shakes.

■ **Mangoes** are low in calories with plenty of beta-carotene, vitamin C, fiber, potassium and even some vitamin E. Let ripen at room temperature until streaked with brighter color and slightly soft.

■ **Papaya** overflows with vitamins A and C and even has a portion of bone-building calcium. Buy papayas when they're predominantly yellow and slightly soft. Peel and halve, then scoop out the seeds.

■ **Passionfruit** is loaded with fiber, thanks to its abundance of edible seeds. The purple type is deeply wrinkled when ripe. Cut the fruit in half and scoop out the pulp.

■ **Pineapple** has more going for it than vitamin C, fiber, potassium, low calories and little fat. It also contains an enzyme that aids digestion.

■ **Sapotes** come in several varieties. The white has thin skin that can range from bright green to canary yellow; it's got smooth flesh and several seeds. Eat when soft as a ripe plum. Black sapotes resemble fat green tomatoes and have creamy, fudge-like flesh; serve when the skin is somewhat blackened.

■ **Starfruit** gets its name from its star-shaped cross sections. Also known as carambolas, the fruits are golden and the size of an egg or longer. An overall golden orange color and browning along the edges indicate ripeness.

A TROPICAL FRUIT BASKET

1 PASSIONFRUIT
Sweet and sour

2 LIME
Tangy

3 STARFRUIT
Flavor ranges from sweet to tangy, depending on variety

4 KIWIFRUIT
A melange of banana, peach and strawberry flavors

5 PINEAPPLE
Juicy with sweet-tart flavor

6 AVOCADO
Delicate nutty flavor and buttery texture

7 MAMEY
A blend of avocado, sweet potato and honey tastes

15 MANGO
Sweet papaya-peach flavor

14 TANGERINE
Sweet and juicy

13 LEMON
Juicy and acidic

12 RED BANANA
A little sweeter than yellow bananas

11 GRAPEFRUIT
Tart, with the pink and red varieties being a little sweeter

10 GUAVA
Flavor depends on variety, such as pineapple, strawberry, lemon

9 PAPAYA
Flavor reminiscent of peaches and berries

8 SAPOTE
Mild sweet flavor with overtones such as lemon, mango, vanilla

ALL ABOUT THE HEALTHFUL HERBS

■ ■ ■ ■ ■ ■ ■ ■ ■ ■ ■ ■ ■

Herbs play a pivotal role in the healthy kitchen. They're absolutely essential for bringing out the best flavors in low-fat, low-salt recipes.

They can even be an unexpected source of vitamins and minerals. Fresh parsley, for example, contains vitamin A, vitamin C, calcium, iron and potassium. Other herbs are also surprisingly decent sources of nutrients.

Granted, most people don't use herbs in large enough quantities to take advantage of this nutritional bonus. But you can look for ways to significantly increase your use of herbs — especially fresh ones. If herb cookery is new to you, start with modest amounts. As you come to enjoy these bold flavors, be more generous. Throw handfuls of parsley, basil, dill or coriander, for instance, into salads, stir-fries, quiches and pasta dishes.

make sure there's not too much condensation in the bag. ▼

KEEP 'EM FRESH

To use herbs to their best advantage, handle and store them properly. Dried herbs retain essential oils that convey their characteristic aromas and flavors. These values diminish with time, so purchase dried herbs in small amounts as needed.

■ Mark the date on jars as soon as you bring them home. Then store them in a cool, dry place away from direct sunlight and moisture. If you use a spice rack, hang it away from the stove and the kitchen sink.

■ Properly stored, dried herbs keep their flavor for about a year. To tell if an herb is still at its prime, use your nose. If you can smell its aroma as soon as you open the container, it's good. If you have to sniff, it is old.

■ Never shake herbs from the jar into a hot pot. Moisture can get into

the jar, causing the herbs to stick together and possibly become moldy.

■ Storing fresh herbs is another matter entirely. Wrap them in a damp paper towel, then in plastic and refrigerate. They'll keep a week. ▼

■ An alternate method is to store herbs bouquet-style. Place stems in a glass containing half an inch of water. Tent the leaves with a plastic bag and refrigerate. Check daily to

A POTPOURRI OF HINTS

■ Chew on parsley sprigs after eating garlic or other strong foods to freshen your breath.

■ One way to preserve the flavor of fresh herbs is to blend them with heart-healthy olive or canola oil. Among the herbs that do particularly well: basil, tarragon, rosemary and sage. Blending in some crushed vitamin C may help keep the leaves green and prevent them from losing their flavors. (Try 250 mg. with ¼ cup oil and ½ pound herbs.)

■ Toss garlicky chive flowers or peppery nasturtium blooms into salads for color and flavor. Use other herb flowers in the same way.

■ Steaming is a particularly healthy way of cooking fish and vegetables. Give them fat-free zip by laying branches of herbs across the food as it cooks. Best bets: dill, rosemary, and tarragon.

■ Microwaving—which preserves vitamins in produce—also retains much more of herbs' natural flavors, so you need less. Reduce the amount of fresh herbs by one-third and dried herbs by one-half.

■ To get the most flavor when roasting meat or poultry, rub its surface well with seasoning before cooking. If preparing poultry with the skin on, loosen the skin and rub the herbs into the flesh underneath. The poultry will absorb the flavors better, and you can then discard the fatty skin before eating without losing the herb taste. ▼

■ Lighten up your tomato sandwiches. Use whole basil leaves in place of or in addition to lettuce. With their full flavor you won't need fatty mayo.

■ When cooking with bay leaves, be sure to remove them before serving. They never soften to the point where you can chew them properly, so you might choke on a piece if you try to eat it.

■ Use mint in pea soup. It not only enriches the flavor but counteracts the tendency of peas to produce gas.

HOW MUCH?

Although most people prefer the flavor of fresh herbs, sometimes the dried form is all that's available. A general rule is to use one-third to one-fifth as much dried herbs as fresh.

If you're unsure how you'll like a particular herb, sample it before you season an entire dish. Remove a small amount of the dish you are preparing and season it proportionately. If this is not possible, mix a little bit of the herb with some cottage cheese. Let it stand at room temperature several minutes before tasting.

If you find you've overseasoned a dish, add a whole peeled raw potato to the dish to absorb some of the flavor. Remove the potato just before serving.

TRADITIONAL KITCHEN MATCH-UPS

While it's true that most herbs go with most foods, there are some pairings that are especially successful, such as these:

Dried beans: cumin, sage, thyme
Cabbage: caraway, dill
Carrots: basil, cumin, mint
Cauliflower: dill, marjoram
Eggplant: basil, cinnamon, oregano
Fruit: anise, ginger, mint
Lamb: bay leaf, mint, rosemary
Potatoes: chives, marjoram, paprika, thyme
Spinach: dill, nutmeg
Tomatoes: basil, oregano, tarragon
Turkey: basil, marjoram, savory

BEST BLENDS

Mix up these all-purpose dried-herb combinations and keep them handy for quick meals. Pulverize the herbs, place in capped shaker jars and use at the stove and on the table. (With fresh herbs, mince only enough for immediate use.)

For poultry: equal parts basil, chervil, marjoram, parsley and thyme

For fish: equal parts chives, celery seed, dill

For vegetables: four parts basil, chervil, chives, marjoram and parsley; plus one part each savory and thyme

A GUIDE TO THE HEALTHIEST GREENS

Lettuce reform. That is, let us reform our salads from anemic wedges of iceberg into vitamin-rich bowls of *health*. It's easier than you may think. Supermarkets today stock an ever-increasing variety of salad fixin's that far outshine the old standby in nutritional merits.

One reason is readily apparent: These new greens are simply alive with color — a sure sign that they're brimming with nutrients. Romaine lettuce, chicory, endive, watercress, spinach, kale, Swiss chard, arugula, dandelion and turnip greens are high in beta-carotene and vitamin C — key nutrients that, among other things, guard against various types of cancer. Ounce for ounce, dark green kale, for instance, has 27 times more vitamin A, 30 times more vitamin C and 7 times more calcium than iceberg lettuce. Arugula has 16 times more calcium and 19 times more iron than iceberg.

All greens are high in fiber and marvelously low in calories and fat. Most have very little sodium. And some — such as cabbage, kale, collards, mustard greens and turnip greens — are members of the cancer-fighting crucifer family.

HANDLING GREENS

■ With greens such as kale and collards choose tender, vibrant leaves. Very large leaves are likely to be bitter. Avoid any that are limp or yellowed.

■ Don't wash the greens before storing them because the added moisture might encourage decay.

■ Wrap greens in paper towels, then place them in a perforated plastic bag. Store them in the crisper drawer, but use within a week.

■ When you do wash them, be sure not to soak greens. Their water-soluble nutrients will go right down the drain. Simply rinse the leaves thoroughly with cold water.

■ If the leaves are sandy or gritty, plunge them into a sink filled with tepid water. Swish them around, then immediately lift them out of the water. Place in a colander and rinse with cold water.

■ If cut with a knife, many types of lettuce discolor at the edges. So always tear the leaves.

■ Many greens will wilt if they're covered with dressing ahead of time, so put everything together at the last minute.

■ If you must assemble your salad ahead, place heavy items (such as tomatoes and broccoli) at the bottom of the bowl. Add the dressing, then top it with the greens. The leaves will remain crisp above the dressing and won't end up crushed. Toss the salad at serving time.

■ For extra crispness place your salad in the freezer for 5 minutes (no longer!) before serving.

■ As for dressing, don't drown your salads in an oil-and-vinegar sea. And use this rule of thumb: The more flavorful the ingredients, the simpler your dressing should be. Choose subtle sunflower, safflower and canola oils for hearty salads. Try olive, walnut or sesame oil and a zesty vinegar (try herb, raspberry or balsamic) for very simple salads.

■ Dressings stick better to dry greens, so whirl them in a mesh basket or salad spinner. Or pat the leaves dry.

THE GREEN GREATS

These salad favorites are bursting with both nutrients and taste appeal.

RADICCHIO
Beautifully veined leaves in shades of maroon; refreshing bittersweet flavor

GARDEN CRESS
Small leaves; spicy hot flavor

MUSTARD GREENS
Slightly sharp, earthy flavor; rough-textured leaves; often cooked

SPINACH
Dark green; mild but distinctive musky flavor; tough stems

MÂCHE (CORN SALAD)
Delicate rosette of leaves; pleasant, grassy flavor

KALE
A strong-flavored green with cabbagelike flavor; dark bluish green; choose tender, young leaves

CHINESE CABBAGE
Includes bok choy, Napa cabbage and Chinese celery cabbage; mild to piquant

ARUGULA (ROQUETTE)
Nippy, light mustard flavor; an interesting change from spinach

TURNIP GREENS
Dark, large, tender leaves; mild cabbage flavor; often cooked

COLLARD GREENS
Large leaves; spinachlike flavor; often cooked

BIBB LETTUCE
A smaller version of Boston lettuce; tender leaves; delicate, mellow flavor

BOSTON LETTUCE
Loose head; large, soft leaves; delicate flavor; also available in a red-tinged variety

BROCCOLI RABE
Bitter-tasting; very popular in Italian cuisine

BEET GREENS
Earthy, beety, chardlike taste; best when leaves are young

SPROUTING GOOD HEALTH

■ ■ ■ ■ ■ ■ ■ ■ ■ ■ ■ ■ ■   ▬▬▬▬▬▬▬▬▬

Growing sprouts in your kitchen is almost like growing vegetables in a garden, but without all the work. You can harvest these little wonders all year 'round, so you can enjoy fresh produce in every season. They grow rapidly and are incredibly economical. Just 1 cup of dried mung beans, for instance, yields about 4 cups of sprouts.

Simply speaking, sprouts are seeds that have begun to germinate. As they grow, protein and vitamins increase. Most sprouts have 12 percent more protein than their original seeds. What's more, their B vitamins jump three to ten times, and vitamins A, E and K also increase. Best of all, sprouting creates lots of vitamin C for protection from infections — even though the dry seeds don't have any.

Sprouts are high in fiber and retain whatever minerals the original seeds have. They are also low in calories: A cup of alfalfa sprouts, for instance, has only about 37 calories. As a bonus, bean sprouts tend to be less troublesome than cooked beans as far as flatulence goes. That's partly because the carbohydrates that cause gas are broken down in the sprouting process.

And get this: Wheat sprouts have been shown to inhibit the genetic damage to cells caused by some cancer-causing agents. You couldn't ask more from a crunchy little food.

A KITCHEN INDUSTRY

■ The best seeds for sprouting are those of the legume family (such as beans, peas and alfalfa) and the grasses (wheat, rye and barley). See the opposite page for favorite sproutables.

■ Buy untreated seeds that are sold specifically for sprouting rather than those intended for garden use. Garden seeds may have been treated with fungicides or insecticides.

■ Although there are many different ways to grow sprouts, here is what's probably the simplest. It's as easy as 1-2-3.

1. Start by soaking the seeds overnight to soften them. The next day, pour off the water. Rinse the seeds and drain well. Place them in a glass quart jar. Cover the mouth of the jar with either a piece of cheesecloth (secured with a rubber band) or a special sprouting lid that you can purchase.

2. Place the jar on its side in a warm place. Tilt it slightly to let moisture drain out. Over the next two to six days — depending on the type you're growing (see opposite page) — rinse and drain the sprouts several times a day using lukewarm water.

3. If desired, during the last day or two of sprouting, put the jar in a sunny spot. Some sprouts, such as alfalfa, will turn a beautiful green as they develop valuable chlorophyll. When they're ready, give the sprouts a final rinse and drain well.

■ Generally speaking, sprouts will stay fresh for a week in the refrigerator. Store them in the coldest part. Always use a container that will protect them from being crushed rather than putting them in a plastic bag. Lining the container with paper towels will help keep excess moisture from building up. Check the sprouts daily to see that they're not turning limp or moldy.

USING YOUR HARVEST

■ Most sprouts can be eaten either raw or cooked. But it's recommended that you cook bean or pea sprouts if you like to eat large amounts. The reason is that raw legume sprouts contain a substance that inhibits trypsin, one of the enzymes we need to digest protein. Simmering or steaming the sprouts for 3 minutes is all that's needed.

■ Very fine, threadlike sprouts, such as alfalfa, tend to mat together if tossed with other salad ingredients. A better idea is to prepare the rest of the salad separately and then serve it on a bed of the sprouts. Or sprinkle the sprouts over the salad.

■ You can also add sprouts to soup. Just toss them into the pot or individual bowls shortly before serving. Lentil sprouts are good this way.

SPROUTS: A GROWING GUIDE

Use this guide to help you grow the tastiest sprouts. Experiment to find the sprout length you enjoy best. And note that sprouts may take longer to grow in cold weather than in the summer.

SEED	SPROUT LENGTH	TIME (days)	COMMENTS
Alfalfa	1''–2''	3–5	Easy to sprout. Light taste.
Barley	Sprout is length of seed	3–4	Chewy texture, pleasant taste, not sweet.
Bean	1''	3–5	For tender sprouts, limit germination time to 3 days.
Buck-wheat	¼''–½''	2–3	Easy to sprout. Buy raw hulled groats for sprouting.
Chick-pea	½''	3	Best lightly cooked.
Cress	1''–1½''	3–5	Gelatinous seed. Strong, peppery taste.
Fenu-greek	1''–3''	3–5	Spicy taste, good in curry dishes. Bitter if sprouted too long.
Lentil	¼''–1''	3	Chewy bean texture. Eat raw or lightly steamed.
Mung	1½''–2''	3–5	Easy to sprout. Popular in oriental dishes.
Mustard	1''–2½''	3–4	Spicy, tangy taste, reminiscent of fresh English mustard.
Pea	Sprout is length of seed	3	Tastes like fresh peas. Best when steamed lightly.
Radish	⅛''–2''	2–6	Taste like the vegetable.
Rice	Sprout is length of seed	3–4	Similar to other sprouted grains. Only whole-grain brown rice will sprout.
Rye	Sprout is length of seed	3–4	Easy to sprout. Very sweet taste with crunchy texture.
Soybean	1''–2''	4–6	Need frequent, thorough rinses. Should be cooked before eating for optimum protein.
Sunflower	Sprout is no longer than seed	1–3	Good snacks, especially if lightly roasted. Become bitter if sprouted too long.
Triticale	Sprout is length of seed	2–3	Easy to sprout. Very sweet taste.
Wheat	Sprout is length of seed	2–4	Easy to sprout. Very sweet taste.

0502-12   Photo: Angelo Caggiano; Food styling: Anne Disrude

WINTER SQUASH: CAROTENE ... AND MORE

■ ■ ■ ■ ■ ■ ■ ■ ■ ■ ■ ■ ■

Hard-shelled squash, commonly referred to as winter squash, have lots of health-building attributes. They're very low in calories, fat and sodium. A half-cup of acorn squash, for instance, has only 57 calories, a trace of fat and 4 milligrams of sodium. Butternut and hubbard squash boast similar figures.

Like other vegetables, squash are cholesterol free — and you can keep them that way if you forgo butter, cheese and cream during preparation and at the table. All types of winter squash are good sources of hunger-appeasing fiber and complex carbohydrates. Fiber also contributes to good digestive health and helps keep cholesterol down.

Vitamin A — and its precursor, cancer-preventing beta-carotene — is abundant in many squash. Deep orange varieties are your best bet. Butternut and hubbard, for instance, are brimming with this nutrient. A half-cup of baked butternut has 71 percent of the Recommended Dietary Allowance of A. But acorn, which tends to be pale yellow, has only 4 percent.

Other nutrients present in many types of squash include immunity-boosting vitamin C, blood-building iron, stroke-preventing potassium and bone-strengthening calcium. For those qualities alone, squash deserve an honored place on your table.

PICKING THE BEST

■ Color is not a sure indicator of quality, especially after the squash have been stored for a while. In the middle of winter, for instance, faded squash may actually have a sweet, intense flavor if they have been properly stored.

■ Winter squash have the best flavor if harvested when fully mature. Select those that are heavy for their size. The rind should be very hard and not easily pierced or scraped away. Beware of gashes, cracks, mold and soft spots. Whenever possible, choose squash that still have firm, fully developed stems attached.

■ When buying cut squash, such as pieces of banana or hubbard, look for crisp, clean flesh. Reject pieces that are discolored, bruised or shriveled.

■ Store squash in a cool (about 50°), dry, well-ventilated area. Most varieties last for months under these conditions, but small types such as Delicata and Sweet Dumpling tend to be less durable. Do not store squash in the refrigerator unless you're buying cut pieces — keep them tightly wrapped and use within a few days.

■ You'll need a sharp, heavy knife to cut winter squash. Softer varieties, such as acorn, butternut and calabaza, are easier to cut than tougher-shelled types, such as pumpkins, kabocha and Golden Nugget. Cut off the stem end first, then halve the squash. You may need the help of a wooden mallet or rolling pin: Place a knife lengthwise on the squash and gently hammer the knife blade (near the handle) until the squash splits open. Scoop out the seeds and stringy fibers.

■ It's easier if you don't peel squash before cooking. But if you must, first cut the squash into small pieces, about 3'' square, then remove the rind with a paring knife.

■ Most winter squash turn out best when baked. Place halves, quarters or large pieces, cut side down, in a baking pan. (Some varieties give off a lot of moisture as they cook, so a baking dish is a safer bet than a cookie sheet.) Bake at 375° until tender, 45 minutes or more.

■ Steaming is a fast alternative. Cut the squash into manageable pieces and place, cut side down, on a steaming rack. Most types will take 20 to 30 minutes. Small, peeled chunks may be done in 15 minutes. Check occasionally to make sure the water hasn't boiled away.

■ Squash can be microwaved. Tiny types can be done whole (pierce in several places and microwave on high for 4 to 6 minutes); let stand for 3 minutes. To do small squash (about 1 pound), halve, remove the seeds, cover and cook for 5 to 8 minutes; let stand for 5 minutes. Larger squash should be cut into pieces, covered and microwaved for 8 to 10 minutes, or until tender.

1 SWEET DUMPLING
Mildly sweet yellow meat; more perishable than most

10 GOLDEN NUGGET
Small with mildly sweet orange meat; has a very hard shell, so best cooked whole

9 BUTTERNUT
Bright orange, mildly sweet flesh; cavity suitable for stuffing

2 ACORN
Mild, creamy, pale yellow flesh; cavity suitable for stuffing; comes in green, orange and white

8 JACK BE LITTLE
Miniature pumpkin with mildly sweet orange meat

3 TURBAN
Flamboyant with creamy, moist, bland flesh

7 BUTTERCUP
Turban shape with dense, sweet, orange flesh

4 SPAGHETTI
Football shape; meat is easily flaked when cooked to resemble spaghetti

6 HUBBARD
Deliciously rich orange meat; comes in blue, gold, red-orange, green and mottled

5 DELICATA
Small with sweet yellow flesh; more perishable than most

HOT STUFF: CHILI PEPPERS

Chilies may be the most widely used spice in the world. They're indispensable for such wide-ranging cuisines as Mexican, Thai, Caribbean and Chinese. And, doctors say, their value exceeds the flavor wallop they give to everyday dishes.

These fiery vegetables are super low in calories, and they're high in infection-fighting vitamins A and C. So you're welcome to eat as much as your taste buds can bear. But even better, chilies may protect against heart attacks and strokes by increasing the blood's capacity to break up dangerous clots that can trigger those problems.

Chilies have other health benefits: They may help prevent colon cancer by inhibiting the formation of undesirable compounds found in cured meats. They can let you burn extra calories by boosting after-dinner metabolism as much as 25 percent. They may lessen the congestion of bronchitis, asthma, allergies and colds. And they may even help clear up irritating dry coughs. Best of all, the amounts needed for these effects are no greater than you'd find in typical Mexican or Indian dishes.

PEPPER PICKIN'

■ First off, accept the confusion that surrounds chilies. There are at least 200 varieties, and many go by several names. Some even have one name when fresh and another when dried. Fresh poblanos become dried anchos, for example. So experiment, then learn to recognize the ones you like.

■ When you can't find just the right chili called for in a recipe, substitute a pepper of the same general size and heat. For instance, you could replace a serrano with a jalapeño, but you wouldn't want to use the larger, milder green Anaheim. Also, it's best to substitute a fresh pepper for another fresh one.

■ When buying fresh peppers, look for firm specimens with tight, glossy, unblemished skins; refrigerate in a paper bag for up to a week. Choose dried chilies with pliable, unbroken skins; store in a tightly closed jar.

■ The flavor of dried chilies is more robust than that of fresh. To intensify it further, toast the chilies briefly at 350°. Use scissors to make chopping easier. Or soak the peppers awhile in water and chop with a knife.

■ You can't always gauge a pepper's hotness by looking at it. But in general, small, narrow, pointed chilies, like cayenne and tabasco, tend to be very hot. Larger specimens with broader shoulders, like poblano and Anaheim, are milder. Don't rely on color for a clue. Although green peppers are often milder than red, a scorching hot habañero may be orange, red, green or white. A red cherry-tomato pepper may have practically no heat, but a red serrano can be fiery.

■ Capsaicin, the chemical that makes peppers hot, is pretty much contained in the ribs and inner membranes to which the seeds are attached. (The seeds tend to become hot when they rub against the membranes.) Capsaicin is not affected by cooking, freezing or the passage of time. One way to reduce a pepper's potency is to remove the inner ribs, membranes and seeds. Another is to soak the chilies in salted ice water or milk for an hour.

■ Capsaicin can cause serious skin irritation. When handling either fresh or dried chilies, wear thin rubber or plastic gloves — or even plastic sandwich bags. If you do get capsaicin on your hands, wash them well in soapy water or a mild bleach solution. Be sure also to cleanse all utensils, and scrub the cutting board with salt and cold water. If there's any chance that there's capsaicin on your hands, don't touch your face, children or pets.

■ When eating hot peppers, douse flaming pain with milk, yogurt or sour cream. Other foods that seem effective are rice, bread and bananas.

■ It's best to sample a chili before cooking so you're not overwhelmed later. One good way is to halve the pepper and use the tip of your tongue to gingerly test a ribless section.

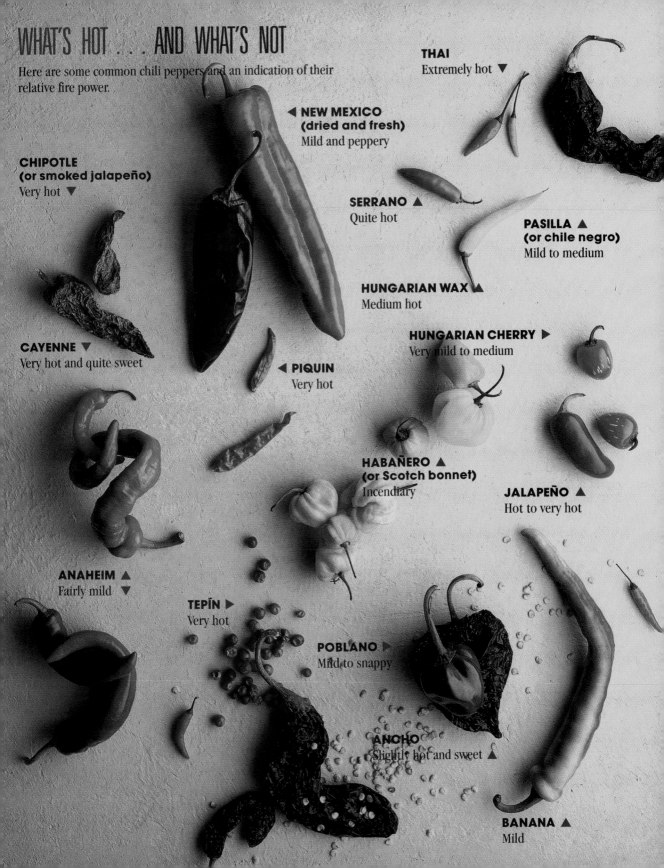

WHAT'S HOT . . . AND WHAT'S NOT

Here are some common chili peppers and an indication of their relative fire power.

THAI
Extremely hot ▼

◄ NEW MEXICO (dried and fresh)
Mild and peppery

CHIPOTLE (or smoked jalapeño)
Very hot ▼

SERRANO ▲
Quite hot

PASILLA ▲ (or chile negro)
Mild to medium

HUNGARIAN WAX ▲
Medium hot

HUNGARIAN CHERRY ►
Very mild to medium

CAYENNE ▼
Very hot and quite sweet

◄ PIQUIN
Very hot

HABAÑERO ▲ (or Scotch bonnet)
Incendiary

JALAPEÑO ▲
Hot to very hot

ANAHEIM ▲
Fairly mild ▼

TEPÍN ►
Very hot

POBLANO ►
Mild to snappy

ANCHO
Slightly hot and sweet ▲

BANANA ▲
Mild

LUSCIOUS, LOW-FAT CHEESES

■ ■ ■ ■ ■ ■ ■ ■ ■ ■ ■ ■ ■ ■

Being both a cheese-lover and a weight watcher isn't easy. As delicious as cheese is, it's one of the fattiest foods around. An ounce of most full-fat varieties runs about 110 calories and 8 or 9 grams of (mostly saturated) fat.

On the other hand, cheese is an excellent source of bone-building calcium as well as vitamin A and the stress-fighting B vitamins, especially riboflavin. And it's a good way to get protein into your diet if you're cutting back on meat.

The secret to having your cheese and a trim waistline, too, is to make your selections with care. For daily fare, try to pick cheeses that are high in protein and calcium and low in fat and salt.

If you have tried low-fat cheeses in the past and found them lacking, give them another try. Cheese makers are heeding the clamor for delicious light products.

BUYING GUIDELINES

■ A good rule of thumb is that hard cheeses, like Cheddar and Swiss, are higher in calories than soft ones, like mozzarella and Brie. Very soft types, like cottage cheese and ricotta, are lower still. Keep in mind that calories and fat can vary tremendously from manufacturer to manufacturer. The figures on the chart shown here, for instance, are only an approximation.

■ Double-check labels that promise light cheese. Sometimes that just means a lighter color or less salt. If you're looking for less fat, make sure the nutrient data confirms the fact. In general, try to buy cheeses that contain 6 grams of fat (or less) per ounce — the lower the better. A *really* low-fat cheese has 3 grams or less.

■ Cut back gradually. Don't make the jump from full-fat ricotta straight to dry-curd cottage cheese, for example. Instead, use part-skim ricotta for a while, then mix in 2 percent cottage cheese in increasing proportions. Over a period of time, you can phase out the ricotta entirely.

■ Look for cream cheese replacements. Start with light cream cheese or Neufchâtel. That can cut your recipe's calorie count up to 25 percent. Or, go to part-skim ricotta, pureed cottage cheese or yogurt cheese.

AT HOME

■ Eat cheese warm or at room temperature. The flavor is more pronounced when the cheese isn't ice cold. So get your selection out of the refrigerator 15 to 30 minutes before serving. Or melt it atop bread, casseroles or tuna burgers.

■ Take small servings. Remember that even with low-fat varieties, calories and fat still add up. If you ate 4 ounces of one diet Cheddar, for instance, that would be 320 calories — practically as much as in a meal. So try to limit yourself to 1 ounce.

■ When snacking, slice cheese thinly and eat it with crunchy, fiber-filled foods that require a lot of chewing, like apple slices or pretzels.

■ To slice really thin pieces of cheese, use a serrated knife, wire cheese cutter or cheese plane. Cut it straight from the refrigerator, then let it warm to develop its flavor.

■ Slim down creamed cottage cheese by placing it in a strainer and rinsing it under cold water. That removes quite a bit of fat and some sodium.

■ To cut even more dairy calories, substitute mashed tofu (a high-protein, cholesterol-free soy food) for ricotta and cottage cheese in recipes. Tofu is milder than dairy cheese, so you may want to add more seasoning.

STORAGE TIPS

■ Because hard cheeses are fairly low in moisture, they store well for several months. Very soft, fresh cheeses keep for only a week.

■ If cheese becomes hard and dry during storage, simply grate it for a topping for spaghetti, vegetables, soups, biscuits or casseroles.

■ If mold grows on cheese, it may be a matter for concern, since some molds contain dangerous aflatoxins. To be on the safe side, discard it.

CHEESE-LOVER'S GUIDE

Want to get the most cheese for the least amount of fat and calories? This table gives a weight-watcher's account of popular types. A range of figures indicates that the cheese varies according to manufacturer. Make your selections wisely.

CHEESE	SERVING	CALORIES	FAT (g.)
Blue	1 oz.	60	4.9
Cheddar, light	1 oz.	65-90	3-6
Cheddar, processed	1 oz.	50-70	2-4
Cottage cheese, 1%	½ cup	93	1.2
Cottage cheese, 2%	½ cup	102	2.2
Cottage cheese, dry curd	½ cup	62	0.3
Farmer's	1 oz.	80-90	5-7
Feta	1 oz.	75	6
Gammelost	1 oz.	52-60	0.1-0.3
Monterey Jack, light	1 oz.	80	6
Monterey Jack, processed	1 oz.	50	2
Mozzarella, part-skim	1 oz.	72	4.5
Muenster, light	1 oz.	85	5
Muenster, processed	1 oz.	50-85	2-5
Neufchâtel	1 oz.	74	6.6
Parmesan, grated	1 T.	29	1.9
Pot cheese	1 oz.	25	0
Ricotta, part-skim	½ cup	171	9.8
Sapsago	1 oz.	66	2.1
Scamorza, part-skim	1 oz.	70	5
String, light	1 oz.	70-90	4-6
Swiss, light	1 oz.	50-97	2-6
Swiss, processed	1 oz.	50-70	2-4
Yogurt cheese	1 oz.	30	0.6

Photo: Angelo Caggiano; Food Styling: Anne Disrude

A COOK'S GUIDE TO CULINARY OILS

■ ■ ■ ■ ■ ■ ■ ■ ■ ■ ■ ■ ■ ▬▬▬▬

Oils are essential cooking ingredients. They lend distinctive character to all types of food, from fruits and vegetables to grains and meats. They even help "carry" flavors so the palate can discern them more readily. But not all oils are created equal. The so-called tropical oils — coconut, palm, palm kernel — contain a lot of saturated fat, which is a major cause of heart disease.

Fortunately, most of the popular oils on the market today are composed largely of beneficial monounsaturated and polyunsaturated fats. Monounsaturates — found in olive, canola, rice-bran and other oils (see the chart on the opposite page) — may help lower cholesterol, control high blood pressure and possibly even reduce glucose levels in those with adult-onset diabetes. Polyunsaturates — prominent in corn, safflower, soybean and certain other oils — also may help lower blood cholesterol.

All vegetable oils are free of dietary cholesterol and contain no sodium. Their one drawback, no matter how good their chemical makeup, is that they're high in fat. Each tablespoon contains approximately 120 calories and about 14 grams of fat. That means you should use them judiciously — substitute these good fats for more saturated ones, such as butter; don't simply add them to your total.

Here are some things to keep in mind when using oil.

FRESHNESS COUNTS

■ In general, light-colored refined oils, such as canola, corn, peanut, safflower, soybean and sunflower, stay fresh longer than dark oils. Under ideal conditions, these oils may last up to a year. Olive oil tends to have a shorter shelf life and may remain fresh for only six to ten months. Dark specialty oils, such as walnut, are the least stable — four to six months tends to be their maximum.

■ No matter what type of oil you use, buy only as much as you anticipate needing over a short time. And mark the container with the date of purchase.

■ If an oil has been stored for several months, check its flavor and aroma before using. Oils that have turned rancid will have an unpleasant taste and smell.

■ Vegetable oils are susceptible to air, heat and light. Store them in tightly capped containers in a cool, dark cabinet. Do not store them over the stove.

■ In summer and any other time your kitchen tends to be warm, refrigerate oil. Most oils will turn thick and cloudy under refrigeration, but that doesn't affect either their flavor or their performance. If they've solidified to the point where you can't get them out of the bottle when cold, let them stand at room temperature until they liquefy.

TOP-SHELF CHOICES

■ Gourmet shops and some supermarkets carry many very flavorful oils, such as walnut, almond, sesame and grapeseed. These oils have such a wonderful, distinctive taste that you don't need to use very much. That helps you cut fat and calories from dishes that would ordinarily contain quite a bit more oil.

■ "Cold-pressed" oils, available from health-food stores, have undergone minimal processing and refinement, so they have more pronounced flavors than their normal supermarket counterparts. To safeguard that flavor, use them in dishes that don't require much heating. They're particularly good in salad dressings.

■ You can make your own specialty oils to give zip to your meals. Herbs, dried chili peppers and sun-dried tomatoes make excellent flavoring agents. If using fresh herbs, lightly crush them to bring out more flavor. Place the flavoring in a jar and cover with a bland oil such as canola or sunflower. Cap the jar tightly and refrigerate for several days. Strain the oil and return it to the fridge. You can discard the herbs or peppers, but keep the tomatoes for future use — they will have plumped nicely.

A WEALTH OF OILS

When choosing an oil, keep in mind both its natural flavor and its intended use. Some oils are very mild and go with practically anything. Others, like olive and walnut, have a distinctive taste that might overpower delicate foods. Some oils are best suited for salads, while others can withstand the heat involved in cooking and baking. Use this chart to help you make the most appropriate choices; M stands for monounsaturated fat, P stands for polyunsaturated fat.

TYPE OF OIL	MAIN FAT	COMMENTS
Almond	M	Mildly sweet with a fresh almond flavor. Expensive. Good on salads, but not really suitable for cooking.
Avocado	M	Sweet, walnutlike flavor. Good on salads, especially those containing bitter greens like radicchio and endive. Not really suitable for cooking.
Canola	M	Light in texture and taste. A good all-purpose oil with a high smoke point. Also known as rapeseed oil.
Corn	P	Light, bland flavor. One of the most popular oils. Good for salads, cooking and baking. Unrefined corn oil has a stronger corn flavor.
Grapeseed	P	Flavor ranges from bland to light grape. Good all-purpose oil. A by-product of the wine industry. Often blended with olive oil and herbs.
Hazelnut	M	Buttery flavor. Good on salads and in nut-flavored desserts. Expensive; can be mixed with blander oils such as corn to make it go further.
Olive	M	Flavor ranges from bland to strong; color ranges from pale yellow to green. Extra-virgin best for salads. Pure olive oil good for light sautés. "Light" olive oil is lighter in flavor, not lower in calories.
Peanut	M	Somewhat bland. Good for cooking, especially Chinese dishes. Nice on raw vegetables and salads. Cold-pressed peanut oil has a nutty taste.
Rice-bran	M	Light in taste and texture. Has a high smoke point, making it suitable for all types of cooking. Also great on salads.
Safflower	P	Bland. Has a high smoke point, making it good for cooking. Wonderful on salads. Of all common oils, safflower is the highest in polyunsaturates.
Sesame	P	Earthy, toasted flavor; amber color. Good in marinades and as a seasoning in Chinese dishes. Not good for frying because it burns easily. Cold-pressed sesame oil is light in color and has a subtle flavor.
Soybean	P	Sweet, beany flavor. Is the leading oil consumed in the United States. Good for cooking because of its high smoke point. Cold-pressed soy oil is darker and has a nutty flavor.
Sunflower	P	Delicate, light flavor. Excellent for cooking, baking and salads.
Walnut	P	Butternut flavor. Expensive; mix with blander oils to make it go further. Excellent in salad dressings, but not really suitable for cooking.

EAT LEAN WITH BEAN CUISINE

■ ■ ■ ■ ■ ■ ■ ■ ■ ■ ■ ■   ■

Beans are an excellent source of hunger-satisfying complex carbohydrates, cholesterol-lowering soluble fiber and digestion-aiding insoluble fiber. And they're high in protein. They do lack a few essential amino acids, but that can be easily remedied by serving beans with grains or dairy foods.

Because they're so rich and filling, you might think beans are fattening. Not so! A half-cup serving of most common varieties averages 125 cholesterol-free calories — and less than 1 gram of fat.

Best of all, beans are nutrient dense. They boast healthy doses of anemia-fighting iron, nerve-soothing B vitamins and bone-building calcium and phosphorus. And being both low in sodium and rich in potassium, they're perfect for anyone with high blood pressure. Further, studies show that beans help normalize blood sugar, which makes them great for diabetics. Here's how to enjoy beans.

■ Look for beans that are uniform in color and size. Faded beans have probably been stored too long. And mixed sizes will result in uneven cooking.

■ Avoid beans with visible defects. Cracked or shriveled seed coats, lots of foreign material and pinholes caused by insects are signs of low quality. But be aware that even good-quality beans may have a little debris mixed in, so always pick through them.

■ Store beans in tightly covered glass jars in a cool cupboard or the refrigerator. Adding a pinch of rosemary or a bay leaf to the jar will help beans stay fresh. Properly stored, they should last a year.

■ The easiest way to sort beans is to spread them out on a clean (preferably solid-color) kitchen towel and look at the whole batch at once. When you've removed the debris, gather up the towel and pour the beans into a strainer to rinse.

■ All dried beans except lentils and split peas (and sometimes black-eyed peas, depending on the recipe) need to be soaked before cooking.

■ Use a container large enough to permit the beans to expand at least 2½ times, cover with cold water and let them stand overnight at room temperature.

■ If you forget to presoak the beans, boil them for 2 minutes. Cover and let stand for 1 hour.

■ Or think ahead: Freeze presoaked and drained beans in a single layer on a cookie sheet. When the beans are hard as marbles, transfer them to a container or plastic bag. They will not stick together and can be used directly from the freezer.

■ Drain the soaked beans, place them in a saucepan and add enough cold water to reach 2″ above the beans. Bring to a boil, then lower the heat, partially cover the pan and simmer until tender (see the table "Who's Who among Beans" on the opposite page).

■ An alternate cooking method: Place the soaked beans in a large casserole dish or small roasting pan. Add a generous amount of water, cover the pan and bake at 350° until tender (anywhere from 1 to 3 hours).

■ Stirring the beans as they cook is apt to break the skins. If stirring is necessary, use a wooden spoon.

■ Pressure cooking greatly reduces cooking time. For best results don't fill the cooker more than one-third. You might also want to add 1 tablespoon of oil to help prevent foaming that might clog the vent pipe. Follow the manufacturer's directions for pressure setting and cooking time. To check the beans, allow the cooker to stand for 5 minutes before opening. That lets the pressure fall gradually so the skins are less likely to break.

■ Beans cook best by themselves. Molasses, fats, salt and acids, such as tomato or vinegar, all harden the beans' skins and lengthen cooking time. Don't add them until the beans are tender.

■ Do not add baking soda to the water to hasten the cooking process. It tends to destroy the B vitamin thiamine and can adversely affect the taste of the beans.

WHO'S WHO AMONG BEANS

There are dozens of types of beans available. Here are some of the most common, along with cooking information.

VARIETY (1 cup)	COOKING TIME (approx.)	COOKED VOLUME (cups)	NOTES
1 Black (turtle)	45-60 min.	2½	Popular in South American, Caribbean and Mexican food; often served with rice
2 Black-Eyed Pea (cowpea)	1 hr.	2½	Pealike flavor and buttery texture; used extensively in southern cooking; also available fresh
3 Chick-Pea (garbanzo)	2½ hr.	3¼	Essential for Middle Eastern hummus; ideal in antipasto and minestrone
4 Cranberry	45-60 min.	2½	Turn creamy white when cooked; distinctive sweet flavor; also available fresh
5 Fava	45-60 min.	2½	Slightly sharp flavor; good in Middle Eastern and Italian dishes; can be used like limas; also available fresh
6 Kidney	1½ hr.	2½	Come in various shades of red; a staple in three-bean salads and chili
7 Lentil	30 min.	2¾	Come in many colors; don't need soaking; essential for Indian cuisine
8 Lima	45-60 min.	2½	Rich, buttery flavor; also available fresh
9 Mung	1½ hr.	2½	Produce less gas than most; good for Indian cuisine; ideal for sprouting
10 Pea	45-60 min.	2½	Smallest of the white beans; used in classic Boston baked beans
11 Pinto	1½ hr.	2	Popular in Mexican dishes like chili and refried beans
12 Soybean	3 hr.	2¾	Contain high-quality protein; higher in fat than other beans; used to make tofu
13 Split Pea	35-40 min.	2¼	Available in green and yellow; classic soup bean; don't need soaking

0201-12   Photo: Angelo Caggiano; Food styling: Anne Disrude

THE WIDE WORLD OF RICE

A re you watching your weight? How about your cholesterol? Maybe your sodium intake? Are you searching for a food that's filling, satisfying *and* low in calories? Rice measures up on all counts, and it's high time you recognized this grain for the exciting, healthy food it is.

Besides being light on calories, rice is incredibly low in fat and sodium (as long as you cook it without added fat and salt). It's free of gluten and is nonallergenic. Rice is also a source of fiber, thiamine, riboflavin, niacin and iron (the exact amounts vary according to the type of rice).

Brown rice is the top gun as far as nutrition goes. It's undergone very little processing, having had only its inedible outer hull removed. Because the brownish bran that gives it its color is intact, there's three times more fiber present than in white rice. Nevertheless, white rice remains an important staple in healthy diets worldwide. That suggests that, even in its refined state, rice is an intrinsically good food.

NAME THAT GRAIN

■ All rice is classified by the length of its grains.

Long grain is by far the most popular. It includes the aromatic varieties, such as Basmati and Texmati. When cooked, the long grains remain separate and fluffy, making them ideal for pilafs, stuffing, rice salad and casseroles.

Medium-grain rice is shorter, plumper and a bit stickier when cooked. It can double for long-grain in many recipes. Just double-check package instructions before making such a switch because some medium-grain varieties require less water.

Short grain is stubby, almost round in shape. When cooked, it's very sticky and somewhat heavy in texture. It's perfect for sushi, croquettes, paella and stuffed peppers. Arborio is an Italian short-grain rice with an exceptionally creamy texture that's used for risotto.

■ Store all rice in tightly sealed containers in a cool, dry, semidark place. Tear the instructions from the original box and place in the container for later reference. Because brown rice is more perishable than white, store it in the refrigerator or freezer.

■ Some recipes call for rinsing rice before cooking. But it's unnecessary, especially since domestic rice is very clean and washing might remove vita-mins added during the enriching process many rices undergo. The sole exception would be wild rice (which is not a true rice and is not enriched).

■ A rule of thumb is that 1 cup of dry rice requires 2 cups of liquid, but exact measurements and cooking times can vary. Here's one foolproof cooking technique that works for most.

Bring the liquid to a boil, add the rice and allow it to boil, uncovered, for 5 minutes. Reduce the heat to a gentle simmer and partially cover the pan (leave the lid just slightly ajar). Cook until all the liquid has been absorbed and the grains are tender. If the rice is not tender, add a bit more liquid and continue cooking.

■ For best results, don't stir rice as it cooks. That tends to release starch within the grains, causing them to stick together and become gummy.

■ You may also bake rice. Place it in an ovenproof dish. Add boiling liquid and any other ingredients. Cover and bake at 350° to 400° until tender. Exact time will depend upon the temperature and type of rice used, but baking often takes a little longer than stove-top preparation.

■ To reheat refrigerated rice, spoon it into a fine-mesh strainer and steam over boiling water until hot. Or warm it in the microwave: Place in a glass pie plate, sprinkle with 1 tablespoon of liquid per cup of rice. Cover with vented plastic wrap and microwave on full power until hot (about 1 minute for a cup).

CHOOSING AND USING RICE

This chart gives approximate amounts of liquid needed for raw rice and estimated cooking times.

TYPE (1 cup)	LIQUID (cups)	COOKING TIME (min.)	CHARACTERISTICS
Arborio	3-4½	25-45	Short-grain white from Italy. Use primarily for risotto. Remains slightly al dente when cooked.
Aromatic, brown	1¾-2½	30-45	Long grain. High in fiber. Has aroma similar to nuts, popcorn, corn bran or hay. Includes the brown Basmati hybrids, such as Texmati, Pecan and Wehani. Good for curries and Cajun cuisine.
Aromatic, white	1¼-2	15-20	Long grain. Same type of aroma as brown aromatics. Includes true white Basmati and U.S. hybrids.
Brown	1¾-3	45-60	Higher in fiber than white. Comes in long, medium and short grains. Pleasant nutty flavor. Slightly chewy. Beige color. Unlimited uses.
Converted (parboiled)	2-2½	20-25	Long-grain white. Bland flavor. Grains stay separate when cooked. Has undergone a special pressure and steam treatment prior to milling that preserves vitamins. Good for pilafs.
White	1¼-2¼	15-20	Comes in long, medium and short grains. Bland flavor. Soft texture. Pure white color. Unlimited uses.
Wild	2½-4	35-50	Not a true rice; it's the seed of an aquatic North American grass. Difficult to produce. Very expensive. Deep brown color, chewy texture. Slightly smoky, nutty flavor. Often mixed with white or brown rice.

1 Arborio
2 Sweet brown rice
3 Wehani
4 Lundburg wild blend
5 White and brown long grain
6 Wild rice
7 White and brown basmati
8 Black japonica
9 Sweet rice

PERFECTLY HEALTHY PASTA

■ ■ ■ ■ ■ ■ ■ ■ ■ ■ ■ ■ ■ ■

Pasta has shed its image as a diet buster and emerged as a respectable staple of both weight-watching and heart-healthy diets. It's now receiving due credit as a low-fat, low-sodium, hunger-appeasing complex carbohydrate. After all, a normal serving (2 ounces dry weight) has only 200 calories and just a trace of fat and sodium.

And contrary to the long-held belief that pasta is "just starch," research has found that it actually retains most of its mineral content after being cooked. In fact, a plateful of pasta serves up a substantial percentage of the Recommended Dietary Allowance for six major minerals.

These noodles have oodles of vitamins, too. Two cups of spaghetti provides almost half of your daily need for thiamine, one-fifth of your niacin requirement and one-quarter of your riboflavin need.

So pasta-lovers can rejoice. Just make sure to dress your pasta for success. That means keeping sauces light in calories, salt and saturated fat.

USING YOUR NOODLES

■ Although regular white pasta is perfectly nutritious, whole wheat varieties have considerably more fiber. A 2-ounce serving of whole wheat spaghetti has 6.6 grams of dietary fiber; the same amount of white has 1.3 grams. If whole wheat by itself is not to your liking, mix it half-and-half with white. Check the package instructions and cook the pastas separately.

■ Just after adding the pasta, stir the water once or twice with a wooden fork or spoon to keep the pieces from settling to the bottom and sticking there. Do not stir again.

■ Cook pasta until *al dente*—tender but still firm. To test, use a fork to remove a sample, let it cool slightly, then bite into it. It should be cooked clear through but still offer a bit of resistance to your teeth. Stand over the pot and test the strands often.

■ To keep long strands from sticking together, remove the pasta from the water with a wooden fork, if possible. If you must drain the noodles in a sieve or colander, pour them in gently so as not to crush them.

■ Rinsing pasta after cooking is not generally recommended—some nutrients are washed away in the process. The sole exception is when cooking pasta for a cold salad. Give it a *very* quick rinse in cold water to cool it off and keep the pieces from sticking together.

■ Leftover pasta will keep in the refrigerator for three to five days. If already sauced, it can be reheated on top of the stove. Or cover it with foil and warm it in the oven. If not sauced, cover the pasta with boiling water for about 2 minutes, then drain well.

■ Cook pasta in lots of water. Figure on 6 to 7 quarts for 1 pound of pasta. And use a pot that's large enough to hold the water without boiling over. Add the pasta gradually so the water doesn't stop boiling.

THE RIGHT SAUCE

■ For healthiest dining, prepare sauces with olive oil or canola oil instead of butter. These oils are high in the monounsaturated fats that are good for your heart.

■ For cream-type sauces, use low-fat milk thickened with an oil and flour base rather than heavy cream.

■ Let your choice of sauce dictate which type of pasta to use: Seafood sauces and sauces with olive oil as the principal fat go best with thin spaghetti. Tomato sauces are ideal for regular spaghetti. Chunky sauces, such as meat or vegetable types, are good for shaped pasta (shells or ones with holes); the openings and ridges in the pasta trap bits of sauce, coating the pasta inside and out. Creamy sauces work well with ridged pasta, such as rigatoni or penne; the sauce adheres to the ridges.

■ When choosing a cheese to grate over the pasta, opt for a robust variety, such as Parmesan, Romano or sapsago. Their flavors are so strong that a bare sprinkling is enough.

A WHO'S WHO OF PASTAS

Is that cappelletti or capellini? With so many sizes and shapes on the market, it's sometimes hard to put a name to the noodle. Here's a guide to a few of the less common types and shapes. (But don't be surprised to find that names — and spellings! — differ according to manufacturer. That's just part of pasta's mystique.) Remember that although pasta is generally made from wheat, varieties like rice and buckwheat are common.

Ramen:
Crinkly Japanese wheat noodles; used in soups

Somen:
Thin, white Japanese noodles, sometimes made of buckwheat flour

Soba:
Japanese noodles usually made of buckwheat

Udon:
Thick, Japanese wheat noodles

Tagliatelle:
¾''-wide ribbons

Acini di pepe:
Little round or rodlike pasta; used in soups

Rice noodles:
Chinese noodles cut into varying widths

Rotelle:
Corkscrew spirals; also called rotini; sometimes shaped like little wagon wheels

Cappelletti:
Little hats formed by curling up triangles of stuffed pasta

Farfalle:
Wide ribbons pinched in the middle to look like butterflies; also called bow ties

Ravioli:
Little squares of stuffed pasta, usually sealed with pinked edges

Vermicelli:
Very thin spaghetti, sometimes sold in nests

Penne:
Medium-thick tubes with diagonal ends

Fettucce:
½''-wide ribbons

Cannelloni:
Large, hollow reeds; also refers to homemade pasta squares or crêpes that are stuffed, then rolled

Capellini:
Thinnest form of spaghetti, also known as angel hair

Photo: Angelo Caggiano; Food styling: Anne Disrude

0301-12

INDEX

W

Y

Z

ACKNOWLEDGMENTS

■ ■ ■ ■ ■ ■

Special thanks to:
Anichini
Ann Gish from Mottura
Annieglass Studio
Carol Gouthro
Claire DesBecker Ceramics
Claire Weissberg from Claireware
Design Imports India
Jabara
Lindt-Stymeist Designs
Luna Garcia from Mottura
Mottura Bronze
New Glass
Palais Royal
Salvatore Polizzi
Swid Powell
The Pfaltzgraff Company
Umbrello
Vietri, Inc.
Windy Hill Antiques